Storytellers of Art Histories

Living and Sustaining a Creative Life

The Living and Sustaining a Creative Life series of books reveal the realities of today's artists and culture producers. These timely publications comprise essays that generously share innovative models of creative lives that have been sustained over many years. Their first-hand stories show the general public how contemporary artists, creative individuals and change-makers of the twenty first century add to creative economies through their out-of-the-box thinking, while also contributing to the well-being of others. Although there is a misconception that artists are invisible and hidden, the truth is that they furnish measurable and innovative outcomes at the front lines of education, the non-profit sector, and corporate environments. Intended to spark conversations across and beyond the arts, each path is an inspiring example that provides exceptional insight.

All of the contributors have been chosen by guest editors who are distinctive and generous in their own lives. It is my hope you enjoy each essay as much as I have. I believe they will surely inspire new avenues for artists to thrive for years to come.

– Sharon Louden, Living and Sustaining
a Creative Life series editor

Storytellers of Art Histories

Living and Sustaining a Creative Life

Edited by Alpesh Kantilal Patel and Yasmeen Siddiqui

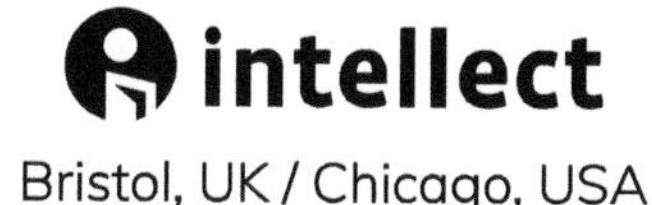

Bristol, UK / Chicago, USA

First published in the UK in 2022 by
Intellect, The Mill, Parnall Road, Fishponds, Bristol, BS16 3JG, UK

First published in the USA in 2022 by
Intellect, The University of Chicago Press, 1427 E. 60th Street,
Chicago, IL 60637, USA

A catalogue record for this book is available from the British Library.

Cover image: Shazia Sikander *Promiscuous Identities*
Patinated bronze 2020 Courtesy of Sean Kelly Gallery
Photo by Jason Wyche
Copy editor: Newgen
Production manager: Tim Mitchell
Typesetting: Newgen
Cover and book design: Holly Rose

Print ISBN 978-1-78938-427-7
ePDF ISBN 978-1-78938-428-4
ePub ISBN 978-1-78938-429-1

Part of the Living and Sustaining a Creative Life series
Print ISSN: 2516-3574 | Online ISSN: 2516-3582

CONTENTS

PREFACE

The cover of our book is a painted bronze sculpture by our contributor Shahzia Sikander. Perhaps well known for her work in manuscript painting, she has worked in a variety of media, such as animation and collaborative performance. We both saw this—Yasmeen in person and Alpesh virtually—in December 2020 when it was first exhibited at Sean Kelly Gallery. On a basic level, Sikander's work brings together two lineages—the Greco-Roman and (South) Asian. The two figures are intertwined—a Greek goddess and an Indian *devata*, or spiritual being.

At first glance, the arrangement of legs and arms suggests that the goddess is carrying the weight of the *devata*. Or is the latter pushing against or away from the former? It is both/and rather than either/or. Indeed, the delicate interplay between pushing and pulling is a profound metaphor for what Gayatri Gopinath writes are the "promiscuous intimacies," a phrase Sikander appropriates for the title of the sculpture, "of multiple times, spaces, art historical traditions, bodies, desires and subjectivities."[1]

Sikander's work challenges our assumptions of division (Greco-Roman, Indian) and thereby opens up a space for the writing of a different history of art—one that is porous, conflicted, antiracist, and not heteronormative. The contributors to this volume boldly disrupt borders and divisions—disciplinary and otherwise—and we dedicate this anthology to them for graciously sharing parts of their lives in their deliberate messiness.

Note

1. Gayatri Gopinath, "Promiscuous Intimacies: Embodiment, Desire and Diasporic Dislocation in the Art of Shahzia Sikander," in *Shahzia Sikander: Extraordinary Realities, eds. Sadia Abbas and Jan Howard* (Munich: Hirmer, 2021), 119.

INTRODUCTION: THE STORY BEHIND STORYTELLERS

Alpesh Kantilal Patel and Yasmeen Siddiqui

IN EARLY 2017, Sharon Louden asked if we would be interested in editing an anthology for her *Living and Sustaining a Creative Life* book series, which focuses on the lives of artists working today. This was to be a book about the lives of art historians. She saw a confluence: Alpesh an art historian and theorist working within the academy, Yasmeen an itinerant writer and curator. Both of us, in our realms, eschew orthodoxies and ready-made interpretations of the ways artists have worked and continue to work.

Alpesh was intrigued because his own art historical scholarship often involves bringing himself into the histories of art he writes. He felt quite strongly that if art historians would make their stakes in the subjects about which they write visible, then it would be clear that these histories are subjective. Yasmeen's practice involves working closely with artists, designers, editors, and authors. She is interested in long-term engagements with a broad array of meaning makers to build exhibitions, books, and conversations. This project caught her attention as an opportunity to examine and, perhaps, expand the application of the subject at hand, art histories.

We realized early on that contemporary art histories were being written by a range of individuals and that we wanted the anthology to reflect this fact. For instance, we discussed how archives become so important as source material for many historians, and yet archivists are rarely brought to the forefront for the integral roles they play in writing histories. Also, artists have increasingly begun to deconstruct histories as knowledge. Of course, curators and art historians have more traditionally been seen as shapers of knowledge. Yet, at the same time, we noted a huge ideological divide between curatorial studies and those shaping the histories of art—despite the fact that the display of artworks and the beginnings of the writings of art history emerge together and are therefore intertwined.

The writing of histories is about storytelling, which is by its very nature subjective, yet histories are usually taught and presented as inviolable truths. We wanted to frame the anthology through the lens of "storytellers" rather than "art historians." As Gayatri Chakravorty Spivak writes, "History is, after all, a storying. The French language has it very conveniently in the word *histoire* which means both history and story."[1]

We focused on those who were actively dealing with issues of gender, race (including Whiteness), class, sexuality, and trans/nationality.[2] We are proud that we have twice as many contributions by women than men. We also felt that we did not want this anthology to somehow appear as something radical that had never been done before. Therefore, we purposefully focused on an intergenerational approach that would bring together individuals who are early or mid-career with those who have been pushing against cisgender White males for decades. We also wanted to make sure that contributors would not only come from the Euro-American monolith. While the dominant art history is a collection of stories of art from Western Europe and North America, it is generally not marked as the regional art history it is.

Once all of the above was in place, we had to figure out who to invite. Following the format of Sharon's previous books, we aimed to have 25 to 30 contributors, each of whom would write up to roughly two thousand words. Our long list of names can readily fill at least two anthologies. In the end, we had 35 contributors in total. The individuals we invited reflect the networks we have both developed through our work. Those we did not know were recommended by colleagues.

Each contributor is actively engaging with producing "art historical futures" impacting a broad range of culture sectors. This term and idea, "art historical futures," was fixating. Our aim is to address the ties that tether futures to pasts. How might we write for the futures we envision without losing sight of what was, what has been? Alongside commissioning this book, we organized the panel "A Reckoning with the Recent Future of Art Historical Knowledge Production" for the 2019 College Art Association (CAA) conference. We crafted a group that would introduce artist Allan deSouza, curator Candice Hopkins, archivist Josh T Franco, art historian Marsha Meskimmon, and director Namita Wiggers in a discussion encouraging a close and honest look at our interdependence as researchers working in and for different types of institutions. In 2021, we continued this inquiry through our moderated panel "Futures of 'Activist' Scholarship" at CAA's annual conference, which invited artist Shahzia Sikander, art historian Jenni Sorkin, and curator Alexandra Chang to reflect on their relationships to art history and their work in its destabilization.

Each individual in this book has provided short, often very personal contributions indicating how they began to become passionate about their practice. Indeed, another way in which histories function more honestly as stories is if the authors become visible and this effectively underpins their subjectivities (even if unconsciously so) and the subjectivity of scholarly writing. This anthology aims to show the highly interested nature of the work the various contributors do while not undermining the rigor of their practices.

It is worth noting that we came across the Spivak quotation in art historian Moira Roth's engaging book *Difference/ Indifference: Musings on Postmodernism, Marcel Duchamp and John Cage*.[3] It is written in a diaristic style and embodies the kind of critical art history that we believe should be written. We kept this in mind when we wrote a "prompt" for our contributors to respond: "Of particular interest to us is your providing a first-person account of your stakes in the field, how you maintain and nurture your own practice in the face of overwhelming odds against the feminist, decolonial, anti-racist, transnational, and queer work you do, the events that led you to this work, and why you chose this path."

The contributors responded in a multitude of surprising ways, appealing equally to people enmeshed in the field through their work and to those simply interested in the field. The stories you will read take various forms—a letter written to a friend, a re-visioned grant application, the pastiche of image and text, children's fables, interviews, coauthored narrative, memoir, manifesto, apology. A number of the essays perform, through a combination of recollected early memory alongside scholarly research, the roots of the theories they explore through publishing, curating, and archival work.

The writings in this anthology reflect our strong interest in amplifying the voices of those who are reshaping art histories. An overwhelming majority of our contributors have fluid practices that make categories like art historian, archivist, curator, or artist moot. Collecting this range of narratives born from different workplaces and disciplines speaks to our belief in the potential boundlessness of the art history that shapes the stories we consume.

Notes

1. Gayatri Chakravorty Spivak interviewed by Alfred Arteaga, "Bonding in Difference," in *An Other Tongue: Nation and Ethnicity in the Linguistic Borderlands*, ed. Alfred Arteaga (Durham: Duke University Press, 1994), 283.
2. Intellect's house style is to capital "W" in "white," however we have left the decision about whether or not to capitalize to each individual author.
3. Moira Roth and Jonathan D. Katz, eds., *Difference/ Indifference: Musings on Postmodernism, Marcel Duchamp and John Cage* (Amsterdam: GB Arts International, 1998).

NANA ADUSEI-POKU

I MUST HAVE been about 8 or 9 years old when my primary school teacher Ms. Wilbrandt took my class on a trip to the Folkwang Museum Essen. It is one of Germany's oldest museums and, as I would learn much later, one of the world's first "Modern Art"-collecting museums, deeply entangled with the history of colonialism and Enlightenment thinking, which degraded people of African descent into the abyss of non-humanness. The art educator—a young white woman, not surprisingly—sat us down in front of the Marc Chagall painting called *Le Champ de Mars* from 1954. We interpreted the painting together, learned about Chagall's exile during World War II and being othered as a French-Russian Jew, and I started to understand that the narrative of his predominantly blue-colored Surrealist painting expressed a deep longing for a notion of wholeness that seemed to have been denied to him. With this realization about the importance and history of art and its contexts, my path wasn't set, but a spark in my imagination about the power of art was seeded in my understanding of the world. I was able to connect to Chagall's longing; being born as a German/Dutch-Ghanaian into a working-class family in the 1980s meant that the notion of difference was ingrained into my understanding of self. Sometimes positive but more often in a negative way (particularly after the Reunification, when neo-Nazis didn't stop yelling "Germany to the Germans" and "Foreigners out"), I knew that I was considered a foreigner; I connected deeply to the notion of unbelonging that Chagall touched on and dreaming oneself into an alternate reality just to not be present in the reality that shaped my otherness. I also did not yet know that I had more in common with Chagall, since Black Germans were equally killed by the Nazi regime, something I understood intuitively in front of his painting that became clearer much later when I learned about Black German history through Black German scholars. This encounter with Chagall's painting came in 1990, the same year I started to go to a local ballet school and take piano lessons, and shortly after, I was enrolled in an old humanist gymnasium, all due to my mother's class uplift aspirations. I would only understand in retrospect how much this kind of upbringing would change my habitus and provide access to people I would never have had contact with otherwise: it was a painful realization how expansive symbolic violence is when I studied Bourdieu for the first time while receiving a master's degree in London.

So much about my process of subjectification is connected to being a Black person growing up in a predominantly white and inherently former colonial society marked and haunted by the cruelties of the Shoah. It wasn't that my desired career as a ballet dancer didn't happen because I was a bad dancer—it didn't happen because my teachers had no imagination for a Black ballerina. My desired acting career didn't happen because nobody could imagine me as a Gretchen in Goethe's *Faust*. What people could imagine for me was to dance in the Moulin Rouge as a showgirl with a bare chest and lots of sparkles; I was told by one of my ballet friend's mothers that she thought I had the right body for it.

I knew that this couldn't be true and that something wasn't right: all of my white friends succeeded and were encouraged in their desired paths, but not me? I came to understand all of these different systemic forms of exclusion and over-sexualization years later, that is, while reading Frantz Fanon and bell hooks when I started my studies. The works that I read with my Black German friends were not necessarily taught in our curricula nor supported by my professors. I was enrolled at the Humboldt University for African Studies and Gender Studies in 2001, and it remained very white until I made my first Black German friends, who introduced me to the Initiative for Black People Living in Germany (Initiative Schwarze Menschen in Deutschland) and ADEFRA (Afro-German Women). I put emphasis on this part of my journey—which was, until that point, a continuous grappling with my identity—because everything changed through the works of other Black German, African American, Afro-Caribbean, Black British, and African thinkers that I was exposed to for the first time through my friends and the two Black adjuncts Peggy Piesche and Grada Kilomba.

After spending a year from 2003 to 2004 in Ghana living with my family and feeling recharged, I finished my BA and knew I needed to go to the place where so many of the thinkers I admired had taught before. A close friend had left his Stuart Hall collection in my apartment when he moved to London, and I was enthralled by Hall's thinking. I knew I needed to study for my MA at Goldsmiths and enrolled in 2008. I returned to the subject of art when I wrote my Ph.D. proposal. I was often asked why I remained in academia around that time, and I knew it was because I wanted to produce knowledge and add something to the ongoing conversations. I was eager to understand how Black artists imagine the world and how I could make sense of being in the world as a Black person, how it shifts and is expressed through art. The graduate program "Gender as a Category of Knowledge," which was initiated by the Center for Transdisciplinary Gender Studies, became the space to discuss and defend my ideas for three years before I moved to the Netherlands, where I held the position of Research Professor for Cultural Diversity—a token position that utilized my otherness in order to blame the project of diversity for its failing. Whereas I was always not academic enough in Germany, I was often turned into the too academic and theoretical person in the Netherlands. I found a possibility to work on my vision through a curatorial fellowship at the Witte de With Center for Contemporary Art, where I was able to work curatorially for the first time. The synergy between artists, theory, giving talks, arranging different formats of programming, and teaching creates the web in which I find a way to express my love for Black people and my admiration for art and allows me to find solace in a world that is still deeply threatened by difference. I am not surprised that I find myself now in the Center for Curatorial Studies, since it encompasses all the different fields that I engage in and is breaking down traditional ideas about disciplines and art history. Curatorial Studies is a field that is constantly in the making and doesn't really fit, which I try to utilize to create ruptures that challenge hegemonic ideas of normativity that are based on antiblackness. I am not surprised that I feel like I have arrived.

MICHELLE ANTOINETTE

BORN IN AUSTRALIA, I'm the child of Mauritian Creole migrants who left behind a context of political upheaval and social turbulence in Mauritius in the early 1970s, arriving in Australia just before the lifting of the infamous "White Australia" policy in 1973. Mauritius became independent in 1968, and the withdrawal of British colonial governance saw rising civil unrest between the country's different ethnic groups. Mauritian Creoles—broadly defined by their mix of European colonial and African slave ancestries, especially after French colonization—feared that their livelihoods and future prospects would be threatened as a now-minority ethnic group in a decolonizing Mauritius that was predominately ethnically Indian after British colonization. This is why, in this period, many Creoles migrated to other countries—chiefly England, France, Canada, and Australia.

Remarkably, as a quirk of Australia's migration history, the discriminatory White Australia policy that had come into law in 1901 was able to be bypassed by some Mauritian Creoles since the early twentieth century as a result of their hybrid, "mixed-race" identity. With their part English and/or European colonial cultural inheritances, they were permitted an easier entry to Australia compared with other "non-whites." Mauritian Creole migration to Australia was at its height, however, after Mauritius became independent in 1968. As with Australia, Mauritius became a member of the British Commonwealth, and English was entirely familiar as the language of British colonial governance. These factors enabled Mauritian Creoles' bureaucratic passing for "White" even if, as it was discovered upon their arrival into Australia, it turned out Mauritian Creoles came in all shades, as is the case with my extended family—a likely mélange of African, French, English, Seychellois, and Dutch heritages at the very least, as far as I've been able to work out through the opacities and obscurations of colonial histories. Different shades of White, Brown, and Black is the typical character of my family's Creole experience.

This inherited history of cultural hybridity and heterogeneity has always underpinned my sense of who I am and how I belong in the world, especially in the context of an ever-changing Australian society and an increasingly globalized world. While my identity has been shaped by multiple generations before me with their Creole histories "over there" in Mauritius, I have also grown up as part of the multicultures of modern Australia "over here," with an increasingly diverse collection of cultures, including from Asia, since the end of the White Australia policy. Likewise, in my intellectual work, my hybrid identity has directed me toward critical explorations and questions about how and why racial and ethnic identities come to be shaped, represented, and essentialized and to consider how we can uphold the integrity of different cultural histories while also respecting the generative possibilities of their complexities, ambiguities, and nuances. It likely also explains my cross-cultural and transnational approach to writing art histories, be they between Australia and Asia, Asia and other places, or within Asia itself—such as in Southeast Asia, my area of special interest.

My initial experiences of Asia are associated with the bodily nourishment I received in my Mauritian Creole familial context. As a Creole cuisine, Mauritian food is a coming together of African, French, Chinese, and Indian gastronomy—the diverse scents and flavors of my family's kitchens. Notably, the closest familial bond I had in my childhood was the one I shared with my maternal grandmother, who was renowned in suburban Melbourne's Mauritian diaspora community for her exceptional culinary skills. Alongside the French-influenced Creole dishes she would make, such as spicy tomato-based *rougaille* plates and *bouillon* (soup), were the Indian-influenced dishes, including curries, *gateaux piments* (dhall-based chili cakes), and her especially famous *faratas* (parathas), as well as homemade *wan tan* (wonton dumplings), fried rice and noodle dishes, *mee foon* (vermicelli), and fish ball soups, all inspired by Chinese cooking. From childhood, I'd accompany my grandmother and mother on their regular trips to the nearby "Asian" shopping hub, which they referred to as the "Chinese" grocers (*la boutique Chinois*), but in reality, these were mostly Vietnamese-owned and operated shops stocking a variety of "exotic" Asian supplies that the mainstream supermarkets didn't supply at the time. Notably, when our extended family had an occasion to celebrate, the venue of choice was always a suburban Chinese restaurant, which actually was very often the only non-Western cuisine you could find across Australian suburbs at that time.

Unconventionally for modern-day Australian society, from a young age I lived between my grandmother's flat and my parents' house. My grandmother's little flat was absolutely chock full of stuff. Maybe it was about migrating to a new place with very few possessions and feeling a certain comfort in accumulating things, but then she wasn't at all materialistic and got much more joy out of giving to others. Whatever the case, I would experience her impulse to gather things, especially during my weekly chores, when I'd have to dust and shine all the rickety photo-stands and other family memorabilia that crowded the flat and sat among an abundance of Catholic religious imagery: saintly clock fixtures; figurines of the much-revered patron saint of Mauritius, Père Laval; a host of other saints pictured on wall hangings; the sacred heart of Jesus beaming from a shiny wall hanging; rosary beads of all kinds; and printed prayers displayed wherever there was a gap to fill. But every now and again, even this domestic shrine to Catholicism would need some extra help when it was suspected that someone's evil eye or envious heart had brought upon serious misfortune and illness to the family; my Gran would turn to non-Christian homely spells from time to time when these forces of evil needed to be properly expelled out of our lives. As a constant, a horseshoe would hang over the front door as a lucky charm, and for good luck of another kind, a humble Laughing Buddha sat on a display shelf, ready to have its belly rubbed in the hope of wealth and prosperity. This syncretic belief is a marker of being Creole, of the coming together of diverse spiritual and superstitious traditions in Mauritius.

In retrospect, while I can see why my journey to being an historian of Asian art might seem like the furthest possible career option imaginable for someone growing up in Melbourne's suburbs as a child of working-class Creole migrants from a tiny, little-known island called Mauritius, in fact, it always felt quite organic. Growing up in Australia in the 1980s and 1990s, I was part of a cultural shift that saw Australians contemplate monumental national issues such as multiculturalism, native title, and republicanism, while also grappling with the multiple definitions and implications of our changing identity and place in Australia, the region, and the world. Australia was seeking to redefine its place in the world, hoping to cut its umbilical ties with the British colonial motherland and become a republic, resituating Australia as part of an Asia Pacific regional imaginary that would have fuller regard for Australia's proximate geographies and cultural histories. Alongside this was a strengthening political consciousness to recognize the Indigenous peoples as the owners and first inhabitants of the land now known as Australia and to acknowledge the violence and traumas inflicted upon them since White colonial settlement, which continue today.

My childhood and teen years in Melbourne in the 1980s and 1990s were also formative in defining what I experienced as regular "Australian" multicultural life. In inner-city Melbourne, we lived closely with Jewish communities, and when my family moved to the suburbs, our nearest neighbors were Chilean, Anglo-Celtic, Italian, and Greek. We all got on well together and welcomed each other into our respective homes. This working-class multi and interculturality also characterized my schooling. I went to primary and secondary schools where there were so many migrant kids or kids of migrants with cultural attachments of all kinds that I never felt out of place, or as if the White kids dominated in any way.

Always academically inclined, I enjoyed and took great pride in my learning at school and I was just ever curious about the world. It was really only at high school that I developed a more focused interest in art, taking it as a study subject throughout my secondary schooling. I was fortunate to have a dedicated art teacher who showed us how art-making and learning about art's history opened up possibilities to learn about so many other things alongside art, including to think creatively *and* critically about the world. I didn't know it then, but this was the start of my art historical training.

As a teenager, every Saturday I would listen to the sounds of the American Top 40—it was the easiest way to tune into the latest R&B and hip-hop tracks, since there really wasn't much of it available on mainstream Australian radio at the time. I'd catch up with others in our "Black–Brown" community to ask if they'd heard the latest tunes or seen the newest dance moves. Black American popular culture provided a huge frame of cultural reference for myself and others at the time, in a context where mainstream popular culture in Australia was otherwise absolutely dominated by images of Whiteness. We sang to R&B tunes and busted hip-hop moves to Salt-N-Pepa and TLC in our brightly colored overalls and oversized hoop earrings.

All through high school, I studied the Japanese language, and in my final year, I went to Japan as part of a school study trip, staying with a host family in Fukuoka. Little did I know that years later, I would reconnect with Fukuoka in my academic work, as the city houses the Fukuoka Asian Art Museum, which holds one of the world's finest collections of modern and contemporary Southeast Asian art.

When I did my undergraduate training in Australia in the 1990s, some of the problems within art history departments had already begun to be identified. There was a concerted push by many to overhaul the sexist, racist, and elite high-art concerns of traditional art history, a push especially influenced by the work of feminist, postcolonial, and visual culture theorists and by new generations of art practitioners whose identities and work challenged art history's traditional biases. Yet from my Australian base, much of this curricular and institutional shift curiously neglected to consider modern and contemporary art histories linked to Australia's nearest geographical neighbors. It was then that I committed to a program of further studies on contemporary Asian art, after becoming increasingly familiar with Asia through my undergraduate studies and backpacking travels. Also hugely formative was working directly with contemporary Asian artists and art when I interned with the Queensland Art Gallery in preparation for the Third Asia-Pacific Triennial of Contemporary Art in 1999.

Today, an Indigenous Australian teacher reminds us that it's respectful to "place" ourselves when we meet with Indigenous people. It's Blackfella way. This means that Indigenous Australians can subsequently position us in the context of the Indigenous lands we live in. It's the "where are you from?" question that I had struggled with at earlier moments of my life because of all the cultural biases it usually encapsulated, but this time, *who's* asking the question and *why* they're asking matters differently. I live and work on the lands of Indigenous Australians whose "place" and "place-making" traditions were ripped from them upon White colonial settlement. Place is quite literally where Indigenous Australian identification resides and finds its agency, but it's something I've personally tended to resist because I don't feel it necessarily tells the complexity of the cultural histories that have shaped me. As is often the case with children of migrant heritage, there is more than one place and culture that shapes us, and for me, being placed into one assumed identity linked to a place label can feel disempowering. For instance, another label I have often had to contend with is being "Australian." What does it mean when I say I'm Australian, as opposed to when someone from a White Anglophone background says it? It's often enough for the White Australian to leave it at that, but I have often found myself having to further explain why I am an Australian with Brown skin and an "exotic" name. So I've tended to dislike the "where are you from?" question, because it's often been asked by those who really want to inquire, "Why are you brown-skinned with a French name? How can I understand your Brownness and interest in Asia in the context of White-settler Australia? Are you Indigenous or Aboriginal? Do you have an Asian connection, is that why you study Asian art? Okay, so you're Australian, but why don't you look like the typical white-skinned, blond-haired Aussie?" Well, actually, lived Australia looks a lot different from this popular-culture stereotype.

My family was "accepted" here on White settler terms as new migrants to Australia and I was born here, so there's an ongoing process of colonization that I contend with in terms of conscious and unconscious migrant complicity in displacing Indigenous Australians and their histories. Like many others of my generation and earlier, I was not given any meaningful education about Indigenous Australia through my schooling, and nor was my family given this information upon migrating to Australia to pass on to me. So in my adulthood, despite being "born into Australia," I find myself continually "becoming Australian" by continuing to educate myself and others where I can about these marginalized Indigenous histories that I didn't get taught about, the real histories of this country, the place from which I began doing art history.

REGINE BASHA

DEAREST YASMEEN,

I have chosen to write to you about my "curatorial origin story" in the form of a letter, to keep the long-lost format of writing between art colleagues alive—in the way that Sol LeWitt did with Lucy Lippard or Eva Hesse. So thank you for giving me a chance to reflect, share, and yes, sometimes rant! To characterize how curating came into my life, I borrow from the title of a Basim Magdy exhibition catalogue I recently wrote for: "Would a firefly fear the fire that burns in its heart?"

With some trepidation, I've opened up the boxes of journals, notebooks, and diaries (stretching decades back to 1988) that trigger dread each time I look at their covers. I have gone through most of them, and in between the chronicles and casualties of many art lives and many love lives, I have sifted various "major themes" out. It has become a process of splitting myself into two and surveying this growing curator from a bit of a distance. I don't think this rereading of my own younger self would be possible to do well, or at all, if not for the work I currently do with MFA students.

A few things I can say right off the top: I wish I had focused more on my own professional trajectory. It appears as though I have, over the years, lived very much in the moment. You know how it can be. Every move or transition was aligned with some love interest or driven by a temporary project. There must be a book in there about the concurrence of art and love à la Kathy Acker driven by a restless rolling, a regular five-year urge to move. Flight is a feeling deeply woven, perhaps tied to family. I am the child of Iraqi Jews who fled.

There is also, of course, the ranting that is throughout the journals: on repeat are cries about seeking "sustenance" in the art world (health care, decently paid work) and, then, of course, the rant about male dominance and bro culture—specifically the remarkable way men tend to breeze through, fuck up, reinvent, and bounce back out of bad situations they've created. I've witnessed this on personal and professional fronts so many times, and it amazes me how so much of this continues to play out. Hopefully with all the light we are shedding on this now, change is on its way.

I can find broad themes when I follow the footsteps set in my secret-unicorn-curatorial-fairy story.

I was always an early bloomer but a latecomer socially—meaning, at 11, I looked like I was 18, and it took time for my inner self to catch up with this outer person. I spent a lot of time in my room rearranging the objects on my shelf as if they spoke to me (true story). I also spent a lot of time staring at things until they looked odd. My mother was a homemaker but painted like Cézanne as a hobby, and my dad was a businessman who played the oud and the violin at parties. I stayed mostly behind the scenes at Beverly Hills High (which I attended only because of my parents' diligent scheming to get me into the right side of that zip code). My friends were either immigrant smart kids or talented misfit dropouts, who were into music, art, and a shared sarcasm about school. By senior year I had finally cracked the code of the place and got invited into an exclusive "popular party," where one of the blond girls, who literally sat next to me in math class all year, turned to me and said, "Hi! OMG, are you new?" This, I believe, was my first training ground for the art world.

More training came out of my own diasporic immigrant family, who performed the classic "two lives" in the United States: one for the home or in the "tribe" and one for the outside world. My parents came from Iraq, and we maintained a strong adherence to the culture—in food, language, and the music we listened to in the house. Though they fled to Israel, where I was born, we moved to Montreal soon after, in 1969. I understood in my bones, my blood, what it means to develop the necessary "public persona" (the "where are you from" question was always too complicated for an Arab Jew to answer). I also developed great observation skills, as I felt like somewhat of an "outsider" most of the time—even at home—so my ability to draw well from observation grew. These observational drawings led me to the studio art program at NYU in 1987. Why NYU? Because I spotted Grace Jones on a street near campus and thought, "That's it—I need to live in New York!" How teens make decisions.

But it really wasn't until one unusual class, taken during junior year abroad in Italy, that I really woke up to a more integrated self. Tucked away in a generic clearinghouse for American students in Florence called Scuola Lorenzo de' Medici were two teachers who went by the combined name of Rosenclaire (Rose Shakinovsky and Claire Gavronsky). They were a lesbian couple, activists from South Africa (close collaborators of William Kentridge), who team-taught art history, theory, and studio art. They argued a lot and had conflicting styles and opinions, which pushed us to think critically. They had a unique ability to discuss, for example, Giotto as though he were an experimental contemporary artist. Upon my return to NYU, I changed my major from studio art to art history and soon moved back to Montreal.

NYU's price tag was exorbitant, and Montreal felt more European—and, well, it had *free education and health care*! One year turned into five unexpected years in which I suddenly became a working curator. It was during this time that I learned everything, A–Z, about exhibition production, fundraising internationally, and running a small nonprofit. This is one story in which unpaid volunteer work actually did amount to a substantial job. I entered as a volunteer, became the assistant to the director, then became the director of the Saidye Bronfman Gallery—a contemporary art space housed in a Jewish Community Center that was built by Phyllis Lambert (a Mies van der Rohe protégé). This gallery (now in a different location and called SBC Gallery) had a great international reputation, weirdly, and was beloved in the Canadian art world thanks to the former director. My coming in at 22 to take the job offended a lot of people locally. The argument the director had for hiring me was that, though I was young, I was familiar with both the (divided) Jewish and French communities and their complicated politics and could move between them easily. My being from an Arabic culture also complicated the Ashkenazi stronghold of the place, plus I had tremendous energy to work hard (and for low pay). Months after the hire, I continued to see the former director socially, which developed into an affair, and despite my hard work, I had to contend with a judgy public that thought my initial hire was purely for that reason. It was a difficult time, with big lessons learned. Luckily, my board believed in me and supported me as I brought in challenging shows, international shows, and cultivated a more mixed and diverse audience for the gallery.

At the tail end of five years, needing to regroup, I heard about a place, you and I share, Yasmeen, the Bard College Center for Curatorial Studies (CCS) Museum, and decided to enter the program's first cohort, which meant a move back to the States. CCS was perfectly suited for the likes of me. The inaugural class was very clearly a petri dish of applicants. Some people had years of art world experience, while others came from other fields: from a poet from Croatia and an anthropologist who was also a Yoruba priestess to a fiction writer in her 40s. Everyone, including the faculty—inspiring people like Vasif Kortun, Norton Batkin, Linda Norden, Ivo Mesquita, Lynne Cooke, Thelma Golden, Peter Schjeldahl, and others—were speculating on what to do with a "Curatorial Program" and how to "teach" curating, especially to a cohort with such varied backgrounds. It was pretty phenomenal to get to witness close-up what Thelma was thinking during her "Black Male" show; watch as Lynne Cooke (then at Dia) developed her show pairing Alighiero Boetti with Frédéric Bruly Bouabré; or learn from Mary Jane Jacobs germinating what is now called "social practice," working hard on "Places with a Past" in Charleston. My own graduate thesis (which was about drawing and mark-making) helped me articulate thoughts about experimentation in general. From this point on, everything changed, and I began to work both more independently and more collaboratively.

There are a few key stages that shaped me—the years 1997–2000 were probably my most wild and raucous, driven by working within exhibition collaboratives (*Mayday* with Anton Vidokle and Christoph Gerozissis, and *The Brewster Project* with Christopher Ho and Omar Lopez-Chahoud, and many others like Rachel Gugelberger and Sara Reisman). I also had a two-year contract working with Michael Krichman and Carmen Ramirez on InSITE 97. InSITE was a binational initiative and partnership formed in the mid-1990s of cultural bodies, institutions, and community centers that collaborated on public, site-specific projects on and across the San Diego/Tijuana border, but that reflected "the Americas." It truly was a phenomenal endeavor that I can't imagine happening today. The organizers and the artists aimed to unpack issues around community engagement, identity politics, and trauma tourism, and—like with many big productions such as these—sometimes the projects were amazing, and other times they suffered from "trying too hard," but the overall experiment was completely worthwhile. I learned a ton, and I can say that I went on to draw from this experience in my own independent projects involving site specificity, such as *The Marfa Sessions*. After this time, I became increasingly interested in artwork that was developed through deep research, consideration of place, and historical revisionism.

Another pivotal period of time came after 9/11, which, of course, overwhelmed everything. One of my journal entries was written when I was working as a cultural affairs officer for the Canadian Consulate General New York, the day I was confirming an appointment for October 11, 2001, with the INS (Immigration and Naturalization Services) to become American. The INS building was completely shut down when I finally did arrive for the appointment in October. Strangely, I was becoming an American and in the position of a cultural diplomat for another country, when the Twin Towers fell, which confounded my own sense of identity in myriad ways. This might have somehow contributed to my choice to move away from (flee?) New York to Texas one year later with my then boyfriend (soon-to-be husband). Many could hardly forgive us for leaving New York and moving to Bush-land! Though I went for love, leaving behind my community and not knowing a single person out there was hard. I had to hope for the best. To my surprise, it was actually during those six years in Texas that I met some of the most genuinely generous and supportive people in my career—patrons, artists, professors, curators—and I became extremely productive. I secured a job as a curator (for Arthouse, now called The Contemporary Austin) and also helped form other new initiatives like Fluent~Collaborative and Testsite, which helped cross-pollinate artists with writers in a salon-style setup in the home of Laurence Miller. In this scale of city, I felt very much a part of a collective effort to seed and advance the whole ecosystem for art.

The six-year mark saw us return to New York for my then spouse's big job opportunity at the Cisneros Foundation. I too was itching to move back as soon as the question of bearing a child came into discussion—I wanted a closeness with family and deeper community ties. But it was hard. Harder than anticipated. I faced a lukewarm reception from my New York colleagues too busy and beleaguered to care about what I did in Texas, and we had to weather a financial crisis (2008) that hit the job market—it was dry for me in New York. Around this time, our son was born and the marriage fell apart: a long story I will chalk up to the challenges faced by two curators trying to make it in a marriage, with the male being more absent, "itinerant," engaging in several extramarital work affairs. It's not the first story of its kind. Yet I was blindsided—mentally, physically, and emotionally—and tasked with having to navigate the NYC special needs educational system for our small child. I felt for a while as though I was timeless and placeless, functioning only in the minutiae of the urgent, moment to moment. I did not see two steps in front of me for a good few years. In fact, those years were a veritable blur of doctors, lawyers, and therapists—for all three of us. To this day, I leap to help others who go through this kind of thing, as I remember how people have helped me along the way.

Somehow, though, a couple of my favorite shows grew out of this otherwise dark period: *Exchange with Sol LeWitt* (at MASS MoCA and Cabinet Magazine), which put out a massive call for artists to gift a work to Sol LeWitt posthumously, and *Speculative Futures*, an all-women series of sculptural interventions at the Bloomberg Financial Headquarters with Julieta Aranda, Beth Campbell, Cao Fei, and Ana Prvački. I also decided to further develop an audiovisual website for my archive *Tuning Baghdad*, narrating the musical parties I grew up around and Iraqi-Jewish musical history, as it seemed apt to work on the past while raising the future (my son Ruben). I discovered valuable methods for self-care, including Ayurveda, which I studied for a year. Eventually, we got through that time, and now many years later, with my son a robust and healthy preteen, we are all stronger and pretty functional as a co-parenting family (with a new stepmom in the mix).

What saved me during that difficult period was a different kind of engagement with the art world: joining the Executive Board of Art Matters Foundation and working with MFA students on their thesis shows (giving me a sense of agency and service to a new generation); collaborating with Michael

Rakowitz and Ella Shohat on the *Dar Al Sulh* dinners (giving me a more collaborative forum to water my Arab-Jewish roots, no longer alone but with others); and becoming more involved with residency programs, especially on the interdisciplinary conversations at Pioneer Works, where I recently worked. The parameters of curating and how it may evolve, in the field and for me personally, are on my mind and in flux, given the great changes afoot globally.

What gives me hope today is witnessing the beginning of an awakening, and I am considering my own version of that at the start of this new decade. As I write this last sentence, 2020 is four hours away, numbers that excite and terrify me. I will be sure to come up for air, resisting a tendency to hold my breath.

With my deepest gratitude,
Xo, Regine

ABBY CHEN

I AM OFTEN asked when I started to develop a sense of feminism. It is hard to say, but one early experience while growing up in Shandong, China, stands out as foundational: As a little girl, I always wanted to have long hair and braids. Both my parents worked, and there was little time to comb my hair every day. So, as a result, I did not have longer hair until high school. During this time, I learned there were several techniques involved in keeping long, healthy hair. Some of these I learned myself through trial and error. For instance, every time I tried to grow it, the hair would get messy, so much so that I didn't know how to deal with it and would have to give up. It was only later when I lived in a dorm that my classmates helped cut my hair in a bob style to allow it to grow out evenly. It was only then that I could start to apply any of the styles my teenager self found fashionable. This was how I learned to ask for help when I couldn't figure something out on my own and to keep on asking until I got the answers needed. It might sound funny, but in retrospect, the way I learned about dealing with hair has helped me be an effective curator and also solve problems outside of the art world. That is, learning on one's own, asking friends and colleagues for help, and finally inquiring again and again until one has answered your query are all traits I feel helped me become gutsy in my curating.

As I noted above, I grew up primarily in China. When I moved to the United States, I initially studied business but found great interest and passion in photography and became a curator focusing on migration and diaspora. It was a path I never would have thought of taking if it hadn't been for the aura of art illuminated by visual image. Art's instantaneity and elusiveness somehow ripped the shield I inhabited in a foreign land. Even to this day, I am still guided by this original instinct I formed around that time, that art is this avenue for us to observe and intervene in the world we live in. I eventually found my way to California College of the Arts to pursue a master's degree in Visual and Critical Studies. Again, a bit similar to how I learned how to grow out my hair. It has been sixteen years since my first project opened at the San Francisco Arts Commission Gallery in 2003. Now, as the head of Contemporary Art at the Asian Art Museum in San Francisco, I have the feeling a new stage of this experiment is about to start.

In this essay, I want to focus on thinking about curating more expansively than within the White cube. Recently, I was involved in helping to create a handbook for ethical treatment of culture workers in the Chinese art world in particular. (While I live and work in San Francisco, I am constantly in dialogue with artists, curators, and others whose work is also based outside of the United States.) More to the point, my exhibitions have always emerged through my engagement with the world around me.

Like species DNA, migration and gender issues create thinking that gets manifested throughout my projects. To be fair and factual, I never curated any women-only exhibitions due to my skepticism about generic groupings based only on specific biological gender. It is also why, in 2010, I launched the Gender Identity Symposium in Guangzhou with Professor Ke Qianting. We invited investigative reporters, public policy scholars, and artists to discuss issues connected to feminism and queerness. This now seemingly rudimentary initiative laid the foundation for WOMEN我們 (a Mandarin homophone meaning both "women" and "we"), which focused on issues of feminism and included women, men, genderqueer artists, and LGBTQ NGOs from China, Hong Kong, and the United States. It was designated as the official exhibition of the Global Chinese Women and Visual Representation Conference organized by Wang Zheng from the University of Michigan, which took place in Shanghai through a partnership with Fudan University. The show was installed in a company showroom; they sell stone to builders. This collaboration was practical, saving on space fees, avoiding censorship, and maintaining curatorial autonomy.

WOMEN我們 was an unconventional exhibition on many accounts, but most importantly, it connected activists and artists. About six months after the show, Shanghai Nv Ai (girl love), artist Gao Ling with her *Hey! TTTTouch Me* (2010), and many who were directly or indirectly involved in the show staged *Occupy Shanghai Subway* (2012), which took the feminist resistance into highly controlled public space, inside both the subway car and the station in Shanghai. This performance/protest, voicing anger against the subway authority putting blame on women for being harassed, went instantly viral across the nation and beyond. The slogans "I can be slutty, you can't harass me" and "It's a dress, not a yes" came out of the protests and have been quoted continuously to this day. The experience further affirmed the curatorial direction I aspire to: Art as a form of expression is like water and air that doesn't need to be confined in a static space. It can also be recognized and curated as a core energy that enables action and movement.

On June 30, 2017, an open complaint was lodged in a WeChat group (China's online message application similar to WhatsApp or Telegram) against a male writer and HB Station Contemporary Art Research Center (HBS 黃邊站)—a well-respected, small alternative space affiliated with Guangzhou Times Museum in China—by a woman artist who had previously collaborated with this institution.[1] This was just a few months prior to the emergence of the #MeToo movement in the United States, which would soon take the world by storm, including China.

HB Station Contemporary Art Research Center has a staff of four, all of whom wear multiple hats: they are writers, artists, and curators. The organization has been an active platform engaging with local culture workers and beyond by organizing exhibitions, talks, publications, and residencies. A WeChat group was among HB's few initiatives that brought about meaningful discourse on feminism. In this group, there were about thirty members involved in art and interested in feminist issues. The institution did not respond to the woman's complaint, so she quit the group. In her absence, there was no immediate inquiry or action taken, or any offer to help her. Some members of the group questioned why she expressed rage, while others analyzed and theorized the incident as if it were abstract or someone not associated with the group. I would learn later that local art organizations took a similar approach, or worse, in response to her complaint. Another art space in Guangzhou, Observatory Society (觀察社), replied in the following way in an e-mail (December 18, 2017):

1. I don't know what happened, and it's not our obligation to investigate.
2. In all honesty, what you said doesn't constitute sexual harassment. But you were probably distressed (by this).
3. Hope you can find a simple and direct means to solve it.
4. If it's serious, call the police or social worker; otherwise solve it by yourself, and be smarter next time.
5. I hope the Guangzhou art scene can be free from all these unnecessary troubles. I am tired of such troubles. Let's focus on art, and focus on how to steer towards a better direction.

Furthermore, the collective United Motion (聯合公告), which advocates for gender equality, responded via email as follows (June 9, 2018):

1. We are volunteer-based. There's no employment relationship among our members.
2. We don't interfere with the members' work beyond our organization, nor are we responsible for their behavior. Moreover, members' behavior doesn't represent United Motion's position. Therefore, your complaint has no direct relationship to United Motion.
3. Although gender equality is an issue United Motion cares about, we tried to learn what happened, and it seems your complaint was responded to and handled by others.
4. On a personal level, we understand your anger, but for United Motion, there doesn't seem to be much we can do, given your complaint is already responded to (by HB). Can you clarify what you want from us? What kind of apology do you want, by whom? In what way?

Such responses are typical of the way victims are treated in China. Any reported incidents are troublemaking, and whoever reports them are troublemakers. You are on your own. Deal with it. Don't come to us for help. Of course, the government normally takes one more step by locking up the whistleblower as a solution.[2]

This woman artist did not give up. Despite all the personal and institutional disregard of her complaint, she continued to bring up the issue on social networks, including WeChat and the popular website douban.com.[3] Because of her persistence in keeping the issue alive, HB not only was under a lot of pressure to respond in a public manner but also needed to address all parties involved.

The woman artist's courage and refusal to let go of the issue presented an urgency for HB as a progressive space to take action. The four staff—Feng Junhua, Li Xiaotian, Liang Jianhua, and Zhu Jianlin—have all previously been active in bringing forward issues of feminism, labor, and community building for the region, largely through an academic lens. Their leadership and involvement for establishing a policy on sexual harassment will be significant in terms of best practices and models for other small organizations, even including those who are independent curators. Being small is not an excuse for lacking principles and policies. Wherever there is power, there is the potential for harassment, and there should be a system of prevention and checks and balances to intervene. As a matter of fact, this small entity presents a huge opportunity and opening to revolutionize how we can all take part in making changes within the harsh reality of disempowerment.

On August 26, 2017, about two months after this public complaint, Liang Jianhua, director of HB, reached out to me, hoping I could help with the situation. He told me all members of HB were under great stress at the time. No one had any experience dealing with such a complaint. On the one hand, they felt the urgency to address it as an institution, but on the other, they felt the accusations were not accurate. Not only did the artist need help, HB was seeking help as well.

For those of us who grew up in China, we never had a policy or brochure telling us what to do in this situation. Not in school, not at work, not from the government. I once told my mom that a doctor touched me inappropriately. Her course of action: I was never to go there again. I don't blame my mom. She probably wouldn't know what to do even if it happened to herself. But having lived in the United States for more than twenty years, I know a bit more now and can approach it like how I curate: first identify a need; then find a way to fulfill that need. I told Liang I was willing to help, on the basic premise that we must all choose to believe the artist as the first step in moving forward. I further explained that the only way to handle this situation is for the organization to clearly declare zero tolerance against sexual harassment. We must all agree to prioritize our efforts to develop a mechanism so there is a channel and a path to seek help.

For decades, feminists, lawmakers, educators, and activists have been advocating for laws and regulations on sexual harassment in China. Very little progress has been made. No victim has ever won a legal case. It was only in 2005 that "sexual harassment" as a term made its first appearance in the Law of the People's Republic of China on the Protection of Rights and Interests of Women. There was almost nothing written about what to do. Having actively participated in the feminist movement in China between 2010 and 2012, I knew well there were hardly any guidelines or implementation processes in place for corporations and institutions. There was no channel to file a complaint or seek protection, let alone address what women have had to endure—slut/victim shaming, double standards, retaliation, bullying, and so on.

One might question why I chose to work on what might seem like a human resource task for a micro-institution that doesn't connect even remotely to curating. My response would be the same one I give every time I'm asked why I do art: I curate because I see a need to participate in enabling visibility on an issue, whether big or small. I curate because art to me is a living thing that requires engaging, more than just observing, in order to arrive at an aesthetic moment. I also view artists as an endangered species in our society. In addition to working with them on exhibitions, curators need to advocate for artists' contributions and needs by studying their mode of creativity and protecting their autonomy as well as survival. Developing this mechanism and policy is about that moment of collective landing on a new ground that is a bit safer and friendlier for the artists.

My motivation to work on this policy comes from feeling both hopeful and hopeless. Having learned about one sexual assault story after another in the academy, the art world, NGOs, government, corporations—literally everywhere—I know we need to act. I knew many of my peers were pushing for legislation and social reform by advocating to pass a bill in the People's Congress, establishing legal precedent, and organizing media initiatives.[4] I was determined to work on this particular case with HB. I can't change the country nor its embedded bureaucratic and corrupted system. But I can start small by making progress in a micro-organization led by people who at least have the will to learn, adapt, and change.

Whether it happens in the subway or at work, we must depart from this so-called norm of viewing the woman victim as a singular incident and think instead about developing synchronized protections. This is closely related to work as a curator because most artists work independently, with hardly anything to protect them against sexual harassment, among other violations.

The process of change takes time, more than I anticipated.

I spent about four months from August to December 2017 discussing with Liang Jianhua how to handle the complaint by seeking a third party as mediator, defining ground rules to prevent further damage to the plaintiff, and even on how to provide self-care for the staff, who were all distressed. On January 12, 2018, we formed a WeChat group with all HB staff to draft policy into a handbook format, rehearse investigations, and discuss how to reach more people involved in understanding and exercising this policy. All this time, I was in California and they were in Guangzhou. Our communication was done online, mainly through WeChat, and from time to time by phone.

Developing a successful mechanism entailed that every step needed to be discussed, thought out, and rehearsed. There were numerous debates, even quarreling and shouting at each other. As China's pioneer city for public intellectuals, Guangzhou had multiple groups and leaders pushing the issue of sexual harassment forward, though many remained at the advocacy stage and very little was done at the implementation stage. This was our chance to act. And we were compelled.

There were times the group was slowed down because the artist retreated from the public forum. It was obvious that pressure was crucially necessary in a process like this to push and motivate progress in action.

By April 2018, eight months after the initial discussion, we came up with the first complete guide. We all agreed on the importance of conducting workshops and outreach to similar-sized organizations and independent curators in the region. The goal was not just about having a handbook on sexual harassment in the workplace but also about getting more people to know and learn about what to do when harassment occurs.

On June 5, 2018, almost a year after the artist lodged her complaint, HB hosted a one-day workshop to launch the handbook and offer training. I was not able to attend, but I knew it was in good hands. The feedback was overwhelmingly positive. Political and social organizing in China is constantly suppressed; during the workshop, a national security officer reached out to Liang Jianhua to get a sense of what we were doing. I hope when they tapped our conversations, they were able to learn something for their own good.

The handbook is now available online.[5] HB continues to offer training workshops for interested parties. Many printed copies of the handbook circulate. We are now at the next stage, garnering more support to make sure the policies and procedures are implemented. To our knowledge, this is probably the first ever handbook on sexual harassment for small organizations in China. The story of the woman artist is the pivot, the point of change. If not for her persistence, this handbook would never have become a reality. Now that the handbook is done, I look back and think of that little girl who desperately wanted braids and how she eventually got them.

Notes

1. The woman artist lodged the complaint with her real name at the time. When I told her that I was about to write this essay, she asked me to use an initial instead of her name. I struggled with this, as I believe if the complaint was already filed with a real name, then it should be quoted so. There has also been a movement started by multiple women, including Itō Shiori (author of *Black Box*, 2019) and Chanel Miller (author of *Know My Name*, 2019), who refused to remain anonymous as rape victims. However, considering this was her wish and the kind of pressure she might undertake, I chose to disclose neither her name nor the initials.
2. When the scandal broke out of a Hainan Province elementary school's headmaster who provided young students, minor girls, to government officials as sex bribes, activist Ye Haiyan and lawyer Wang Yu went to investigate and help the victims'

families, and Ye was threatened and arrested. Emily Feng, "'Hooligan Sparrow' Fights for Justice for Sexually Assaulted Schoolgirls," *NPR*, October 17, 2016, https://www.npr.org/sections/goatsandsoda/2016/10/17/497697103/when-6-girls-are-sexually-assaulted-hooligan-sparrow-seeks-justice.

3. The artist used douban.com to post her story. As of the time of this writing, the link is still valid. See artist's statement (in Chinese, revised multiple times): https://m.douban.com/note/665259940/?bid=M6JpZ_DIPQo&from=singlemessage&isappinstalled=0.
4. As a region, the Pearl River Delta has been home to artists and culture workers, who are historically progressive, open-minded, and nonmarket driven. It was home to the forefront of China's investigative journalism by Southern Weekend and Southern Metro (although they all were shut down in recent years). New Media Women's Network was first founded in Guangzhou by veteran journalist Li Sipan, who was instrumental in the in-depth reporting on the case of the large family enterprise owner Song Shanmu, who was eventually found guilty of raping his employee (there were allegedly many victims, but only one chose to come forward). In fact, my first WOMEN我们 symposium on gender identity was launched in 2010 in Guangzhou with SYS University professor Ke Qianting and the then young student Irene Guo.
5. HB's handbook (in Chinese): http://fuben.org/hbs/guildline_and_procedure_hbs.pdf. HB first published this on WeChat on August 8, 2018.

DELINDA COLLIER

I'M OUTING MYSELF, having attended Brigham Young University (BYU) in Hawaii for my BA in studio art. There in the 1990s, I learned up close and in real time about the Church's current and historical relationship with colonialism. I lived in a dorm next to the Polynesian Cultural Center, a sort of Disneyland of performative Polynesia, made up of villages that correspond to the islands. Young Mormon Pacific Islanders work their four years of college on contracts that exchange their labor for tuition. Every night at 9.55 p.m., I fell asleep reading to the sound of a fake volcanic explosion at the evening show, the capstone performance of the Luau that included fire dancers and bikini-clad women who told legends of six island cultures. Customers were served decaffeinated coffee and no alcohol. Performers at the Polynesian Cultural Center were temporarily allowed to be minimally dressed—despite the clothing regulations of BYU's "honor code"—in order to play the part of the native for the crowd of mostly mainland Haole and Asian tourists. It was a strange place, where postings for the good jobs read "must look Polynesian," and the White students were relegated to working the snack bar or janitorial services unless they were sneaky. Sneaky: my White roommate from American Fork, Utah, spent every day at Waimea Bay and became tan enough to work a "must look Polynesian" job; she wore a small "Tahitian" grass skirt as a greeter who took pictures with tourists, some of whom would grope her as they posed.

I chose Hawaii, at age 25, because I was running from a series of turbulent relationships that brought the unavoidable knowledge that I was gay—a knowledge initially so unthinkable that I could not function as a young student and had to drop out of college. I was stifled by a family desperate to fix me. As I achieved my freedom from them, far away in the middle of the Pacific, I began the long process of extricating myself from all of the other stories I rehearsed about the meaning of (my) life. As a studio art major, I dug, looking for raw material in piles of junk at the physical plant, on the beaches and in urban Honolulu, in my journals, and especially at the library. I dug through my family history, my 1820s British settler colonial ancestors in South Africa, a country I would go on to study. On the other side of the family were Scandinavian and English converts who immigrated to the United States to join the wagon train with Mormons who were driven out of the Midwest, called "Indian" or "Mohammedan" because of their practice of polygamy. With their special brand of millenarian religious zeal and "erotic noncompliance," my ancestors helped colonize a chunk of the West, determined to be considered White.[1] During that same period of 1850–90, the Church bought and settled the North Shore of Oahu with a sugar plantation, a temple, and a college—where, much later, I found myself learning postcolonial theory and art history.

My ambivalence about this history—my own historicity—came into sharp view when, by chance, I pulled a large, brand-new book off the library shelf in the Joseph F. Smith Library on campus: Dan Cameron's and Carolyn Christov-Bakargiev's catalog for William Kentridge.[2] The work was a revelation in the 1990s. It confronted the art world with its own Whiteness, and for me, it was on the same affective register as my inner life: Kentridge's raw, frantic, and violent rendering of a self-portrait-cum-historical type. His work connected precisely to the violent imposition of European culture in Africa and also to the subsequent Leftist critique of the bourgeoisie. Excavating this long history of European culture, my family history, including all of the untruths I had been given about the history of South Africa, the Mormon church, and the history of the gay struggle, was painful and exhilarating. I also realized I was a much better writer than a painter, and I decided to go to grad school for art history and write about the art of political struggle in Africa. I began to leave the closet and the Church;

9/11 happened in my second week of grad school, and my first major paper was on Okwui Enwezor's ground-shifting catalog essay for Documenta11, "The Black Box."

In grad school, it felt at times as though I were trading one religion for another—as Latour says, trading fetish for fact.[3] Initially, I needed academia, with all of its rules, rigor, and codes, to replace the structure of a worldview that I lost as I broke from Mormonism. Throughout grad school, however, I came to be more uncomfortable with what I saw was an overdetermined, overconfident secularism in the academy. It bothered me, as I began to seriously study African art, that most methodologies relied on Enlightenment-derived notions of autonomy and evidence, even when ostensibly critiqued from the scholars of Continental theory, the then-dominant critical paradigm in art history. I started to determine that the very notion of critical distance was incomplete and could be imperialist; some criticisms of postcolonial theory by Islamic and Black Studies scholars were influential on me. A lot of the critical theory I read was simply uninteresting to me as someone doubly outside the liberal tradition: a queer (former) Mormon. As I began to write my dissertation, I borrowed and historicized the extant scholarship, attempting to critique critical distance.

What I also faced as I started my career was the death of my sister, who was also gay, genderqueer, uncooperative at every official job she ever had, and a genius practitioner of empathy with everyone she met. She was seven years older than me, but we occupied two different generations of queer history—hers as struggle, mine as beneficiary. She died of alcohol addiction in the first year of my tenure track. The weekend of the funeral, my dissertation was being reviewed by my committee, and I had been waiting to hear if I would be able to defend it the following week. It was the middle of my second semester teaching a 3/3 course load; I created and taught six new courses in my first year. As the other now openly gay member in the family, I delivered my sister's eulogy because my parents were uncomfortable saying the word "partner" over the pulpit at the church service, even though her partner sat and mourned with us. That weekend, I realized that conflict and contradiction would be a feature of my life and career; I allowed myself to really feel it as being a matter of my survival.

In the immediate term, I relaxed about the fate of my dissertation and career because it was suddenly minor. In the long term, as part of the ongoing making of sense of her life and death, I've started to understand that she was unable to live with an impossible irony about the Church. The Church's founding prophet was dedicated to (and arguably assassinated for) his divergent sexual and familial practices. The noncompliant theology created in the nineteenth century remained in the scriptures that we read, despite the institution being increasingly correlated with the state. It refigured itself as a "normal" Christian church, disavowed its gay members, and never looked back. There was something deeply perverse about the Church's fight against gay marriage (raging in the few years before she died), a visible political battle that tore families like ours apart. As I returned home to my partner from the funeral, I felt committed to maintaining my alterity as a scholar and not giving in to the despair of being excluded by my community of birth.

I leave BYU-Hawaii off my CV in an act of protest against the Church's politically motivated views on gender and sexuality, but I wonder if I would've felt as urgent a need to address the practices of colonialism that still go unnoticed if I had gone somewhere else. My struggle to fit in culturally with academia is probably recognizable to many artists and writers who have wanted to escape the sureties of the academic endeavor and to leave open the possibility of exceptional existence. My two lives, the previous one and this one, have both been structured around methodologies of Utopia, "Celestial Kingdoms." If I were to try to map what I think are my stakes in the field, it would be the legacy of the Left in art history and criticism, as well as the fiction that critical theory does not practice its own "magic" in mediating the world for its adherents. If there is a chance to write global art history, it would have to proceed with the admission that we are in the hands of speech and do not, as we often think, shape it (as a proverb from a lineage of West African Griot storytellers, the Mandé, says). But to the extent that language is quotidian, it can be utopian by our desire for small acts of transformation.

Notes

1. Peter Coviello, *Make Yourselves Gods: Mormons and the Unfinished Business of American Secularism* (Chicago: University of Chicago Press, 2019), 2. See also W. Paul Reeve, *Religion of a Different Color: Race and the Mormon Struggle for Whiteness* (Oxford: Oxford University Press, 2015).
2. Dan Cameron, *William Kentridge* (London: Phaidon, 1999).
3. Bruno Latour, *On the Modern Cult of the Factish Gods* (Durham, NC: Duke University Press, 2010).

PARUL DAVE-MUKHERJI

I WOULD NOT have been an art historian if I had not met E. H. Gombrich and B. K. Matilal or read their books at the start of my career. More accurately, if I understand my practice today as Janus-faced, doubly oriented toward the past and the present, it is due to the early impact of this art historian and this philosopher. The one book that got me started was Gombrich's *Art and Illusion* (1960), which I chanced upon in the library as an MA student at an art school in Baroda. It is not that often that I get obsessed by a book. From the time I opened this book, I felt an urgency to read it from cover to cover. This book offered to me a riveting history of illusion in European art: it kept bringing back to my mind a memory, or rather an epiphany, of a sandstone statue from Mohenjo-daro of the Indus Valley Civilization that I saw on a slide in a darkened art history classroom as an undergraduate in Kalabhavan, Santiniketan.

I recalled that it was through this slide of the male torso that my art history teacher had introduced us to the Viennese art historian Stella Kramrisch. Kramrisch was, in fact, invited from Vienna by the founder of my university, the poet Rabindranath Tagore, to set up the country's first art history department. What was of greater interest to me was her use of this statuette to illustrate the *prana* or breathing quality that she claimed some of the best works of Indian art embodied. To me, the sculpture's magical quality of transforming itself from stone to human flesh, so that the viewer could almost "see" the figure breathe, was a form of "Indian" illusion. In the art history discourse in India,

Gombrich's "illusion" would correspond to "naturalism"—a term that has a contested history in the colonial/nationalist art historiography. According to this discourse—driven heavily by binary logic—Indian art had to be diametrically opposite to Western art. If Western art was considered to have a high quotient of naturalism, Indian art is taken to have culturally rejected it to make a way for transcendentalism—a dichotomy that has never stopped troubling me and which underlay my long-term obsession with decolonizing/denationalizing mimesis in premodern Indian art and aesthetics.

It was this visual memory of the pulsating torso from Harappa that would keep returning to my mind, as if to rebel against the commonsense view of Indian art as otherworldly and divorced from the experience of visual perception. I was busy looking around for an alternative take on representation when I stumbled across B. K. Matilal's *Perception* (1986). I was intrigued by the fact that its author, Matilal, a well-known philosopher teaching at Oxford University, was also contesting the commonsense view of Indian philosophy as being transcendental, a view made popular by another philosopher, S. Radhakrishnan. Matilal engaged instead with analytical schools of Indian philosophy such as the Nyaya and the Vaisesika schools. His groundbreaking book *Perception* opened my eyes to epistemology and the theories of visual perception in early India, which ranged from idealism to a staunch realism (that the world exists whether there is someone viewing it or not). I was sure by then that I wanted to pursue my research with Matilal as my advisor and explore if there was a meeting point between aesthetics and epistemology to work as a new lens to view Indian art.

Once in London, I was trying to find my bearing in the city, clutching onto my London A–Z. At some point, I found myself standing in front of the Warburg Institute and decided to take a chance at meeting Prof. E. H. Gombrich. Six months ago, it was the art historian Partha Mitter, formerly one of Gombrich's students, who had put me in touch with this art historian regarded as a leading authority on Western art. Incidentally, the book through which he is most widely known even outside the West is *The Story of Art* (1950), an early foray into what today we like to call the global art history. Prof. Gombrich and I had exchanged letters and postcards, and in one of them, he casually mentioned that if I were to make it to Oxford, we must meet.

Landing up without an appointment was frowned upon by the receptionist, but when Prof. Gombrich not only agreed to see me but also came down to receive me, it left her startled and overwhelmed me. I recalled that afternoon as feeling dazed, being given a tour of the library by the director of the Warburg Institute himself.

It was later, when we started to chat in his office about the relevance of *Art and Illusion* to my research, that I realized how much his own position on illusion had shifted; he no longer subscribed to the perceptual relativism that had been an inspiration for me as a graduate student but now held the view that naturalism was quintessentially a phenomenon specific to the West: that only twice in world art history was naturalism in art accomplished convincingly—once by the Greeks and the Romans and then at the time of the Italian Renaissance. His response to my excitement about many classical Indian theories of visual perception, Sanskrit textual sources, and terminologies that implied a notion of illusion in art was to direct me to E. Kris and O. Kurz's *Legend, Myth, and Magic in the Image of the Artist.*[1]

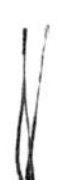

I returned to Oxford dejected but decided to refer to the book he had recommended. When I revisit this moment in my mind, I remember being troubled by its skepticism toward textual material and its association of magic with non-Western representation. More bad news awaited me at the Oriental Institute: Indologist Prof. Richard Gombrich, incidentally E. H. Gombrich's son, urged me to change my advisor from Matilal, who had been diagnosed with a terminal illness, to Alexis Sanderson. Apart from the personal shock of losing an advisor who was the reason for my being in Oxford, it meant a loss of a stalwart in the field. Sanderson, a renowned Sanskritist and an authority on Pratyabhijña philosophy of Kashmir Shaivism, took me on as his student on condition that I abandon my ambitious project and work on a critical edition of the *Citrasutra*, a classical Sanskrit text on painting of *c.*fifth to ninth century CE. My initial resistance transformed into excitement about working with primary source material, daunted though I was by the challenge of learning Sanskrit in the way Latin is taught in Oxford. The text I was editing had less to do with epistemology than with what I today understand as applied aesthetics.

My conversation with Gombrich continued to haunt me. Recently, I became aware of David Freedberg's critique of the book by Kris and Kurz, which made me reflect on why

Gombrich had recommended the book to me at that time. Was he consigning the Sanskrit treatise and all the textual references I had discussed with him to a primitivist space, or that of people of childish mentality who said one thing and did something quite different, whose art and theory did not quite match?[2]

Right in the middle of my research, reading Edward Said's *Orientalism*[3] was an eye-opener in the way he underlined the collusion between power and knowledge and the fraught terrain of representation itself. Moreover, art historian Norman Bryson's trenchant critique of Gombrich vindicated the British philosopher Nelson Goodman's linguistic model.[4] By this time, I had gradually shifted my loyalties to Goodman, on one hand, and to Said, on the other; if Goodman alerted me to distrust similarity as one of the most slippery terrains in representation,[5] Said cautioned me about the possibility of Eurocentric claims around modes of representation (for me, mimesis was one such mode) as a way of creating a hierarchy between self and others. It is in this context that Matilal's contribution to Indian epistemology opened up a way for me to grapple with the question of decolonizing mimesis in Indian art.[6]

Another story of serendipity related to my other foot anchored in modern and contemporary art. I owe my interest in global art history to, again, a chance encounter with *Stories of Art* (2002) by the Chicago-based art historian James Elkins, in a bookstore in Oxford. On the flight back to New Delhi, I obsessively read the book, especially the chapter on non-Western art history, which profusely referred to the very text I had edited as a D.Phil. student: the *Citrasutra*! While I admired Elkins's attempt at a multicultural art history or art history in the plural, meant to be a broadening of E. H. Gombrich's *The Story of Art*, I found his coverage of non-Western art history and its textual sources unconvincing and springing from a lack of awareness about non-Western art history. And at the next global (CIHA) conference in Melbourne, I vehemently critiqued the book.[7] It was through the convenor of the session, Professor Thomas DaCosta Kaufmann, an art historian from Princeton University, that the news of my presentation traveled to Elkins. Elkins's reaching out to me through an e-mail offering to clarify his position may itself be taken as a facet of global art history in the age of internet communication! Even if it opened a place of dialogue between the scholars of Global South and Global North, in which we agreed to disagree, *Stories of Art* did trigger my interest in the impact of globalization on art theory and art history. When I look back to where I had started, my chance encounters with books and people make me think of serendipity as part of research.

Notes

1. Ernst Kris and Otto Kurz, *Legend, Myth, and Magic in the Image of the Artist: A Historical Experiment* (New Haven: Yale University Press, [1929] 1981).
2. See Gombrich's defensive review of David Freedberg's book *The Power of Images: Studies in the History and Theory of Response* (Chicago: University of Chicago Press, 1989) in the *New York Review of Books*, February 15, 1990, 6:

   > Anyone who can consult my book *The Story of Art* will find that the first chapter deals with what is there described as "the power of image making." It is true that this power is exemplified in a discussion of primitive art, but far from confirming Freedberg's charge that the relevance of these observations to our own response is habitually denied, the chapter also says, "Instead of beginning with the Ice Age, let us begin with ourselves."

3. Edward Said, *Orientalism* (New York: Pantheon, 1978).
4. Norman Bryson, *Vision and Painting: The Logic of the Gaze* (New Haven: Yale University Press, 1983).
5. Nelson Goodman, "Seven Strictures against Similarity," in *Problems and Projects* (Indianapolis: Bobbs-Merill, 1972), 437–46.
6. Parul Dave-Mukherji, "Who Is Afraid of Mimesis?: Contesting the Common Sense of Indian Aesthetics through the Theory of Mimesis or Anukaraṇa Vāda," in *The Bloomsbury Research Handbook of Indian Aesthetics and the Philosophy of Art*, ed. Arindam Chakrabarti (London: Bloomsbury, 2016), 71–92.
7. Parul Dave-Mukherji, "Putting the World in a Book: How Global Can Art History Be Today," in *Crossing Cultures: Conflict, Migration and Convergence*, ed. Jaynie Anderson (Melbourne: Miegunyah Press, 2009), 109–15.

JANE CHIN DAVIDSON

I WANT TO begin this essay by explicitly asking this question: As a researcher who says she researches subjects of feminism, performance, and Chinese identity in relation to artists, how exactly am I doing this critical race/gender work when the norm of art historical objectivity requires that my own embodiment play no part in the methodology of research?

For as long as I can remember, I was surrounded by artists and the arts, especially growing up in the progressive education system in the Pacific Northwest during the 1970s, a moment when art programs were flourishing and when the National Endowment for the Arts actually funded visual artists. My elder sister would become a well-known poet, and I eventually went to work in small nonprofit art galleries. I didn't really comprehend the nature of an academic or intellectual life until I went to university. I had waited until my three children left to attend college in the late 1990s before I decided to go myself, which is how I first entertained the idea of becoming an "art historian," a job title I still use with hesitancy. For me as a first-generation immigrant from Hong Kong, and thus a first-generation student, going to college was transformative. I saw an opportunity to study my own cultural history, something that I could hardly talk about with my mother and grandmother (my parents). When they both died, however, I felt that the very "self" of culture died with them. I don't think I would have become a researcher of Chinese contemporary art if my parents were still with me, and yet, this research is assumed to be *objective* and detached from my Chinese self.

On the other hand, the contradictions of cultural attachments became a way to question being Chinese, especially my decision to complete a senior thesis on the work of Zhang Huan and Yin Xiuzhen and other artists in China. Looking back, I see now that the decision was a conflicted endeavor under the cover of research: I chose the subject of my so-called nationality, but not really of my *Chinese American* identity. I have been obsessed with the meaning of *Chineseness* ever since, because the term addresses the distinctions among subjects of China, Hong Kong, and Chinese America through its study of creolization, hybridity, and cross-assimilations.[1] As defined in my monograph on these issues, the term Chineseness "puts to the test the very premise of the genealogical inscription for Chinese contemporary art and the ways in which cultural objects are attributed to territories, usually through the status of residency, homeland, or citizenship of their makers."[2] The categorization of art in the global context is still dependent on the identity of the artist, and I have focused on the performative and bodily oriented works by Chinese artists because they often reveal those contradictions in revelatory ways. The discourse of *Chineseness* confronts the ambiguities of being Chinese and the sort of fetishizations that are particular to Chinese women.

Academics must navigate the paradoxes of embodied and disembodied subjects, and in returning to methodology, the tension exists between the identity of the historian and the feminist, raced, queer subjects she writes about *objectively*. I have addressed the significance of this tension in my advocacy work, particularly in regard to the lack of women of color in the hiring practices of university faculties.[3] Although it would never be polite to say out loud the things I have witnessed, such as the White male art historian getting the job offer for the Asian Art position over the Asian female candidate, these experiences always leave an unsettling silence. The standard explanation for White males getting the majority of academic positions is, of course, because they are evaluated *objectively* as being *more qualified*. I always wondered what Chinese embodiment serves in those specifically Asian Art competitions.

Donna Haraway addressed the "inescapable term 'objectivity'" as the constant problem for "academic and activist feminist inquiry" by exposing its privileged form of *dis*embodiment under the conquering gaze of "Man and White": "the imagined 'they' constitute a kind of invisible conspiracy," while "the imagined 'we' are the embodied others, who are not allowed *not* to have a body, a finite point of view, and so an inevitably disqualifying and polluting bias in any discussion of consequence outside our own little circles."[4] Based on Haraway's assessment, as a Chinese female in the academic community, women like me are "not allowed *not* to have a body," and intuitively, I am quite sure that I both substituted my own subjectivity and took cover through the bodily oriented subjects of my study of China's contemporary artists. Of course, there are complex reasons why I initially focused on the performative artworks of Yin Xiuzhen and Zhang Huan. Maybe not consciously, but I was initiating a plan for both my activist and academic lives, a decision I want to understand better.

Haraway rejects simplistic subjective/objective conclusions. Her strategy for a "feminist objectivity means quite simply *situated knowledges*," an approach engaged thereafter by many feminist researchers in different fields. The inspiration of feminists that came before always feels like the work of a coalition in which activist writing does not seem like a solitary practice because of its longstanding model of resistance. For instance, Marsha Meskimmon took Haraway's idea of objectivity to illustrate feminist activism by suggesting that knowledge is fluid—a theory in which ethics, aesthetics, and female subjectivity converge.[5] In fact, the way in which an art historian is able to conduct feminist, decolonial, anti-racist, transnational, and queer work is presumed to be quite opposite from the self-reflexive confessions and critiques by *artists* whose biographical methodologies constitute an artistic form of power. Situated knowledge is embodied knowledge, and its feminist production in the visual arts is often meant to express something radical but intimated through ideas that are personal to the artist, no matter from what cultural tradition. So, when Meskimmon suggested there is a need for an ethical engagement in the epistemology of art history, her critical activism was toward a body of knowledge that is *always* biased and subjectively from the *historian*.

By the mid-2000s, art history's function in constructing the idea of Western civilization was being intently challenged; as an epistemology, art history was always less a discourse than a grand European tradition, a mythological story. When I define art history for my students today, I explain the European myth and then teach how to use the methodology for the study of art in global cultures. In fact, the notion that art history *is* storytelling represents the reason why this collection of essays is so on point. Thinking about this fiction/fact context had me searching for examples of subjective and objective writing by other art historians in order to find an insightful model. The disembodied and embodied forms of storytelling by Partha Mitter and Suzanne Preston Blier exemplify contrasting strategies for redressing art history. The writing of discourse and history remains, of course, considered as an objective practice.

Mitter's approach to research is convincing, especially his 2008 essay "Decentering Modernism" for *Art Bulletin*, focusing on twentieth-century modern art and avant-gardism in India. He skillfully conveys his own activist position through an objective contextualization of art history's "pervasive hold of 'hegemonic' universality."[6] Mitter argues that, even when discussing a particular period for art, "a qualifying epithet becomes necessary to speak of any other: East European modernism, Chinese modernism, Indian modernism, and so on."[7] This is how he illustrates the hegemonic, and to cite an example of the "universal" as the cultural dominant, he chose *Art Since 1900*, "the magisterial volume on the avant-garde published in 2004," authored by Benjamin H. D. Buchloh, Hal Foster, Rosalind Krauss, and Yve-Alain Bois—because these gatekeepers of the field ignore the world outside the United States and Western Europe.[8] Mitter's critique of *Art Since 1900* was daring; all the while his method and tone were "objective" as he delivered a decolonial model for writing art history. Mitter's approach is considered as rigorous scholarship, associated implicitly with theoretical and evidence-based work.

In contrast, Blier took an entirely subjective approach when she wrote her 2001 essay "Autobiography and Art History: The Imperative of Peripheral Vision" for the journal *RES: Anthropology and Aesthetics*. Her first-person storytelling connected her Peace Corps experience in Yoruba with her eventual Ph.D. work in the field of African art. Blier wanted to tackle the blind spots in relation to "how the meanings of the related artworks are shaped through this process" of intellectual journeys in art historical subjectivity.[9] I appreciated the way in which Blier begins with a frank discussion about a 1945 photograph of her parents at the Zanzibar Café in New York with its logo of an exotica black female on the souvenir cover.[10] The author makes herself vulnerable, confessing that when she first encountered the image in her teenage years, it did not seem at all troubling: "The most important feature of the photograph and cover for me today is the blindness that I (they?) had to its racial and sexual subtext."[11] Perceiving she was speaking from the subject position of the "white norm," her honesty provides an emotional template for how one could contextualize past experiences with race in writing autobiography and art history. But in the end, I was not able to use her writing to make sense of my own firsthand experiences with discrimination. Growing up among the white populace of Portland, Oregon, my personal context for race was based on being embarrassed by it—and to paraphrase Fanon, the racist shame is placed on the shamed.[12]

It is hard to see beyond the negatives when remembering the immigrant past that informs my academic present. Then it occurred to me that the major difference for academics of color is that they are never afforded the possibility of "blindness" to the racial-plus-sexual subtexts, which corresponds to Haraway's explanation for "embodied others, who are not allowed *not* to have a body." The artistic representation of nationality and cultural identity remains central to art but not necessarily to the embodied identity of the art historian. This conflict will always be part of storytelling, and that is why the stories told by bodily oriented artists might convey something closer to the reality of race and gender in life experiences that are volatile and difficult to define or pin down. Ultimately, when this kind of artist's subject becomes the researcher's subject, the goal of activism becomes very important because it marks the difference for the self as other who is still not allowed *not* to have a body. And to a certain extent, "objective" analysis had paradoxically enabled me to disavow my embodied, raced self (for better or worse). In reflection, this project has challenged me to think about my own practice and to reconsider the act of writing. Going forth, my goal is to tell stories from my own gendered Chinese subject position and work toward being more subjective in doing so. After all, that's exactly what my poet sister is still doing.

Notes

1. See Jane Chin Davidson, *Staging Art and Chineseness: The Politics of Trans/Nationalism and Global Expositions* (Manchester: University of Manchester Press, 2019).
2. Ibid., 4.
3. See my essay, cowritten with Deepa Reddy, "Performative Testimony and the Practice of Dismissal," in *Written/Unwritten: Diversity and the Hidden Truths of Tenure*, ed. Patricia A. Matthew (Chapel Hill: University of North Carolina Press, 2016).
4. Donna Haraway, "Situated Knowledges: The Science Question in Feminism and the Privilege of Partial Perspective," *Feminist Studies* 14, no. 3 (Fall 1988), 575–99, at 575, 581; original emphasis.
5. Marsha Meskimmon, *Women Making Art: History, Subjectivity, Aesthetics* (London: Routledge, 2003), 80.
6. Partha Mitter, "Decentering Modernism: Art History and Avant-Garde Art from the Periphery," *The Art Bulletin* 90, no. 4 (December 2008): 531–48, at 532.
7. Ibid.
8. Ibid., 531.
9. Suzanne Preston Blier, "Autobiography and Art History: The Imperative of Peripheral Vision," *RES: Anthropology and Aesthetics*, no. 39 (Spring 2001): 24–40, at 25.
10. Ibid.
11. Ibid.
12. Fanon explains the emotion of "shame and self-contempt" in Frantz Fanon, *Black Skin, White Masks* (London: Pluto Press, 1986), 116.

ALLAN DESOUZA

MY ART PRACTICE, much like my name, bears the imprint of dual colonial legacies. I was born to Goan parents in Kenya, a then-British colony, with Goa then being a Portuguese colony. While I don't consider my work as autobiographical, I do draw upon familial histories as practices of self-positioning and located criticality, similar to how Mary Louise Pratt, invoking W. E. B. Du Bois's concept of double consciousness, describes an autoethnographic text as one "in which people undertake to describe themselves in ways that engage with representations others have made of them."[1] My focus, then, is often on "hauntings," preexisting narratives, representations, institutional structures, and institutionalized practices. I trace these from the late nineteenth-century "high" periods of both modernism and colonialism, whose aftermaths continue to *impress* upon the body (including leaving impressions within), and which "assign" different bodies differently.[2] My larger intention is, in Ariella Azoulay's terms, to "unlearn imperialism."[3]

While I maintain that all artworks proceed from their makers' histories (then to now, there to here), my work is never about my "identity." My territorial and temporal claim is a broader one: the world in which we live, though I defer to others who are better placed to speak from their own positionings. I mention these questions of who has the right to speak, and what they can speak of, since they often arise around my work and in our cultural moment. Once, when teaching about protests against artworks,

I told my students that I was reticent to project the image of Dana Schutz's painting *Open Casket* (2016), because it registered upon me as a physical assault (the students understood, but nevertheless immediately looked up the work on their phones and laptops). I'm not easily "outraged" by artworks (there are other, much worse things in the world), though I accept that one role of artists is to test boundaries of knowledge and acceptability; I can overlap intellectual criticality and aesthetic pleasure; I can hold more than one viewpoint—*against* censorship and *for* the (albeit symbolic) destruction of a particular work; I can deploy critical thinking even as my body refuses, including and especially when violence and its representation are activated to promote the freedoms of one group over another. It might not be the work itself as image or object that becomes objectionable, but how it participates within and activates white supremacy (in this case). Any blanket insistence on artistic freedom and against censorship should lead one to ask whose freedoms are being called for, whose dissent is quashed, and whose interests are being ultimately served.

Within such contexts, what is it to be an artist, a storyteller, and of what stories? How does one responsibly transfer and translate—in their original meanings of *to bear* and *to carry across*—the membranous vestibule between the world "outside" and an "interior" life, and how are these implicated by making and writing within the system of another's language, another's viewing of that world? One might say that this is already to write within translation, to write from a self that is itself *in* translation (carried across), and to write from that condition of mobility "betwixt and between the positions assigned and arrayed by custom."[4] Susette Min quotes Victor Turner's description of liminal space to examine the political positioning of Asian American culture, and I want to reiterate her questions of how culture can act as dissent within, between, and betwixt the spaces to which one is already assigned. My work functions in the liminal, membranous within–between–betwixt spaces that separate (and connect) outside and inside, present and past, colonizer and colonized.

I'd like to call upon one project in particular, *Ark of Martyrs* (2014–20).[5] *Martyrs* uses the medium of text and works within, between, and against another text: Joseph Conrad's *Heart of Darkness* (1899), a text that assigns bodies by race and racialized gender. In its assignation of how someone like me can be in the world, that work became unavoidable despite the damnations by such scholars as Chinua Achebe, who considered it irredeemable while acknowledging that Conrad, as "one of the great stylists of modern fiction," is precisely what makes him so widely read (and so insidious). Achebe identifies Conrad as a "bloody racist," whose racism is so normative that "its manifestations go completely undetected."[6] I agree, but for the same reasons remain hesitant to dismiss Conrad. It's not that I seek to redeem his work, but I can't escape its effect within that world to which we are forcefully returned (in case we ever imagined otherwise), where we can be told to go back where we came from (I take this to mean less to a geographical location and more to a social position, our "proper" place).

In my rewriting of *Darkness*, my primary intent is not, on the surface, to provide a literary or political critique, since those are already available. Nevertheless, Conrad's nineteenth-century, *fin de siècle* pronouncements on race and racialized gender, on the threatening "horrors" of Blackness, on the façades of whiteness, his liberal criticism of "bad" colonialism and his equally liberal justification of "good" colonialism—all these are still with us, and resurgent.

Another reason for my pull toward *Darkness*: Conrad's tale (to speak only of its surface) of a ship journey on the Congo River opens and is narrated from a ship anchored on the River Thames in London. After my family's emigration from Kenya, we lived in London near the Thames (close to where the MI5 secret service's fortress-like headquarters now stand). Relocated to the one place, we recalled others left behind. Conrad similarly imagines geography in relation to time, but in his telling, the past is the primitive and the barbaric—and for him, Africa is always the past (this racist-imagined Africa, as it can only ever be, is worth comparing with an equally racist-imagined America, as it "should" be, as it once apparently was). How then to tell stories and make artworks that are always in the becoming, unmaking and remaking pasts, making and changing futures, or what José Esteban Muñoz describes as potentialities? Again, through Susette Min: "unlike a possibility, a thing that simply might happen, a potentiality is a certain mode of nonbeing that is eminent, a thing that is present but not actually existing in the present tense."[7] Using Achille Mbembe's proposition that the present is an entanglement of absences, my work utilizes time as hybrid and malleable.

I should mention linguistic constraints on my rewriting of Conrad's text. It employs the school method of dictation in language classes whereby the teacher reads aloud a text and the students write it down, like the archaic boss dictating to a secretary. What might appear as seemingly physical, linguistic, social, or cultural inabilities, as forms of mishearing or mistranslating, are instead activated into forms of dissent and talking back. I would carry over such questions of mistranslation and dissent to the disciplinary processes of racialization and gendering, so that they can be highly mobile, resistant, perhaps *chosen* conditions even as they are assigned fixity.

I use homophones and different strategies of rhyme, so that both texts sound similar when read aloud. I have largely maintained Conrad's grammatical structures, pacing, and so on. Mine is a(n un)sound work that readers are required to translate and sound out for themselves. If anything, it is indebted to the Black multi-vocalities of Creole, Santeria, gospel, toasting, and rap, rather than to the denigrated Blackness that haunts Conrad. The story consists of the mental chatter, the unspoken and unspeakable desires, avarice, anxieties, and political resentments of guests at a wedding party on a cruise ship that, unknown to the guests, is adrift and under quarantine. A time of selfies but with limited opportunities for self-reflection. Formally, the writing is also adrift, flitting across psychohistories and psychosocialities, similar to psychoanalysis but with no trajectory toward a cure, pulled instead in multiple directions and intersections by (pre) dominantly human—lunatic rather than lunar—tides.

I may be out on an art historical limb here, but through my work I want to retell Kazimir Malevich's painting *Black Square* (1915), which marks the seemingly nonracial, but pigment, medium, and ideologically based birth of Suprematism and a pivotal moment for the development of Euro-modernism. The 2015 discovery that Malevich's canvas, under its top coat of black paint, contains a racial inscription, "Battle of negroes in a dark cave," makes it even more overtly—and subtextually—a foundational moment for modernism. *BS* (if I may) has been variously discussed as the death of painting and as the birth of a new art. We might see it instead as a racialized haunting, similar to how Blackness was a perennial antithesis of Conrad's notion of civilization.[8]

Like Malevich's racist joke, I'm peeking under the white sheet (in Malevich's case, it's a black sheet, but grant me this license), poking under the "top coat" public (ad)dress of Conrad's text. I'm not looking for a subtext as such, since Conrad is already explicit, all (sur)face. Malevich's *BS* is the undercurrent of a seemingly aesthetically neutral (although highly politically charged) surface (the *ur*-face of Blackness within Euro-modernism, a thin wash over the indelible stain on the social and canvas fabric). Conrad's is also a stain, but whitewashed within a canon of "great literature."

In "light" of Conrad's colonialist configuration of time, I take the *liberté* to propose that my text prefigures his, that mine is the undertext of his, the clean dirt of the world, the dissent of an assigned body, the underwriting before the whitewash, that mine is the joke (*avant la lettre*, pardon my French) beneath his racist, misogynist, xenophobic exterior.

A further "joke," though more of a play within and between meanings: *Ark of Martyrs* is subtitled *An Autobiography of V*. First, if there is *an* autobiography, presumably there can be other versions, and that any one version refutes claims of being authoritative. Second, how does one write an *auto*biography of another? Is the other, then, a version or reflection of oneself? Who is the author, and who is authorized? V, of indeterminate and mobile gender, tells their story "less as a process of coming out and more one of coming together: a multiple self as a complexly accumulated meshing of histories, experiences, and imaginings."[9] V is a fabulous confabulation, an imagined I, or more correctly an imagined us, made flesh through the word. V is also a historical legacy, a matrilineal inheritance of my mother's name, *Visitaçao*, the Visitation. How else to unlearn the imperialism of a singular history, or to tell stories within, between, and betwixt the spaces to which one is already assigned, if not as a multiple self?

Notes

1. Mary Louise Pratt, "Arts of the Contact Zone," *Profession* (1991): 33–40, at 35.
2. My use of "impression" is from Sara Ahmed's writings on how emotions circulate; see her *The Cultural Politics of Emotion* (Edinburgh: Edinburgh University Press, 2004).
3. See Ariella Aïsha Azoulay, *Potential History: Unlearning Imperialism* (London: Verso, 2019).

4. Victor Turner quoted in Susette Min, *Unnamable: The Ends of Asian American Art* (New York: NYU Press, 2018), 22.
5. First exhibited as a single-channel video at the California Museum of Photography, 2014. Published by Sming Sming Books, 2020.
6. Chinua Achebe, "An Image of Africa: Racism in Conrad's *Heart of Darkness*," *Massachusetts Review*, 18 (1977): 782–94.
7. Min, *Unnamable*, 28; quoting José Esteban Muñoz, *Cruising Utopia: The Then and There of Queer Futurity* (New York: NYU Press, 2009), 9.
8. I would further argue that much of art history is haunted by its omissions, cover-ups, and overt depictions of race. Similar arguments apply to spaces of education and exhibition: which bodies does one see and not see in them; from which bodies were profits taken to enable those spaces?
9. Allan deSouza, *Ark of Martyrs: An Autobiography of V* (San José: Sming Sming Books, 2020), 95.

CLAIRE FARAGO AND DONALD PREZIOSI

Collaboration

We speak of collaboration as if it were a readily available mode of working, but in fact collaboration is not widely practiced in the humanities. Nonetheless, collaboration across disciplines is absolutely essential to reimagining art history in the grip of the climate crisis. The art historian as narrator traditionally emulates the imagined singularity of the artist. Artists are in turn treated as objects that embody the spirit of the times. The art historian in her turn is the singular expert on whatever subject. That is how disciplinarity functions in the academy and the marketplace, but neither disciplinarity nor the format of the autonomous creator is conducive to the collaboration that is needed for the future.

Our previous collaborations are many—we have published in different venues, delivered joint papers, offered advice, taught seminars together, and so on. There have also been two formal collaborations, from which we draw the following observations. The first was *Grasping the World: The Idea of the Museum* (2004), an edited volume with critical introductions that grew out of a graduate seminar and a symposium that we co-taught and co-organized at University of California, Los Angeles: Art as Institution: Race/Nation, Aesthetics, and the Fabrication of Modernity (1997–98). The second was *Art Is Not What You Think It Is* (2012), a volume commissioned by Wiley-Blackwell for their "Manifesto" series of short provocations addressed to existing disciplines by leading experts. In the first project, Donald had developed a reader for an earlier graduate seminar on museums. Claire contributed her knowledge of scholarship on the Early Modern period. The second project proceeded the same way, with each of us contributing our own distinct specialist areas: Claire provided expertise on Early Modern art and art theory, while Donald provided expertise on semiotic theory. We worked jointly to develop research on Indigenous Australian art and anthropology during two extended research fellowships at the University of Melbourne, Australia (2007 and 2008). Together we visited museums in Europe and Australia, and art centers in the Australian Outback. Most importantly, we read theory together and discussed the issues among ourselves and with colleagues, giving numerous talks during our time in Australia.

The most important element of our collaboration has always been the conversation between us and with friends and colleagues. At first, we tried to coauthor the same short text, but we quickly abandoned the attempt and instead wrote sections individually, then edited each other's work. We combined short sections into longer arguments that we typically rehearsed in conversation. However, we want to emphasize that the kind of collaboration we developed—sharing ideas and expertise, writing and editing each other's texts—is only the first step in the prolonged period of dialogue that is necessary to bridge the methodological and linguistic differences between the sciences and the humanistic disciplines effectively. Meaningful collaboration across subdisciplines, and across the arts and sciences, raises conundrums that only practitioners can address moving forward.

Donald Preziosi

As this anthology is part of a series of first-person narratives of the many ways in which creative people "nurture[d] a creative practice while trying to survive," I'm asked to provide a first-person account of my stakes in the (art historical) field and how I might be maintaining and nurturing my own practice in the face of "overwhelming odds against the feminist, decolonial, anti-racist, transnational, and queer work [I] do."

My first reaction is that "first-person narratives" are a deceptively simple fiction: a literary abstraction that isolates persons from their social and cultural lives so as to fabricate "essences"—the familiar ethnic, gender, moral, religious, racial distinctions that our co-constructed modernities situate in the individual—a term that refers to purportedly undivided and purportedly unique singularities.

For as long as I can remember, I've never really believed in such singularities. Growing up in New York City in the 1940s, I always felt myself as living simultaneously diverse selves. Maybe because I never really fully believed in absolute distinctions between what in English are called "subjects" and "objects." Maybe because I grew up in a household inhabited by diverse role models: my dad was an artist, his dad was a poet and journalist, and my grandfather's books were on the shelves in the living room, below my dad's artwork on the walls. Maybe also because my dad was a twin; he was Romulus, and his twin brother—Remus, of course—was a musician and songwriter. Art and music, visual and verbal artistries.

For me, this evolved into a kind of schizophrenic oscillation between visual and verbal interests throughout my professional life. I tried to "resolve" or at least more fully understand this through an early fascination with semiotics, and in general a fascination with *how* things mean, not only *what* things meant or were seen as representing—an awareness that renders "representation" itself far from simple or unproblematic. If art history traditionally sought to ground cultural objects—artworks and their "style"—in the personality of persons ("You are your stuff" and the form of your work is the figure of your truth, who and what you are), then critical art practice (understanding art history as an artistic practice) must trouble or queer dominant hegemonic notions of practice, andro- or gyno-centrist practices, as well as any other centrisms. And for me personally, this has been and always will be a *dancing* practice, a choreographic unfolding as its object of attention or critique itself evolves and changes.

I've been "reimagining art history" since I first imagined being an art historian, and examples of how it is possible to reimagine art history have existed since the field first imagined itself into existence in Europe some five centuries ago. Moreover, the notion that art *had* a history, that it existed and was worthy of intellectual and critical investigation, came into existence along with its opposite or antithesis—that "art" (however defined) was timeless or "transcended" the spatio-temporal coordinates of its creation and reception. And the notion that art was a *kind* of thing existing in contrast to *non*artistic or merely utilitarian or functional artifacts was itself related to the rise of commodity capitalism in early modernity. In other words, neither art nor its putative histories were originally, nor are they now, distinct from their co-constructed social, philosophical, ethnic, ethical, or erotic natures and functions.

To put it more starkly, art, artistry, and artifice are *deponent* phenomena: their meanings, significance, or consequences and implications essentially entailed a wide range of other cultural practices and processes. In addition, art—and, by extension, any mode of human fabrication—has always entailed religious or "spiritual" beliefs and practices. Art and religion are co-constructions, both in the various Western traditions and in countless other societies and communities. Art as a religion coexists with religion as an art, as an artistic practice.

My queering practices had a number of early origins; I'll close by mentioning one catalyst that comes to mind. A lecture I gave in Manchester, United Kingdom, in 1994, "So Is Art Queer, Then?" began from the idea that art—by which I mean *artistry*, the practice of making or fabricating in whatever palpable form it may have taken or will take in the future—*fundamentally troubles*, *opposes*, or *queers* canonical or conventional truths or legitimized realities: all that may be taken as given or acceptable/permissible/proper, and so on. Just before that, in 1993, I was walking out of a very boring semiotics conference in San Francisco, and seeing an equally bored and frustrated academic colleague, Rosalind Krauss, I engaged her in conversation, and we agreed on the importance of "making trouble" as the strategic necessity of what a responsible "art historian"/critical theorist/citizen might be and do. And that practice—call it artistry or history-writing, by which I mean, in the most general sense, the practice of *worlding* or world-making—is radical enough and terror-inducing by nature.

Art is itself a *queering*: the problematizing of what given social orders promote and not infrequently terrorize its populations into believing as natural, real, true, or divinely inspired and in sync with the cosmos. Artifice or artistry in its most general sense is fundamentally an activity of queering—that is, of foregrounding the constructedness or mediatedness of human activity: a radical problematizing of hegemonic power in purporting to fabricate collective realities. Queerings as fundamentally skeptical, deconstructive relationships to institutional hegemonies of various kinds. As hegemonies and their terrorisms evolve, so too must our queerings.

Claire Farago

I didn't choose a path of resistance—it chose me. My career has unfolded in two main areas: Leonardo da Vinci manuscript studies and cross-cultural studies. The connections may not be obvious, but for me, they developed as two sides of the same coin. Leonardo was not university educated, and his readings of sources were sometimes idiosyncratic—that is part of his appeal today and an important aspect of the methodological challenge that interested me as a doctoral student in the 1980s. Long before that, as an undergraduate, I had become interested in the history of the creative process, that is, how the creative process has been conceived historically in the Western tradition. Leonardo's writings on painting were a formative part of that history, as I came to appreciate in some detail at a time when studies by art historians exclusively focused on the literature on art were rare. In fact, they were discouraged in the United States. We operate in a field that discourages the study of intellectual trends if they do not arise from the examination of individual objects. What justifies these assumptions? What justifies the methodology? The history of the discipline's highly esteemed empirical practices has received some attention (notably from historians of science such as Peter Galison, Lorraine Daston, and Caroline Jones), but it has not changed the way art historians generally operate. My methods of analysis are based above all on what I learned from my dissertation advisor, David Summers, who encouraged me to focus on Leonardo's *Paragone* because the text is, as he once put it, "a can of worms." In the course of my studies, I stumbled upon the complex phenomenon of "intertextuality" and, almost without realizing it, intertextuality became central to the way I think about history relationally by de-centering the author or artist, or whatever the object of study as an autonomous, singular entity would be in an empirical study designed to produce positive information. Throughout my career, I have practiced a kind of intertextuality on myself by working collaboratively: a dialogic structure enables multi-vocal historical perspectives that foreground *how* things mean, rather than purporting to dictate *what* things mean. Significance is always a function of many interdependent factors open to interpretation. There is no way to arrest the movement of semiosis permanently.

My interest in cross-cultural studies began roughly the same way as my study of Leonardo's writings, in trying to understand the history of the discourse. In the case of transcultural processes, the European discourse was always about the classification of the arts as knowledge. Were painting and sculpture "liberal arts"? What kind of theoretical knowledge did they each require? Which is more challenging? Having focused on Leonardo and the European literature of art, I began to ask how complete our historical understanding of Western aesthetic theory was. Did extra-European culture play a role in the formation of European categories? I adapted feminist strategies to ask new questions about the history of categories such as "Renaissance" and units of analysis such as "national culture" and "period style." My queries led to an anthology, *Reframing the Renaissance: Visual Culture in Europe and Latin America, 1450–1650* (1995). The response to this collaborative publication, consisting of fifteen authors in different subfields of Early Modern art history, has been overwhelming—the field of "cross-cultural" or "transcultural" studies did not yet exist. We were lucky to be in the right place at the right time, but I had a difficult time getting it published. The first peer reviewer complained that there was nothing Eurocentric about the Renaissance. When I rewrote the prospectus to explain more fully why that was not the case, the reviewer erupted in rage, complete with four-letter words and a vicious personal attack that left me shaken, angry, and resolved to publish the study. Fortunately, the press did not abandon the project, and Latin Americanists in particular embraced the publication. Its most enthusiastic readers have been graduate students and young scholars.

My next big project was another collaboration, *Transforming Images: New Mexican Santos in-between Worlds* (2006), a case study of a "contact zone" where previously unrelated cultures coexisted for an extended period of time. It grew directly out of the *Reframing* project, as I had become very interested in *how* things mean—the process of semiosis itself—how images and material objects enable people with different beliefs to coexist. This study of material culture in the margins of the Spanish

Empire conceived as a center in its own right was also difficult to publish: the first peer reviewer recommended excising all the theory and increasing the number of color illustrations to make it into a cocktail table book (the reviewer's words, not mine). Eventually, I found a new publisher. Pennsylvania State University Press did a beautiful job, and the Andrew Wyeth Foundation through the College Art Associaton provided a generous subvention that enabled us to have 250 color illustrations of material that was either unpublished or known only in the regional literature. Yet the book, which was the product of a decade-long collaboration among thirteen scholars from different fields combining their data and knowledge, fell between the cracks. To my dismay, *Transforming Images*, which explicitly took up the problem of systemic racism, never received much critical attention.

What was even more discouraging is that my university colleagues did not welcome my pedagogical efforts to revise the curriculum to be less Eurocentric, more pluralistic, no longer racist. Twenty-two years after the publication of *Reframing the Renaissance*, they decided to eliminate the collaborative introductory course I had spearheaded a few years earlier with their help and that of graduate students, supported by university grants to make the course more diverse, in favor of an introductory course in World Art that used Kenneth Clark's *The Nude: A Study in Ideal Form* as its only text. That administrative maneuver took place in November 2016, a week after Trump's election, and it was when I decided to retire, to write for a broader public about how we humanists can motivate action to address the dual threat of the climate crisis and populism.

So now I have used up nearly half of my allotted space with stories of how I have *failed* to thrive in the face of overwhelming odds. I've always picked my projects for the issues they enabled me to explore, and I've never given up, but I have not thrived. I've questioned authority and called for major changes to the status quo—like Donald, I've been reimagining art history since I first imagined being an art historian. The complaints I voice here describe how I experienced privilege operating in a patriarchal field of cultural production. It has been an ethical commitment rather than a savvy career choice to study the history of our inherited categories and to work collaboratively so that the specializations formed by those categories do not keep reproducing the same essentializing, culturally and historically specific assumptions about identity. And regardless of one's social position, as an author, changing the structure of the field is far more difficult than contributing new studies that leave the structure intact.

In my earlier work, I was interested in recovering the voices of the culturally dispossessed. I am not sure where that desire originated—maybe from my father's stories about life in Nazi Hungary during the Second World War when he worked for the underground recruiting other dissidents, maybe from my own experience as a teenager and college student in the 1960s protesting social injustices: the Civil Rights movement, the war in Vietnam. Or maybe as a second-generation feminist impressed by Judith Butler's critique of essentialist defenses of "woman" and bell hooks's and others' objections to white privilege in the women's movement. But times and priorities have changed. Climate disruption/crisis/emergency is an existential threat facing the entire planet. At the same time, populism is surging. Its effects are frightening, destructive, and cruel.

We humanists have the responsibility and possibly the power to change this discourse, to encourage responsible global citizenship. As Donald observed in his statement, as hegemonies and their terrorisms evolve, so too must our queerings. It is time to reimagine the cultural history of the planet in terms that bring us together, terms that encourage everyone to marshal all their resources into a multipronged effort to mitigate the ecological and humanitarian disaster in which we find ourselves. Every research project today needs to be framed with the current world situation in mind and the need to act responsibly as global citizens. Today's world calls for collaborative efforts because the problems that need to be addressed exceed any one discipline, field, or expertise. We need studies that are aware of the histories of their inherited categories, studies diachronic in their framing so that Eurocentric categories are not unintentionally reproduced, studies that span existing geographical categories for the same reason. It has never been more critical to understand how media affects behavior.

Initially, I conceived collaborative studies because the breadth of the questions driving my research also required a depth of knowledge that exceeds any one specialization. I wanted to articulate what would be involved in reframing our discipline to focus on cultural interaction. Our existing categories of period, style, national culture, and individual biography (to start with an obvious but partial list) discourage such self-reflection. To articulate the issues requires expertise in a range of Early Modern specializations, so I invited scholars in a variety of subdisciplines with an interest in historiography and methodology to contribute case studies in areas (such as collecting practices and theories of images) that would have to be considered critically if cultural interaction and the formation of identity—rather than the taxonomic exercise of classifying existing identities—became the main questions driving research.

Reframing the Renaissance led me to undertake an extended case study of cultural exchange in one location, the decade-long project that was published in 2006 as *Transforming Images*. Again, the depth and breadth of this study's research questions necessitated collaboration—above all, unpacking the conventionally assumed direct relationship between the appearance of objects and the ethnic and/or biological identity of their makers and users. I was and am still asking how to conceive relationships between artistry and agency that do not fall back on essentializing assumptions about subjects and objects. Art history reimagined to serve contemporary needs in order to create an educated civil society has an important role to play in mitigating the climate crisis. Literally, nothing else matters if the oceans run out of oxygen and the global food chain breaks down. The world needs humanists, artists, critics working alongside scientists whose studies of climate disruption and pollution are predicting this dire outcome if the planet does not change course now. This is not a drill.

JOSH T FRANCO

HOW DID I end up an art historian, a storyteller with pictures? Below, in the main body, is a version of my story in just under 2000 characters. This was the limit set on the application for a recent funding source I sought as an independent art worker. It is under consideration at the time of this writing. It is my voice in a button-down shirt and a suit jacket. For this writing, I have added endnotes, which are me in my underwear on a Saturday, halfway through the morning's coffee. Maybe I am hungover, and maybe you spent the night. This seemed a rare opportunity to exercise both voices simultaneously. Any good storyteller is multivocal. And, let's face it, in today's saturated art worlds, the application for which I wrote this narrative will likely be unsuccessful. Only two or three people may ever see it otherwise.

(This is called economizing, folks, and it is key to an art worker's survival.)

Here it is:

Josh T Franco is an artist and art historian.[1] *His West Texas upbringing critically informs his scholarly and studio projects, and the methods with which he approaches them.*[2] *He is currently based in Washington, DC, and serves as National Collector at the Smithsonian's Archives of American Art.*[3]

Franco's investments in the discipline in which he would eventually earn a PhD began in high school, while taking an introductory art history course.[4] *He continued this pursuit at Southwestern University in Georgetown, Texas, where he completed two capstone projects.*[5] *One interpreted a disciplinary genealogy leading from the early foundations of the field established by Austrian and German scholars to the emergence of social art history, as demonstrated in Thomas Crow's "Painters and Public Life in Eighteenth-Century Paris."*[6] *His second senior thesis was an analysis of representations of sexuality in Hellenistic sculpture, culminating in a comparative study of this work with contemporary popular culture and a focus on mass market advertising imagery.*[7]

From 2006–2008, Franco served as Service-Learning Coordinator at Our Lady of the Lake University in San Antonio, Texas.[8] *During this transformational period, he underwent the process Guillermo Gómez-Peña terms "Chicanization," of becoming Chicano.*[9]

In his dissertation, Franco unpacked his 2009–2011 performance/installation project MARFITA.[10] *In order to articulate the complex minimalist and rasquache character of Marfa, Texas—where his ancestors have long dwelt—he worked closely with primary advisers from art history, philosophy, and anthropology as well as a global network of artists, scholars, and activists self-identified as the Modernity/Coloniality/Decoloniality network.*[11]

Franco's two years as an Artist-Guide at Donald Judd's preserved home in NYC inspired his interest in artists' legacies, central to his current work and proposed book project.[12] *Ultimately, he wonders: What is the story of the first human-made mark?*[13]

Coda in real time (writing from August 2020): It is always a risk to write from a present moment. A present-tense voice goes against the grain of the editing process. This coda comes much later than what you have read above. The application for which this version of my bio was drafted was unsuccessful. I found out while this sat in my inbox, accompanied with the first round of editors' notes. Good thing it is useful anyway. (Like I wrote months ago, economizing is key.) I allowed myself to be upset for exactly one evening. (This is called compartmentalizing, folks, and it is key to an art worker's survival.) Then I applied for two more opportunities, one major, one less of a mutual commitment, but special in its way. One of these was successful, and I look forward to participating in the Risograph Residency at the Future, a gathering place for witches and weirdos in

Minneapolis, in December. Residencies punctuate my ongoing work—the "day job"—at the Archives of American Art. I realized recently that I make art for art historians, which is why my studio practice and professional life complement rather than compete with one another. Storytelling is the purview of both writers and makers.

Notes

1. It is only in the past three or four years that people, including me, seem to have dropped the skepticism that it is possible to be both. I am gauging this based on external affirmation. I wish it wasn't so, but at the end of the day, I am quite happy to tell you about the awards, exhibitions, and funding opportunities that validate each position. Am I a gross title and money chaser? Maybe. But I have been able to research, make, and write things that I couldn't have dreamt of doing alone. And damn, audiences are nice.
2. I often feel like I am exploiting my upbringing. But it is *mine*, right? Or did I give up access to those roughneck oilfield and vaquero virtues inch by inch as I stacked degree on degree? Am I making a caricature of West Texas in my work? Is that what all artists and scholars do to their subjects?
3. Yes, this job is rad! I won the art historical independent study lottery they never told us existed. The account of this country's art history that I've received over coffee and many, many pastries is so stunningly rich compared to that delivered in most textbooks. There was a whole other version of this piece you are reading now where I planned to list brief summaries of the stories I have heard from the veteran American art workers I meet with regularly. But too many were shared in confidence, and they are theirs at the end of the day. What I can offer is this pro tip: Go visit your elder artists. Every hour with them will be worth a week in your studio. I promise.
4. This was also traumatizing. I was accused of cheating because I passed a note during a test. The note had nothing to do with the test. It was a dirty love note. The teacher—who I have not forgiven—maintained that it was still somehow cheating, even after she invaded our privacy and read it. Now I wonder if this is why I am obsessed with the overlaps of personal intimacy and art historical labor. I am certain this moment confirmed for

me that Roald Dahl was spot on: Adults are evil. And I earned a 4 out of 5 on the Advanced Placement Art History exam and got a Ph.D., so there.

5. As a high school senior, I applied to only one college: Williams. If you are 17 and already know you want to be an art historian, why apply anywhere else, right? And I was admitted! However, at the last minute, the isolated Berkshires simply felt too alien for this West Texan, especially after my younger brother had recently and unexpectedly passed away. It was a scramble. Thanks to my English teacher, Mrs. Hobbs, I found Southwestern. I would not change this decision. I am still unpacking the gifts this school gave me. And though I never attended Williams, I happily attend symposia and other gatherings there now as a fully-fledged art historian. I wistfully, but not regretfully, imagine what it would have been like to be 17 there.
6. I still revisit the boys on the regular. The boys are: Alois Riegl, Erwin Panofsky, Heinrich Wölfflin, Johann Joachim Winckelmann, Aby Warburg, et al. You have to know what the foundation is made of if you want to burn a house down.
7. This I have never revisited. I think I was just a horny, repressed college kid. I really love that professor, so I cringe now when I think of him reading it. Sorry, Dr. Howe!
8. What is a service-learning coordinator? I designed and oversaw collaborations between university courses and community organizations throughout San Antonio. I was based in a school of social work, and my theoretical interests in artmaking and investment in art's long history could no longer be my priorities on a day-to-day basis. Instead, I was consumed with the logistics of moving students to and from work sites and assessing the immediate pedagogical value of, for instance, participating in public mural creations. This job changed my life. I learned not only to value but also to really see, for the first time, art's capacity to meet immediate needs.
9. I recently realized that I was an art historian before I was a Chicano. I was always well aware that I am a Mexican American, but "Chicano" is a political choice I didn't make until my early twenties. Being immersed in the long artistic and political history of San Antonio brought this out in me. I am grateful to that city and my beloveds there for midwifing the early process. I will point out that while Gómez-Peña's formulation is indeed helpful, there's a crucial difference from my own

story: immigration. Gómez-Peña writes from the experience of moving to the United States from central Mexico. As a Tejano from a family that has largely resided in what is the Chihuahuan Desert region for millennia, I have no significant immigration story or recent ancestral memories of movement in my constitution. The nearest significant immigration is that of the Iberian branch hundreds of years ago, long before the United States or Mexico was constructed in its present form. The Indigenous were already in the region thousands of years before that. We didn't cross the border. The border crossed us. My Chicanization came from this realization, rather than from any experience of physical diaspora, exile, or immigration. Now, my move to upstate New York for graduate school is a different story …

10. I loved critic Jeanne Claire van Ryzin's review. She is a stalwart of Texas contemporary art criticism, and it was an honor to be visited and considered by her. She wrote: "For 'Marfita,' Franco and his collaborators juxtapose [Donald] Judd's rarefied vision along with its resultant exclusivity against another pilgrimage site in Marfa: The home of the late Hector Sanchez, who in 1994 saw an apparition of the Virgin Mary in his backyard. Sanchez lived less than a half mile from Chinati and the shrine he built at his house is still a destination for the faithful. Though they may literally cross paths, the pilgrims headed to the Sanchez shrine and those headed to Chinati never connect and, Franco surmises, have virtually no knowledge of each other. […] 'Marfita' troubles the boundary between two distinct groups that treasure Marfa with the same depth of reverence. Franco and his cohorts have neatly raised questions, and smartly left it to us to ponder possible answers." Jeanne Claire van Ryzin, "A little take on Marfa's Culture Clash," October 26, 2011, https://www.austin360.com/entertainment/arts—theater/little-take-marfa-culture-clash/5aoCYkWkYLCBcJAOyv1eUI/. I am also eternally grateful to the three other artists who created this installation, environmental, and performance artwork by my side: Natalie Goodnow, Alison Kuo, and Joshua Saunders.
11. What is rasquachismo? How do I reinterpret minimalism? How does my deployment of decoloniality operate? There's a dissertation for that: Josh T Franco, "Marfa, Marfa: Minimalism, Rasquachismo, and Questioning 'Decolonial Aesthetics' in Far West Texas" (Ph.D. dissertation, SUNY Binghamton, 2016).

12. I once took a nap on the fifth (top) floor at 101 Spring Street. I wanted to wake up naturally to the light of Dan Flavin, *untitled*, 1970, a series of overlapping human-scale rectilinear forms composed of red and blue neon lights that span the long side of the room. The work sits inches from the emulated poured glass windows that look out on the intersection of Spring and Mercer in Soho. It was one of those sleep experiences where waking up is the dreamy part. More prosaically, this job was an unexpected perfect bridge from inward-facing academia to the public scholarship I now undertake at the Smithsonian. Groups of visitors did include the die-hard Judd aficionados, but as press coverage expanded, audiences began to include tourists with little previous knowledge. Articulating the history of the building and the collection in the context of Judd's practice and postwar American art history for this audience was precisely the kind of training that prepared me for working in our nation's cultural memory holder. Here, my work is beholden to *all* Americans, be they plumbers or Ph.D.s.
13. I am genuinely consumed by this question. It is the ultimate art historical project. I tend to imagine a scar. It is not exactly an accident, this minor wound. By nature, it could not be accidental. I see a girl, sitting just within the luminous zone of the campfire that cooked a kill from that day. She has eaten her fill and is left with a precious few minutes to let her mind wander. Her eyes wander too. She spots one of the sharpened stones that brought down the beast. Curious and empathetic, she puts it to her own skin. A substrate. A tool. Pressure. Intention. Motion. Then a bright red line, the first drawing. The blood spreads (the line diffuses). The first paint. A thousand other curious moments will lead her to dyes, pigments, cave walls, and cliff sides. The thought of the first mark keeps me going. What do you imagine? Speculate this art history with me. Tell me a story.

CHITRA GANESH

I WAS BORN and raised in New York City in a tight-knit bilingual immigrant community, speaking English and Tamil, studying Indian classical music and dance, traveling regularly to India over summer holidays, while memorizing the NYC subway map to explore the city and its cultural institutions as a young New Yorker, from CBGB to Museum of Modern Art. My earliest field trips revealed to me how art objects on view from my region of the world—the South Asian subcontinent—were often considered artifacts rather than art.

Objects on view were invariably thousands of years old and relegated to a frozen past, compared to the nuanced chronology and display of eighteenth- to twentieth-century Euro-American art. I was struck by this representational void between eighth-century Chola sculpture and Steve McCurry's war-torn "Afghan girl" on the cover of National Geographic that I encountered on line at the supermarket. I wondered why certain stories easily proliferated and accrued power, while others remained absent or even actively suppressed—questions which still animate my practice and appear today in the form of critical analysis of museum collections, the restitution of looted objects, and more. My encounter at age 9 with Pablo Bartholomew's iconic 1984 World Press photo of a dead young girl's mask-like face lying in the dirt awakened me to the scale and reverberations of the environmental atrocities of India's Bhopal gas tragedy, and how such events, in what was then called "the Third World," were used as a way to visualize the non-West as abject and backward. This was also the first time I ever saw someone like me represented in American media, and I was shaken. I often meditate on this moment as an augur of what I've grown to understand about how hierarchies of visual representation still privilege certain body politics and subjectivities over others, how some parts of the world are always represented as impoverished or war torn. For example, I often think of that picture in relation to the surprising consistency in the representation of Afghanistan in the mainstream American media over 25 years and to how deeply images can stir us and make us think.

These early impressions sparked a lifelong interest in trying to make sense of representational contradictions and lacunae, both in the imaging of everyday politics and current events and in the economies of visibility and absence within the canons of art history. A commitment to visualizing absence continues to be a key impulse that guides my drawing practice, and it extends to the projects and content I pursue across media. I am drawn to the iconography of mythic, literary, and popular narratives that have been historically considered minor literatures and genres, such as science fiction, song lyrics, comics, and graphic art, as a means to bring forth alternate representations of female subjectivity and power that I felt to be so acutely missing. Drawing on the comic form as a complex system of signification in its own right, narrative devices of epic myth, and the visual vocabulary of psychedelic and protest posters, I probe familiar, collectively held stories for moments of rupture, dissonance, and new narrative possibilities. Collage and automatic writing have been a central part of my process, as a means to form nonlinear and surrealist narratives, populated by unreliable narrators, new female subjectivities, and unexpected desires. Oftentimes, the medium is also the message. I often integrate mass-produced and vernacular objects into my site-specific wall drawings as focal points in drawings that often tower over the viewer to extend off the wall into three-dimensional space. Once located within my drawings' frames, quotidian objects such as shower curtains, marbles, toys, or shards of broken glass are transformed, signifying lush vegetation or adornment for mythic creatures. I work with such defamiliarized found objects, rich with traces of everyday life, as dish sponges and hair extensions. I see this as a means both to comingle radically different and historically segregated object histories and to provide viewers with additional points of entry into the work. These sculptural elements animate the visceral, erotic undercurrents of my mythic imagery and offer a visual experience that binds or links the monumentality of epic texts to the objects that ground us in life's daily labor and rituals.

In 2004, I began working with artist Mariam Ghani on Index of the Disappeared, a collaboration that continues today. Our work developed as a response to a post-9/11 political landscape and has evolved into a physical archive and a mobile platform for dialogue and interventions. Between the fall of 2001 up through the summer 2004 Republican National Convention in New York City, Mariam and I separately noticed a meta-narrative forming around disappearance and shaping the nation's political discourse. Initially this was abundantly visible to us in the form of flyers posted across New York City of missing persons who were victims of the events of the 9/11 tragedy. At the same time, we noticed a parallel narrative of disappearance emerge, one that was targeting members of our own communities. Post-9/11 American exceptionalist policies were systematically, disproportionately disappearing men of Muslim, South Asian, and Arab origin, mobilizing policies such as indefinite detention, deportation, special registration, and acts of state-sponsored brutality under the guise of fighting terrorism. Index of the Disappeared organically evolved out of a shared commitment to archive around the absences and erasures that struck us and affected our communities deeply. As an archive, Index of the Disappeared foregrounds the difficult histories of immigrant, "Other," and dissenting communities in the United States since 9/11 and how these continue to shape subsequent US military and intelligence interventions around the world. Collecting and connecting official documents, secondary literature, and personal narratives, the Index archive traces the ways in which censorship and data blackouts are part of a broader shift to secrecy that allows for disappearances, deportations, renditions, and detentions on an unprecedented scale.

Figuration and the erotic

I work with figuration to shed light on feminist, queer, and previously unconsidered narratives typically absent from canons of history, literature, and art. I'm interested in both the body's materiality and its place within a larger set of social and cultural significations; for the duration of history into our present moment, the female figure has served as a flashpoint of geopolitical conflict and domestic political struggles. Take, for example, the continued fight on the part of conservative lawmakers to police women's decisions around their bodies, to deny women access to the right to have an abortion; the invisibility and disturbing regularity with which Black trans women continue to be murdered in the United States; or the revolutionary and inspiring role that women across India have taken in courageously standing up against the violence of the nascent fascism and Hindu nationalism of the ruling government.

Anthropologist Mary Douglas's thinking around the body very much echoes the impulse behind my work: "The body is a complex structure. The functions of its different parts and their relation afford a source of symbols for other complex structures. We cannot possibly interpret rituals concerning excreta, breast milk, saliva and the rest unless we are prepared to see in the body a symbol of society, and to see the powers and dangers credited to social structure reproduced in small on the human body."[1] I hold the Brown femme body and its attendant histories of representation as a potent site for transformation and subversion. I first read *Sister Outsider* 28 years ago. Too young to fully grasp the meaning behind what I was reading, I nonetheless felt a door open ever so slightly and sensed myself wanting to step into that crack of light that emanated from within. Revisiting *The Uses of the Erotic* directed me to Audre Lorde's legacy as part of a movement that took on the project of writing alternative femininities into being, a shared impulse that was also at the heart of my own approach to making. A writing that was not reactive, or interested in replacing a pure image with a denigrated one, but that sought to flesh out the possibilities of bodily and affective resonance as a legitimate, and critical, and intellectually robust mode of communication, power, and change. Such writings have been crucial in making the space for contemporary conversations around race, sexuality, and power. Lorde's erotics on the page are part of a larger feminist discursive strategy that gave me permission to take that leap into the unknown. Walking straight into black holes, feeling myself to be on ever-shifting ground, seeing beauty near the abyss, and acknowledging the violence of certain erasures as I walk in the valley of the shadow of life.

Lorde's notion of the erotic as a signifier of unclaimed and unattended forms of knowledge resonates for me in the multiplicity of visual languages that continue to lie beyond, outside, or beneath Euro-American contemporary art discourse. Growing up in an everyday-people household, my very first visual with art and aesthetics was via the beauty of fridge magnets depicting Hindu gods and goddesses, children's book illustrations, the melodrama and excess of Bollywood movies, or the graphic design on the packaging of my dad's cigarettes—Alive with Pleasure.

Lorde's notion of unclaimed or unattended knowledge resonates in my own practice via the aesthetics of children's comics published in India in the 1960s and 1970s, the visual idiom of horror and Bollywood movie posters and painted covers of pulp fiction novels, the shapeshifting power and potency of both X-Men and song lyrics that hit you differently every time, depending on your emotional temperature at that moment. Everyday mark-making such as the scratching and scrawl on the walls of a public girls' bathroom also provided inspiration for writing. There is no question I received inspiration in equal part from the stacks of books I borrowed at the Brooklyn Public Library as I did from the writing that covered those bathroom stalls: meditations in their own right on sex, longing, desperation, self-loathing, self-love, violence, and transcendence.

Accessing the erotic could also offer a potent exit strategy—where you, I, and we can gather ourselves and exit left stage from the polarizing set of discursive terms that shape art history and contemporary art: inside/outside, theory/practice, conceptual/figurative, abstraction/decoration, painting/drawing, drawing/illustration, genius/unrecognized, and so forth. There is a messiness about the affective experience, about an artwork that stuns you into silence or stops you in your tracks, pulls you out of your body for a second only to send you crashing right back into yourself, that has the potential to interrupt all of this, to disrupt existing boundaries and reconvene them in more pluralistic, polymorphous ways. It could even be that you look at a work of art, and it stares right back at you, touching you with its piercing gaze, as you touch it with your eyes, and you and it, for a moment, become one.

The erotic's capacity to form a bridge between sharers is another intervention that sheds light on my own experiments with figuration and narrative. My works often integrate image and text, to offer parallel visual and written narratives that occupy a singular frame. In this process, I hope to provide an opening of sorts, a third story or position that the viewer may inhabit, a dream which the viewer may step into and walk down the streets of. I aim to invite my viewers to share in the subjectivities of, and questions posed by, the bodies that inhabit my work. Dark skinned, feminine, possessing both an intellectual and an erotic articulation.

Bodies are road maps, repositories, constellations of stars, albeit ones that some are not willing to read. Black and Brown bodies (or their outlines in chalk once they are violently disappeared from our material world) signify so much beyond the visual presentation of that particular body on the screen/canvas/page. What secrets and histories do these bodies know? Which bodies are legible, and why? Ultimately, the body holds a certain kind of responsive knowledge, be it traumatic or ecstatic, that can't be found anywhere else.

Friendship as life support

These days many of my professional spaces, and the politics shaping them, appear as a series of darkened labyrinths, far too daunting to navigate. Who else walked these roads? Why does my flashlight keep disappearing? In this foggy journey, friendship has been everything: a torch, a support system, my outbreath.

It feels natural as the child of immigrants to seek translators, guides, and kindred spirits to navigate machineries of opaque institutions that one never imagined entering. On alien soil, it was a matter of survival to cultivate ties beyond geographic origin, our primary bonds no longer locked in place by the immutability of blood. And so I need our nuanced conversations and abiding trust to walk hand in hand as we traverse art's hallowed grounds: those institutional/discursive spaces where so many of us were never even meant to exist.

One task at hand is facing down representational annihilation in a country that still struggles to acknowledge visual languages and aesthetic histories animated by anything other than Euro-American art history. In these hierarchical art worlds, it's through friendship that we are able to enunciate ourselves into existence in the sidebars of everyday life, hear criticism with love, and amplify our voices to speak truth to canons, mechanisms of production and distribution, and representational regimes that constrain and exclude us. Years were devoted to tending spaces of reciprocity and care, a vital affective anchor for the intellectual, phenomenological, and psychic terrain I navigated as a young artist whose interests and subjectivity were rarely reflected in the art I studied or saw. We enunciated ourselves into being and collectively emerged, developing visual grammar and art-historical lineage, illuminating that which was previously invisible/illegible/unseen—in museums, galleries, literatures, lexicons, and perhaps even within ourselves.

New York City, my scrappy childhood stomping grounds, is now a shark tank of ambition, a space of addiction to being busy. It demands a punishing pace of work, measuring every moment according to vague and unexamined notions of productivity and success. Failure is too expensive, meandering explorations too inefficient. This harms both art and ideas, which require time and an absence of measuring sticks or one-way mirrors in order to thrive. Friendship gives me the armor, gentle push, shared sense of vision and politics, permission to fail, and radical acceptance that I need to claw my way out of the twenty-first-century New York state of mind. Pushing beyond the transactional and strategic, the cheers rising up from the depths of friendship's echo chambers reaffirm my values and enable radical shifts in thinking and making that I never imagined possible. When I find myself in a traffic jam of thoughts, a cacophonous insecurity of competing and receiving ideas, I start a conversation with you in my head, and the spinning slows. Thoughts exhale, and begin to unravel themselves. Eventually these ideas will manifest in ink, object, moving image, or more words between us. But for now, it is in our connection that seeds of my thoughts can begin to form themselves, long before they become whole.

Note

1. Mary Douglas, *Purity and Danger: An Analysis of Concepts of Pollution and Taboo* (London: Routledge, 1966), 116.

DAVID J. GETSY

I NEVER INTENDED to study art history; I had no exposure to it. I was a first-generation college student, and the most important thing to me was queer activism and the AIDS crisis. My first job, as a high-school student in upstate New York in the late 1980s, had been working at Binghamton General Hospital delivering food to patients. I still remember the first time a patient was there due to AIDS-related complications. I could barely see his face behind layers of protective curtains, and I was told to wear a special mask and gloves before entering this room that looked so different from any of the others on my route. I was 16, and I saw myself for the first time. Soon after, I started volunteering at the Southern Tier AIDS Program (and met my first queer mentor, Laurie Bennett, the volunteer coordinator who took me under her wing and whose example and guidance helped me more than she ever knew).

I went to college with these experiences and the determination to do something. Art was not really part of the plan, but in my first year at Oberlin College, I became swept up (as many did) by the powerful teaching of feminist art historian Patricia Mathews. She modeled a mode of engagement with culture that was political and critical.[1] She taught me the importance of looking beyond and beneath the observable to visualize resistance and respite. Still, I couldn't help but see a contradiction between my work on queer issues in campus politics and the excitement of wading into academics and art history.

One of my other Oberlin professors, the inimitable William Hood, would—every time I saw him in subsequent years—remind me how I cried in our methodology seminar. My reasons were good. We were talking about Ernst Gombrich's oblique writing about the Holocaust, and it led to a question of personal responsibility to history and to the world. Bill told a story about his own past and explained his conflicted experience of taking a leave from graduate school during protest movements against the war in Vietnam. I lost it. What was the point, I thought, of doing something as effete as art history in the face of all that needed to be done? My crisis of faith hit me in that seminar, with Bill looking incredulously but supportively at me (shocked, I think, that his own story had such an impact).

I didn't leave art history, however, but this event made it clear to me that I needed a sense of purpose greater than I had given it. Art history, for me, became a place where I could make a case for finding positions outside and against the expected or the "natural" ones—that is, queer positions. I still feel ambivalent about letting my activist energies wane, and only years later did I come to balance that feeling with a recognition of how important it has been to do the often unseen work of supporting other scholars and students of transgender and queer topics. Or, at least, I hope it makes up for it a little.

I emphasize this formative undergraduate moment because it comes back for me often when I ask myself (as we all do), what's the point of all this effort? Scholarship is rarely activism, but it does make a difference. Whether in the classroom, in the reader's report, or in a publication, I can facilitate a conversation with far different horizons than were available to me or to those who came before. We need to be in those conversations for them to happen, and they can happen anywhere.

My attempt to contribute has been to ask about the ways art history can address the determining role of the visual for queer and transgender people. We don't know a person when we see a body, and trans and queer people have to negotiate (differently) questions of disclosure and exposure daily through the navigation of scrutiny, surveillance, camouflage, defiant spectacle, and the searching look. For me, this is why there is an organic relationship between art history's ongoing debates about the human form and transgender and queer histories and politics.

I started on this path out of frustration with the ways in which a queer art history was limited (by both its advocates and its detractors) by a demand for visual evidence. This came down to an exclusive focus on bodies and sexual acts, and "gay and lesbian art history," as it was just beginning to be called when I started graduate school, remained largely focused on the figure, often nude, perhaps coupled. From the beginning, my work has been about thinking about queer experience more broadly, with the understanding that outlawed desires and ways of living are about much more than just sex. This isn't to avoid or deny sex, but to decry the narrow taxonomy of allowed visualizations of its effects on the ways we live and love. For those antagonistic to a queer art history (or for a scholar who thinks it is merely "niche" or auxiliary to art history), there is a persistent demand for visual confirmation. If they cannot clearly see evidence, it must not be there. Traditional historical methodologies demand evidence but have no way of redressing the erasures and suppressions of histories that made evidence of homoeroticism, queer desires or nonascribed genders impossible, unarchivable, or invisible. In particular, it was my dissertation work under Whitney Davis on the queer forebear John Addington Symonds that laid the foundation for me.[2] I struggled with Symonds's coded ways of arguing that queer experience mattered and that history offered a means of being seen in a culture that refuses to do so. His desire to find evidence of homoeroticism outside of the easily recognizable and identifiable became mine. I also began to see how much a queer or transgender history was a history not just of self-evident objects of study but also of others' disavowals, refusals to recognize, and condescending silences.

I also had to face my own refusal to recognize, however. Soon after I started teaching, I was afforded the opportunity to teach queer theory and queer art history. I was excited about this, but teaching is not reading. It is a conversation. Through the conversations with my students about how to wrestle with these ideas, I kept stumbling on my own language.

It became increasingly clear to me that my received accounts of queer experience (including my own) had been hampered by a presumption of binary genders. I came to see how the queer theory I was reading made transgender subjects invisible or, at dubious best, deployed stereotypes about them. This was over fifteen years ago, and it was then that I committed myself to learning the literature on what was then coalescing as transgender studies. I remember thinking at this moment about my undergraduate crisis of faith, and I resolved to do something.

This was a risk, as is any attempt to write about an identity that one does not share, but I also understood that I was in the position to be able to contribute. When I started learning from and eventually contributing to transgender studies, you could still count the number of tenured transgender studies scholars in the humanities on one or maybe two hands. The fabled "transgender tipping point" was still to happen. Work was being done in literature, film studies, and popular culture, but there was no sustained work in art history about transgender issues. I asked myself how I might support its growth. My answer to this was not to write from an experience I did not have, but rather to ask how gender's multiplicity had been obscured from historical narratives. I came to study abstraction, with its avoidance of figuration, as a test case to discuss the limitations of binary ascriptions—and how to imagine what might be beyond them.[3]

For the first few years of graduate school, I always got embarrassed when I remembered crying in my undergraduate seminar, but now I recall that moment when I need to keep myself honest or on the path. That conversation was about the question of personal responsibility in the face of forces beyond control or even comprehension. I didn't take from it the answer about what to do, but I did take the conviction that I had to keep asking myself the question.

Notes

1. This is exemplified in Mathews' and Thalia Gouma-Peterson's coauthored state-of-the field essay "The Feminist Critique of Art History," *Art Bulletin* 69, no. 3 (1987): 326–57, and her book *Passionate Discontent: Creativity, Gender, and French Symbolist Art* (Chicago: University of Chicago Press, 1999), which I have often used in my own teaching.
2. The result was my article "Recognizing the Homoerotic: The Uses of Intersubjectivity in John Addington Symonds' 1887 Essays on Art," *Visual Culture in Britain* 8, no. 1 (Spring 2007): 37–57. During this time, Davis was working on the book that became his *Queer Beauty: Sexuality and Aesthetics*

from Winckelmann to Freud and Beyond (New York: Columbia University Press, 2010).

3. See "Capacity," *TSQ: Transgender Studies Quarterly* 1, nos 1–2 (May 2014), 47–49; "Introduction: Trans Cultural Production" (coauthored with Julian B. Carter and Trish Salah), *TSQ: Transgender Studies Quarterly* 1, no. 4 (November 2014): 469–81; and *Abstract Bodies: Sixties Sculpture in the Expanded Field of Gender* (New Haven and London: Yale University Press, 2015).

ROSELEE GOLDBERG

INTERVIEW CONDUCTED ON January 17, 2020, via phone.

ALPESH KANTILAL PATEL (AKP): You were born and raised in South Africa and eventually received degrees there as well. Can you share a few anecdotes from that period of your life? Specifically, in hindsight, are there any moments you think probably helped shape the kind of art historian you've become today?

South Africa

ROSELEE GOLDBERG (RG): I would say that growing up in South Africa is absolutely fundamental to who I am and, yes, also to my understanding of art history. From a very young age, I was aware of the politics of the country, of the inhumanity and inequities of Apartheid, of police brutality, of special branch police imprisoning people who objected to this horrific racism and holding them illegally. Not a moment of a day went by without awareness of that system. That sense of politics underlying everything, shaping every aspect of our lives, whether art, architecture, education, personal relationships, is always with me.

I grew up in subtropical Durban, on the Indian Ocean. Up the coast, waving hills of sugarcane fields, and further north, Zululand. I grew up listening to Zulu songs on the radio, hearing various African languages spoken on the street as groups of people walked down the hill where we lived, playing the guitar and harmonizing as they went; observing women wearing traditional dress with its patterns of intricate Zulu beading and large marital headdresses. Being woken by the sound of hadeda birds. In Durban, there was also a large population of Indians who were brought to South Africa in the 1860s from India as indentured workers on the railways and in the sugar fields. There was a strong sense of their culture, with Indian temples and festivals and a large Indian market in the center of town. And, of course, Gandhi lived in Durban for 21 years from 1893. So, it was a society of many different ethnicities, languages, cultures, despite the government's vigilance at keeping everyone separated.

I was also a dancer from a young age. I started with tap around 5 years old, then classical ballet, classical Spanish, also Bharatanatyam, which was taught by a young Indian dancer at the back of her uncle's photo studio in an area of town reserved for Indians. It was not exactly illegal for me to be there, I don't think, but it was somewhat hidden from view. My mother would take me and wait for the lesson to end to take me home.

Art history

I began studying art history at 13 years old, in my first year of high school. I had an amazing teacher who made art history riveting. I tried to never miss a day of her classes, which alternated between art history and painting and drawing classes. I clearly remember the very first lesson: we began with imagining how to build a Zulu hut, the beehive-shaped thatched structures that dotted the hills around Durban the moment one left the city on drives into the countryside. Clay pots, Zulu beadwork, cave paintings of the San people in the Drakensberg Mountains, the oldest dating to around 73,000 years ago. She built our understanding of art and culture through the ages, one layer at a time: the painted sculptures of ancient Greece, the rhythms of classic columns and their distinct capitals from Athens to Rome to Florence. Art history was the lens through which I viewed the world early on.

I left Durban for Johannesburg to attend the University of the Witwatersrand, where there was an exciting art history department made up of several very strong, politically aware professors. Interestingly, the art history department, fine art studios, and the

Architecture School shared the same modern building on campus, Bauhaus style, with students from the different disciplines attending some of the same foundation classes and lectures. My majors were fine art and art history, as well as political science, which only confirmed my belief in the importance of understanding the politics of a period as underpinning the history of art. My political science and art history papers were almost interchangeable, each illuminating the other. I was always cross-referencing the two and then taking the ideas being discussed back to the studio. I was also running a dance studio at the university. I was all about mixing these different understandings of practice and politics and history and research.

AKP: You describe such a rich background in the arts and politics, being very aware of politics when you're doing art. And then when you went to England, you went to the Courtauld Institute. I'm curious what kind of experience that was like. This must have been a huge shift.

London

RG: The Courtauld was an extraordinary place to be a university student in London in the late 1960s. In those days, it was located on Portman Square, in a breathtakingly beautiful mansion designed by Robert Adam in 1777, with its famous helix stairway. I initially intended to research Medieval and early Spanish Romanesque architecture and had plans to explore connections between late Romanesque and architectural styles in North Africa, but after a semester, I switched to "modern," eager to study with art historian John Golding, an amazing writer and lecturer whose book on Cubism I had read in South Africa, and which is probably still the main touchstone on Cubism. It was very evident from his book that he must have been a painter, and for me as a fine arts student, his parsing of space and the relationship of flat planes and how surfaces are broken up was a fascinating guide. I was still attending dance classes regularly in London, trying to decide my focus, dance or visual art, when I discovered the work of Oskar Schlemmer at the Bauhaus, which became the subject of my dissertation at the Courtauld. It would be the beginning of my writing and research on the history of performance.

AKP: Very soon after the Courtauld, you became a director of a gallery at the Royal College of Art. What did the contemporary art scene look like in England at this time? Was your work at the gallery how you ended up getting very interested in curating?

The Royal College of Art Gallery

RG: After completing my degree in London, I lived in Paris for almost a year, from where I applied for a position that had been advertised at the Royal College of Art (RCA) for director of exhibitions. To my surprise, I got the job, even though I had absolutely no experience as a curator nor any knowledge of contemporary art. At the interview, I extemporaneously came up with the idea of finding ways to work with all departments at the RCA, not knowing that inter-departmentalization was a major concern there at the time, and described the gallery as a meeting place for them all, a hub for discourse, performances, events, and exhibitions, that would connect the departments: graphic designers would design catalogues and flyers, interior design students would help install exhibitions, general studies students would be engaged in research and writing. I am sure I was inspired by my close attention to the Bauhaus with its integrated curriculum connecting so many disciplines.

I accepted the position, and suddenly, I had to ask myself, "Oh, now what?" The first thing I did was head to the Venice Biennial, and on the first morning there, I met people whom I would stay close to over the next decades—Vito Acconci, Joseph Kosuth, Joan Jonas, Germano Celant, Giancarlo Politi, Ileana Sonnabend—sitting in the café in St. Mark's Square. The art world was quite small in those days, everyone pretty much fitting into one café on the square, moving in the evening to the other side, whichever was the shadier. I remember a boat ride to Torcello with Roberto Matta (Gordon Matta-Clark's father), meeting French artist Daniel Buren, even César with his gravelly voice. I will always remember Gerhard Richter's black-and-white portraits, installed just below the dome in the German pavilion in 1972. Next was Documenta, where I would meet Kounellis, Dorothea Rockburne, Mel Bochner, and Marcel Broodthaers. I also went to Los Angeles and New York City. I visited the Watts Towers on my first day in Los Angeles, taken by a very good friend, an African American sociologist and activist whom I had met in London, who had been involved with the Studio Watts Workshop. He also took me to the Women's Building and introduced me to many artists.

So that was the beginning of my curatorial education! From the start, I was looking across media, across disciplines. My first exhibition at the RCA was by Giulio Paolini, another was "Record as Artwork" curated by Germano Celant, and later "A Space: A Thousand Words" of fifteen artists and fifteen architects, curated with the architect Bernard Tschumi. The gallery had a very tight budget, but I wrote to artists whom I had met in New York and elsewhere: "If you're in London, please come and join us for a talk and presentation." Many came! So, the program of exhibitions and events was incredibly exciting for the students but also for the London art scene of the time. Visitors included Christo and Jeanne-Claude, Carl Andre, Willoughby Sharp, Anthony McCall, Christian Boltanski, and Marina Abramović.

AKP: What compelled you to move to New York City, which is where you went to next? From South Africa to England to New York City. What got you to New York City? This was also when you become a curator at the Kitchen in New York City. It seems like such a pivotal moment in terms of performance for you. Can you tell us more about that?

New York

RG: During my first trip to New York, I was struck by the high energy of the city and the high energy of Americans in general, and felt the irresistible pull to stay. After three years at the RCA, where the program received terrific critical recognition but where the established painters and sculptors within the school wished the gallery to focus more on work created internally and less on the newest international developments in contemporary art, it was time to move on. New York was beckoning. My final exhibition at the gallery, "A Space: A Thousand Words," would travel to the Institute for Architecture and Urban Studies in New York and the USC gallery in LA. I continued writing on performance for *Studio International*, on the downtown scene and women artists for *Spare Rib* in London, and wrote my first article for *Artforum*, on Schlemmer and the Bauhaus, in 1977. I became close friends with artists Robert Longo and Cindy Sherman, and many others including Laurie Simmons, David Salle, and Eric Fischl, who had all recently moved to New York around this time. Longo was then the video curator at the Kitchen and suggested that I take over his position, since he didn't wish to be curating anymore but wanted to focus on his own work. I became curator of video at the Kitchen, soon adding performance to the title and building a gallery and video-viewing room. The program used the same interdisciplinary framework that I had instigated at the RCA.

The Kitchen

I had just submitted the manuscript of my book *Performance: Live Art 1909 to the Present* to my editor at Thames & Hudson in London, which would come out the following year in 1979. (The title would change to *Performance Art: From Futurism to the Present* with the second edition, when it became part of the World of Art series in 1988). I was intrigued by the possibilities of curating this material that had always been so untamable, artist driven without curatorial overview, but I decided that it was possible to work within an institution yet retain a radical position. Indeed, it became my mantra as a curator and as an art historian: I still believe that it is essential to unravel given histories, to approach both roles from a radical place, always rethinking both the meaning and the presentation of both historic and contemporary developments. I was the first art historian-curator at the Kitchen. Up until then, programs had been run by artists: actor and performer Eric Bogosian was in charge of the dance program, musician Rhys Chatham was the music director, and Longo curated video. I introduced analytic group exhibitions and performance series with a particular overview, such as "Made for TV?" which included artists working on the edge of TV, video art, and early cable TV; or "The New West," with Eleanor Antin, Bob & Bob, and other West Coast artists; or "Imports," which included artists with whom I had worked in the United Kingdom, such as Brian Eno, the Kipper Kids, Anne Bean, and Bruce McLean. I also organized the first solo shows of Cindy Sherman, Robert Longo, Sherrie Levine, Thomas Lawson, and Jack Goldstein in the gallery. It was an extraordinary couple of years (from 1978 to 1980). For my book launch in May 1979, it was especially meaningful to present it at the Kitchen, with live performances, and with so many members of the art community in attendance. We also held book launch events at Fiorucci with Klaus Nomi and at the Mudd Club! The book became very much a reference to the lives we were living.

AKP: Ah, okay. Are there any pivotal moments for you in the 1980s? Is this also when you began teaching in New York University's Department of Art and Art Administration?

Teaching

RG: I've always been teaching, ever since I graduated: in London at the Architectural Association, through the gallery at Royal College, and in New York at the School of Visual Arts. I have taught at Steinhardt NYU since 1987. I feel an obligation to teach, to download my firsthand experience of watching history unfold since the 1970s, and to provoke a different kind of thinking about what art history is capable of, to rethink art history as an investigative tool, as a way to inform, inspire, and entice. There's no better way to understand art history than to be deeply immersed in contemporary art. As I explain to my students, the more deeply you understand the present, the better you will understand the past. To really feel art history, it helps to recognize how all parts of the art world work, right now, today. This knowledge and awareness will give you a good idea of how it possibly might've been in the 1500s. There were power players then as there are now.

It is extraordinary how many different fields you can enter through art history, whether it's philosophy, sociology, political science, or gender studies. There's a radicalism to art history that is always in motion. I think to be an art historian is to have a huge imagination and to make sure that your imagination is at work at all times. To be a good historian is to sit at the feet of the people about whom you're writing: imagine that moment in time, recognize that art history is the story of ongoing invention, breakthroughs, political, cultural, social shifts. For me, Performa is a way to animate art history in the most exciting ways, to "refresh" the ever-changing ways that we understand the overlapping threads that make up the cultures of the world.

AKP: Any other anecdotes about the 1980s?

RG: For me, the 1980s was an intense, accelerated decade. It seemed to be a real swing of the proverbial pendulum from the 1970s: the obsession with money, Wall Street, Reagan, Thatcher. Some part of me was somewhat in shock; belief systems of the 1980s art world seemed to be entirely at odds with the noncommercial, highly conceptual work that we cared about so much in the 1970s. At the same time, the artists to whom I was closest—whom I call the first media generation, since they came of age with rock 'n' roll, 24-hour television, *The Twilight Zone*, punk music, and B movies, and who were critically looking at the ubiquity of media, the "mediatization" of experiences—provided entirely new ways of examining and articulating American culture through their art, which was completely absorbing. I continued teaching and writing.

I also had two children in the 1980s, which seemed an incredibly radical thing to do then in the downtown art world. Sarah Charlesworth, Laurie Simmons, Louise Lawler, Jane Kaplowitz, Elizabeth Murray, among my friends, also had children in the 1980s. And, yes, I was working as an independent curator. In the 1990s, I organized several performance series at the Museum of Modern Art and one at the Guggenheim.

AKP: This seems like an interesting moment where you got a major mainstream institution to acknowledge performance.

RG: Mainstream institutions largely ignored the history of performance. Even though they presented performance from time to time, performance was considered outside of curatorial thinking. I wanted to see it integrated into art history. I was close friends with Kirk Varnedoe, an extraordinary art historian and curator at MoMA, and when he told me about the exhibition he was preparing on the role of non-Western art in shaping early Modernism, I reminded him about the fact that Steve Reich's *Drumming* was based on Reich's exploration of African drumming in Ghana and that it would be an exciting addition to his exhibition, which it was. That was followed a few years later by a performance series that I organized to accompany Kirk's exhibition, "High and Low: Modern Art and Popular Culture," in 1990. Once again, I curated a complementary series to the work in the exhibition, including Laurie Anderson, Eric Bogosian, David Cale, Brian Eno, Spalding Gray, and Ann Magnuson, all of whose work existed on that edge between "high" and "low." At the Guggenheim, I would organize a performance by Daniel Buren to accompany his retrospective.

First commission

I was in Venice in 1999, and I saw Shirin Neshat's installation *Turbulent* (1998) in the Arsenale of the Biennial. There were two films, the man on one side, the woman on the other, projected on two facing screens, and the most beautiful surround-sound from the singers in the films linking the two. I was stunned, almost in tears. I sat there thinking, "What if this were live?" The work had all the qualities I felt would make for an amazing live work: cinematic choreography, a rich story, visual storytelling. It was a time in the 1990s when quite a few artists were producing beautiful installations—large film projections in white spaces that were visually stunning and dense with meaning. Isaac Julien, Steve McQueen, Douglas Gordan, Gillian Wearing, Stan Douglas. There were probably other projection-based works that year in Venice, but all I can remember is Shirin's.

I returned from Venice and met up with Shirin. "Would you ever think of creating a live performance?" I asked. "I feel your work has all the ingredients to make an extraordinary live production." She said, "What a fantastic idea. Yes, I'd love to do it." So the project was on! I had no idea what it would cost to commission this performance, whether the budget would be $20,000 or $200,000, or even what a production would entail. And neither did she. But we both ran with the idea, found some funds for an initial workshop at the Massachusetts Museum of Contemporary Art (MASS MoCA), and went forward from there.

We presented *Logic of the Birds*, based on a twelfth-century Persian poem, in its almost finished form at the Kitchen in October 2001, just three weeks after the tragedy of 9/11, which made it additionally heart-wrenching and profoundly relevant. Propelled by a series of films, recorded and live song, and live performance, it was thrilling. I had invited the head of the Lincoln Center Festival, Nigel Redden, to join us for our first full run-through of the production, and at the end of the night, he said, "We'll take it." The following year, *Logic* was presented at Lincoln Center. It was everything I had dreamed of.

It took a while to think about what I wanted to do after that. Obviously, the model of commissioning and producing new live work by artists was very tempting. But as an art historian, I couldn't imagine presenting material separate from a larger cultural context; it was essential to me that such work expand to include an education program and publications, and that it engage a community of artists, curators, architects, musicians, dancers, curators, writers, and museum directors as part of the start-up vision. And so it took me a while before I decided, in 2004, to create the Performa Biennial.

Performa

At that time in 2004, the art world was very much about big institutions and about big institutions expanding and getting even bigger. Attention centered on the huge spaces in Chelsea that looked more like car showrooms than galleries. I felt there was no place for young artists. There was no place for totally different ways of operating. And so I decided to create a biennial. It began with a public series that I presented in the Einstein Auditorium at Steinhardt called "Not for Sale." In the first discussion with Marina Abramović, Chrissie Iles, and Rob Storr, we talked about the importance of going back to artists' ideas and not just talking about the marketplace, which seemed so prevalent at the time. The mood was definitely a reaction against the explosion of art fairs, too. Another reason for starting Performa was to finally give the history of performance a highly visible, public platform. My book on the history of performance art was first published in 1979; for me, it was a necessary revisionist history of the twentieth century that inserted performance into all those places where it was a critical turning point in the history of art ideas and where it had been left out. Performa was committed to exploring, live and through research and archives, the history of performance, whether performance of the Renaissance, Russian Constructivism, or 1920s Paris.

Also, I felt we needed a community again. The New York art world felt too grown up, too top heavy. I wanted to create an environment where we could capture new ways of thinking and find new ways of producing artwork. Performa from the beginning was about working with artists, creating commissions from scratch. Many of the artists would make live performance for the first time. Shirin Neshat had never done performance before, yet all her work was performance driven, except audiences were on the set with her, behind the camera. Performa has always been about realizing an artist's wildest imagination; giving them full license to try something utterly new; and providing the necessary curatorial, technical, and financial support for them to do so.

Performa is about rethinking, remaking, and reimagining art history and bringing it to life in the present in the most public way. For every Performa Biennial, we spend two years in a very exciting research phase into a variety of historical periods or performance in select countries, such as in South Africa, Taiwan, or Sweden. We're always creating new outlets for putting this material into the world, for bringing the public into our research and conversations. To do this, we have established the *Performa Magazine*, Performa Institute, Performa Publications, and Performa TV and Radical Broadcast, both on our Performa website. We are a production house and a hands-on training ground for the next generation of curators and producers, who, not surprisingly, are in demand. So yes, we're much more than the biennial!

Art is a way to change people's hearts and minds and to make us better human beings. It's the only totally free space, a radical space. It cannot be contained. Art historians have a responsibility to be radical, too, as radical as the artists about whom they write.

AMY HAMLIN

Note to the reader: This is a letter I wrote to a former student, who was at the time considering Ph.D. programs in art history. The events I describe—both my own and Molly's—are true to life. Though conceived as a private correspondence, with prompts from this anthology's call for submissions, I have her permission to publish this letter.

September 21, 2019
Dear Molly,

In the time that has passed since our last exchange, I've been reflecting on your interest in pursuing a Ph.D. in art history. It seems so much more than a leap of faith to set yourself on this path, as I've observed from afar these recent years your steady dedication to your art and studies since you graduated college; you've been active in the feminist zine community, you've interned for a famous artist, and you've completed your master's degree in critical visuality studies, among other achievements. I trust you're making this decision to continue your education with eyes wide open, not only to what it augurs for you personally but also to the changes that must occur in art history for it to survive. You already know that the discipline risks obsolescence, if not extinction. Owing to the persistence of Whiteness in the field, growing anti-intellectualism in higher education, and the adjunctification of the professoriate, to say nothing of the rise of global fascism and the threats of climate collapse, this risk could also be a valuable opportunity to shape a more humane and sustainable discipline. This brings me to your questions about how I came to art history and my stakes in the field. Although it does not come naturally to me to write about myself, I will try.

For a long time, my response to the first question was a bit of confabulation crafted to meet whatever I thought my petitioner expected. I imagined them awaiting a dramatic story of epiphany before a well-known work of art in some exotic location. And so my story turned on a close encounter with Michelangelo's frescoes in the Sistine Chapel. It is true that I had a unique opportunity, with financial support from my grandparents, to spend a summer month in Italy in 1986, when I was in middle school. But the terrifying sight of airport security guards with automatic weapons left a more lasting impression than did Adam's index finger or the Libyan Sibyl's big toe. Impressive as those details are and remain, Michelangelo's storytelling in Rome left me cold. There was something about his totalizing narrative of human creation that contradicted my already deeply skeptical intuitions about the world. Nevertheless, I do suppose this encounter opened a door to a lifelong interest in art history.

I walked through that door several years later as a junior in high school in order to feed a growing curiosity about art and artists. Every Thursday evening, I volunteered at the Minneapolis Institute of Arts, as it was then known. My post was the information desk, and so I was expected to familiarize myself with some of the museum's most storied objects: the Doryphoros, Rembrandt's Lucretia, the Qing Dynasty Jade Mountain, and Vincent's Olive Trees. Sometimes I arrived early to spend time in the galleries, and it was not long before I developed an uneasy but rapt rapport with Max Beckmann's wartime triptych on the third floor. Packed with brightly colored figures and forms in a stage-like space, the painting with its flirtatious and arcane title commanded the viewer's attention. *Blind Man's Buff* was arguably just another crowd pleaser in the modern galleries. But it was Beckmann's apparent fear of empty space—his horror vacui—that drew me to the picture. I stayed for his allegorical storytelling.

Allegory had a similar effect when I first encountered the work of Kara Walker. I was living in New York City in the spring of 1998, when Walker was included in a group exhibition at Wooster Gardens in SoHo. I went alone to see the show and distinctly recall the sucker punch of her silhouetted antebellum fantasies/nightmares. These life-size tableaux, rendered in cut black paper against a white background, said one thing. And they meant something else entirely. At first glance, I registered the genteel Gone-with-the-Wind mythology about our nation's past. Closer inspection, however, revealed her characters engaging in the unspeakable violence and dehumanization of American slavery. I was put on notice. It was the first time I truly felt racialized as a viewer.

This is remarkable, shameful even, given the fact that I had already had the good fortune of seeing the 1993 Whitney Biennial. I was in college at the time and tasked with writing about a work of art in the show (I chose *The Ballad of Sexual Dependency* by Nan Goldin). When I teach that exhibition now, I'm galled by the fact that Daniel J. Martinez's brilliant intervention didn't fully register in my White consciousness. His mantra, parceled out on the brightly colored metal museum tags for that exhibition, read: "I can't imagine ever wanting to be white." As a Minnesota transplant—of settler colonial ancestry—in New York City, why couldn't I imagine the implications of my own Whiteness? And what did this mean for my study and practice of art history? Because art history as I had experienced, and would continue to experience, was more or less free of any racial or racist implications.

But I digress from Walker's work and its lasting impact. Art, as I have often encountered it and in the spaces of those encounters, always accommodates bodies like mine: especially White, but also able-bodied, cisgender, straight, young, thin, and female. At the 1993 Biennial, I couldn't imagine my own racial objectification, much less my complicity in art history's racial/racist status quo. Walker's allegories finally awakened my awareness, though the lessons have been slow to take root. I've returned to her work over the years, to her allegorical tales with no discernible resolution, only the complexities, desires, and violence of human entanglements birthed in the abattoir of modern colonialism. As you know, I wrote about Walker's work in graduate school and even gave a paper on her at my first academic conference in the fall of 2001. The title of my talk betrayed the entitlement and ignorance of my unacknowledged racism: "Looking Back, Talking Back: Reclaiming a Black Female Subjectivity in Kara Walker's Works on Paper and Writings." Although I don't believe that White scholars have no business writing about Black artists, I now question the all-too-often unexamined motivations for this work. In my case, I left unattended my own desires and assumptions about Black female subjectivity. Who was I to speak on that aspect of my topic that I—literally—knew nothing about? And why did I wish to speak about her work in this way? Was I not, in bell hooks's terms, guilty of "eating the Other"? Progressive White women are nothing if not persistent, and this is not always a virtue. Given our deep reluctance to examine our complicity in White supremacy, the implications for art history are tremendous. White scholars are rarely taught to examine their own racialized positions and privileges within a field that, at least since the new art history, sees itself as politically progressive. As a young White scholar, you are better equipped now with the resources and the expectation to examine your own training, your own desires and assumptions. Find friends, mentors, and colleagues to help you in this discernment and education.

As for Beckmann, you know that I wrote my dissertation on what I have occasionally described as his ineffable modernism. Anchored in what his contemporaries had to say about his pictures, my research looked for answers where there were only questions. This realization kept me coming back for more, not only from Beckmann but also from Walker. You see, I believe that both artists tell us something about race and art history, about art history as a racialized practice with inevitably racist consequences. Where Beckmann's critical engagement with art history reveals its unbearable Whiteness, Walker's engagement lays bare its unbearable racism. But it goes deeper than this. For Beckmann's vaunted status relies on the myth of the modernist underdog, the White male genius whose career and reputation were both vilified and affirmed in the Degenerate Art exhibition. Walker's genius is rooted in her parrhesia, her willingness to make herself vulnerable in speaking truth to power. Expressed like Beckmann's in an allegorical doublespeak, her work intervenes in the history of art because it assumes that race and racism have long shaped master narratives.

What, you might be asking, does this testimony have to do with my stakes in the field? Stakes are posts that demarcate boundaries to establish ownership. Whereas I do not presume to own a piece of art history, I am nonetheless a beneficiary in its vast landscape of Whiteness. My challenge as an educator, scholar, and advocate is to leverage my privilege to disrupt the status quo. I have a deep interest in art history's transformation as a condition for its survival. To my mind, the works of both Beckmann and Walker—the former by accident, the latter by design—shine a conflagratory light of accountability on art history and its practitioners. In its two hundred years as a discipline, art history has perpetuated an allegiance to a culture of White supremacy and ultimately to its peril. Let this be a dramatic story of epiphany, but know that there is no eschatology for art history. There is no story of salvation that will redeem its sins, only hope in the construction of new narratives and habits of mind. Knowing that you are further on in your process and much younger than I am, I do believe that you are already a storyteller in the future of art history. Feed your critical awareness and capacity for self-examination daily, because it is so easy to slip into the familiar behaviors that perpetuate White supremacy. I am excited for you and ready to write a recommendation letter in full support of what you have to offer. You are a bright star.

With much love, support, and admiration,
Amy

BEÁTA HOCK

A FEW MEMORABLE encounters with art, art history, and art criticism are building the backbone of the story i am telling.[1] My attempts to reimagine art history emerge from a *noncore European* location, from the position of a "close Other," as the late Polish art historian Piotr Piotrowski once identified Eastern Europe's intricate position between the Western and non-Western worlds. "Close Others" are both reminiscent of and different from the "real" Other of postcolonial theory in that the East European Other is almost, yet not quite, like the "Self" (Western Europe and the broader Euro-Atlantic constellation). Crucially, the East European difference lies in the subordinate position that close Others occupy vis-à-vis the dominant "Self." Also, the Eastern European experience typically remains invisible in traditional master narratives, and this relative obliteration has hardly been alleviated by recently emerging postcolonial and global perspectives. In an attempt to move away from a longstanding Eurocentric bias in scholarship and beyond, these cutting-edge new approaches have prioritized extra-European areas, whereby the distinction between Europe's western and eastern halves has often been overlooked.

The first episode i am relating takes us back to 2010, when i attended the fourth annual Stone Summer Theory Institute at the School of the Art Institute of Chicago (SAIC) in 2010. I was a fresh postdoc with a degree in Comparative Gender Studies from the Central European University of Budapest, the institution where i became acutely aware of the existence and salience of the above "rule of European difference" (which is, of course, a wry retake on the "rule of colonial difference," the term with which Partha Chatterjee captured transcontinental power relations). I was thus prepared to be speaking in a doubly marginalized voice: as an Eastern European and as a feminist. (2010 does not seem to be that far back, yet the pertinence of gendered perspectives was not yet necessarily acknowledged by the broader academic community, despite the occasional superficial bow to the need to "have more women" in the room, in the curriculum, in museums, and so on, and the slippery ground beyond the two sexes was still the reserve of gender outlaws.) The five days of the "institute" remain a tremendously rich and formative event for me, including the experience of being the only peripherally Western participant at a professional gathering where the faculty and rest of the fellows all came from the United States and Western, Northern, or Southeastern Europe. To my surprise, however, most participants coming from currently or historically dominant countries like the United Kingdom, Germany, France, Portugal, or Spain felt similarly sidelined as the conversation increasingly revolved around issues whose centrality could be perceived and commented upon only from North American or, more precisely, East Coast and, even more precisely, New York–based positions. What was convened to be a broad general discussion about one of the central puzzles of contemporary art boiled down to a local, if not parochial, dispute.

This international gathering also gave an incisive example of how the self-assuredness of dominant centers might backfire. The central theme in 2010 at SAIC was "Beyond the Aesthetic and Anti-Aesthetic," and Clement Greenberg, the originator of the master narrative of modern art, featured prominently in our discussions. As it transpired, Greenberg's views seem to have made waves only within the Manhattan art scene until the *October* group's seminal and widely reviewed publication *The Anti-Aesthetic* (1983) started to disseminate the Greenbergian model worldwide.[2] Although the authors in the volume harshly opposed Greenberg, they evidently made him more central in their writing than he actually was—so much so, as a seminar participant from Portugal confirmed, that it was eventually through *October*'s writing that Greenberg became reified in her country, where art historians had not formerly known of his existence and never before understood their own modernism in terms of Greenberg's purist theory. This accidental reality check made Hal Foster, a central figure of the *October* group, also present at the institute, "want to jump out the window."[3]

But let me return and linger on the Central European University (CEU) in Budapest, an English-language college issuing both US and Hungarian-accredited degrees, where i pursued my MA and Ph.D. studies. Thanks to CEU's uniquely multinational faculty and student body[4] and to its location in semi-peripheral Hungary, the university's curriculum contests at the same time as it disseminates knowledge produced mainly by Anglo-American academia. Despite the use of one common mediating language, no single national culture or narrative framework comes forth as dominant in this intellectual context, as members of the scholarly community are constantly exposed to many different and sometimes opposing perspectives. In this environment, not only universalist master narratives were deconstructed and their exclusions exposed on a theoretical level, but also the voices of history's various Others were eagerly heard. A subaltern dream come true, really.[5]

In my own case, this inspiring milieu also involved some theoretical challenges. One of them was the need to come to grips with the question of to what degree and in what ways the analytical tools of a Western-developed feminist criticism can be deployed to the social and cultural context i am inhabiting. When translated into my curatorial work, trying to avoid the possible trap of appropriating "Second World" realities by "First World" formulations meant keeping an open eye (and open mind) for artists, artworks, and, equally importantly, issues that might not be familiar from a gradually forming feminist artistic canon. Along this road, i was happy to come across—literally discover—Judit Kele and her multipart art project *I Am a Work of Art* (1979–80).

Kele left her native Hungary shortly after the final performance of this body of work. Her departure was an effect and a logical, yet unexpected, consequence of this performance in which she auctioned herself off as a work of art at the Paris Biennale. The bidders at the auction were selected from among respondents to a matrimonial ad the artist had reportedly published in the French daily paper *Libération*. As the ad stated, she hoped to gain more freedom of movement through the marriage:

> Young and successful Eastern European female artist seeks gentleman for marriage. This marriage would enable her to freely move around and accompany her exhibitions to the West. In exchange accommodation in her home country and local art contacts are offered. Respond to the following address: [...]. Meetings possible after July 10.

Some of the replies Kele received offered help out of comradeship, and rather than requesting a photo of the future bride or inquiring about her looks or any other personal details, the respondents communicated their own attitudes toward the particular status of an Eastern European woman in Cold War Europe. These ranged from idle curiosity to appended quotes from Marx and Hegel to intriguing narratives of pro-Leftist cultural activism in France. After the auction, Kele's new "owner" insisted that the purchased "work of art" stay physically with him, that is, in his possession. At the time, this was possible only if he married his far-from-freewheeling Eastern European "artwork," so Kele moved to France. The groom was a prominent member of the Parisian dance world and a gay man. Thus, for him, marrying a woman artist from somewhat exotic Eastern Europe was an act that could advantageously pass in his raffish bohemian milieu, not to mention the tax reduction for which he became eligible by becoming his wife's supporter.

Kele abandoned art practice in 1985 when she turned to filmmaking, and this is how her scarcely recorded oeuvre became forgotten and practically unknown even to local art historians. When reconstructing and exhibiting her work in my *Agents and Provocateurs* show (2009), i suggested that *I Am a Work of Art* is a peculiarly gendered piece in the bold tradition of body art in which the artist exposed not only her physical body but her entire existence to an unforeseeable process—perhaps a new category is required here, possibly called "*social* body art."

Gender Check, the first comprehensive "Eastern European gender show," on view in Vienna's MUMOK at the end of 2009, missed this old but "latent" work by Judit Kele. Bringing Kele's superb art project back to light for my own parallel running exhibition required following up some initial innocuous-looking clues—a small pile of handwritten and typewritten sheets and a newspaper cutting—found in the Artpool Art Research Center, Budapest. A great reward of this research for both artist and curator is that, since its first presentation at *Agents and Provocateurs*, *I Am a Work of Art* has traveled to various cities across Europe, and the Ludwig Museum Budapest has purchased it for its collection. Kele's piece arouses extraordinary fascination each time it is put on display, and the artist occasionally adds further sequels to the complex body of work. Most recently, and as a celebration of her fifth divorce, she staged a sologamist wedding ceremony in which she finally married—herself.

Notes

1. The use of the lowercase pronoun "i" signifies my reservations about a unique convention in the English language, wherein the first-person singular is capitalized and thus prioritized. It comes across as a remarkably self-centered characteristic and, as such, may deserve to be denaturalized.
2. Hal Foster, ed., *The Anti-Aesthetic: Essays on Postmodern Culture* (Port Townsend, WA: Bay Press, 1983).
3. This memorable moment is recorded in James Elkins and Harper Montgomery, eds., *Beyond the Aesthetic and the Anti-Aesthetic* (University Park: Pennsylvania State University Press, 2013), which emerged from the scholarly encounters at the Stone Summer Theory Institute.
4. The faculty and the comparatively small student body (1448 students in AY 2016–17) come from over 110 countries on five continents.
5. During the preparation of the present volume, the university moved from Budapest to Vienna, following a 2017 legislative change introduced by Hungary's current "illiberal" government, which aimed at terminating the operation of the school in Budapest.

CLAIRE HSU

THE COMMUNITY GATHERED around the 250-year-old banyan tree in Hollywood Road Park to hear the Sheung Wan elders recount stories sown by an archive[1] that had once occupied the eleventh floor of a neighboring building, now demolished. The archive had moved out of Sheung Wan over 80 years ago, sometime in the 1920s, but the stories it held and shared had been retold for many decades by those who had spent afternoons among the bulging library shelves. As the full moon illuminated the tree's octopus-like tentacles gripping the single jagged rock protruding from the park's cement floor, several of the children called out, "Please tell us the story of the yellow man."

"So be it," whispered one of the elders, who vaguely recalled her youth as a volunteer in the archive's library.

"Once upon a time in Singapore, whose name is derived from Singapura, which in the ancient language of Sanskrit means Lion City, there was an artist who called himself Wen. He grew up increasingly feeling as if the world he had been brought into could not accommodate him. After six years of working in a bank, he decided he could no longer follow the conventional path that society so encouraged, nor ignore the voice in his heart."

"One night, he packed his bags and followed the many other artists who had come before him, crossed the passages of oceans to what was then one of the most important art capitals and the former mothership of an empire that had once controlled vast lands, including Singapore and our very own city of Hong Kong. In fact, the British landed in Hong Kong in 1841 and took possession of Hong Kong on that very road," the elder said, pointing over the wall gently embracing the park. The group turned their head in unison to stare at the wall, with its layers of paints, washed-out posters and faded graffiti, with nothing but the faded words "Free Hong Kong" legible.

"Wen had hoped that his new life would help him find the peace he was looking for, but instead, he was constantly mistaken for being Mainland Chinese because of the shade of his skin and the shape of his eyes. While his appearance told one story, his upbringing spoke of another. And so he decided that he would paint his entire body yellow, from the tips of his toes to the top of his bald head, a canary yellow that sang from every inch of his skin, and that he would go through life directly facing the pains and prejudices of the world to address the pains he felt inside. From England, Yellow Man traveled to India, Japan, Thailand, Mexico, Australia, China, and back to Singapore, keeping a journal and sketching everywhere he went, each time painting another layer of skin, until the yellow shone so bright that he was visible even on a cloudy winter night and, some say, from the moon."

"Where are the journals?" asked one of the children.

"The journals were all digitized by the archive and are housed on the website, but there is a myth that the originals were buried in this very garden, beneath this tree, on the request of the artist," replied the elder, as she gently unfolded a torn page with a pencil drawing of the goddess Lakshmi seated on a giant lotus flanked by Tang blue and green mountains. She had carried it close to her since finding it under this very tree. For a moment, they all looked toward the ground, some gently pressing their hands to the earth, as if collectively remembering all that lay buried beneath its soil.

"Please tell of another story," called out one of the older children, "one we have not heard before."

"Yes, well, okay, we have time for one more," the elder conceded, mindful that the potluck picnic dinner had run late and that it was a school night.

"As a child, Nilima loved nothing more than to go on long treks with her parents in the lush, pristine hills of Kashmir. Little did she know that these glorious mountains, and troubled territory, would become so integral to the artworks she would go on to make as an adult. Nilima decided that she wanted to study art from a young age, not a conventional path for girls at that time. While so many of her fellow male artists were unabashedly using oil painting, bright colors and abstract forms that spoke to a modern time, a new India, and a new world, Nilima sensed that there was a contemporary art language out there that could still be impregnated with all that had come before. Following her heart's truth, she enrolled in the University of Baroda, under the tutelage of teachers who were exploring Indian craft traditions as equal to the new art being made."

"Nilima loved walking around the halls of the Baroda Museum just before the crowds arrived in the morning. The museum had been built in 1894 based on the famous Victoria and Albert Museum in London, when India too had been part of the British Empire. It was home to an extensive gallery of reproductions of European oil paintings and sculptures; rooms dedicated to the arts of Tibet, China, and Japan; an Egyptian mummy; traditional Indian weaving looms; and the skeleton of a baby blue whale. Nilima at once understood that she wanted not only to study and reclaim India's traditions but also to put them into conversation with the histories of other places whose connections had long been forgotten. Nilima was awarded a prestigious prize to travel, and while other artists went to Paris, New York, and London, Nilima decided to go to the ancient caves of Dunhuang in China: caves whose walls whispered the stories of Gautama the Enlightened One and were firsthand witnesses to the flow of ideas and goods along a once pulsating Silk Road."

"While crushing a cinnabar red pigment in her studio one day, Nilima was shocked to learn of the death of her daughter's friend, who had been burned to death by her in-laws. She had been horrified when hearing about dowry deaths growing up and never imagined this would happen to someone she knew. From that day on, Nilima vowed to include the voices of Champa and others like her in her work. She would be with women artists and paint her children. She increasingly recovered an artistic language that could speak to these pains."

"Nilima devoted the rest of her life to challenging the norms of art being produced by painting histories that had been forgotten and voices that had been silenced ..." The elder's voice tapered off as a meandering cloud covering the moon distracted her gaze toward the sky. "I'm afraid that's all we have time for tonight."

By now, the children knew that there was no point in asking for another story but still let out a collective groan. They would have to wait until the next full moon to hear the heroic stories of their ancestors first told by an archive that had once stood next to this very park.

Note

1. The founding story of Asia Art Archive has been recorded in various interviews, and so I will keep it brief. The idea was born during an internship at Hanart TZ Gallery in 1999 in conversation with Johnson Chang as we lamented the lack of documentation of the explosion of creativity happening in the art scene across Asia. I finished my MA in history of art at SOAS London University in 2000, came back to Hong Kong, and cofounded the AAA. I was 24 at the time. I am not exactly sure where the voice came from to do this; all I knew was that the stories I had grown up with did not encompass the intensity, abundance, complexity, or depth of experience around me. My parents met on an airplane flying somewhere over Germany, and maybe it is because I am half Chinese and half Austrian, so instantly belonging to two very different cultures from birth, that I was most interested in telling the stories of others. While taking a gap year in China in 1993, I stumbled across the experimental artist village Yuanmingyuan, and it was this moment that sparked my interest in the power of art to give voice to expression less perceptible in mainstream society. The seed was planted and activated some years later. That being said, the seed could only be germinated through the hard work and passion of so many others—it is this incredible community of artists, thinkers, patrons, teachers, scholars, friends, and family that have enabled AAA to sprout and grow into one of the most active and valuable resources and catalysts for the writing of a more generous global art history.

   There are a few guiding principles to how we do our work—an AAA DNA, so to speak. We don't, for example, buy archives; instead, we digitize archives and make these accessible online. We want to make sure we do not extract knowledge from its place of origin, but use our resources to amplify this knowledge from multiple sources. This is possible in the digital age. We are interested in bringing different histories and geographies next to one another, and while we work on the recent history of art from Asia, we do not see history as linear but as cycles of knowledge shining light on the present at different moments in time. Our contribution to a more generous history means shining light on less visible histories and focusing on practices like performance art or the representation of women, as two examples. I decided to respond to this invitation in the form of a children's story as it is often hard for my three daughters to relate to what I do in the current form the archive takes. There are a number of great new kids' publications that we read together chronicling the lives of inspiring women and lesser-known heroes/heroines. The hope is that the archive will inspire many stories to be written and rewritten, and that from these stories, a diversity of role models like Lee Wen and Nilima Sheikh, who stand for freedom, bravery, and generosity, will be widely circulated. It is the contribution of these incredible individuals who challenge the norms and limitations of the way that we see things that have inspired me for the past twenty years. And finally, I have set this story in Hollywood Road Park in Sheung Wan, which is home to an extremely wise banyan tree that the archive looks down upon from the 11/F. I often sit under her beard-like branches and imagine all that she has witnessed, humbled by the magnitude of knowledge held within her roots, trunks, and branches. A microcosm of our majestic cosmos.

ALICE MING WAI JIM

The first time I was mistaken for being Indigenous, notably by an Indigenous person, was in 2017 at a conference in Dublin, Ireland. "What community are you from?" she asked. Taken by surprise, I stuttered back, "Uh, Chinese? My parents are both from Hong Kong, but I was born in Tiohtiá:ke/Montreal." She apologized immediately, "I thought you were Indigenous; I didn't mean to offend." I was not offended at all. In fact, feeling quite the contrary, I ventured to ask, "Why did you think I might be?" She replied, "Oh, because of your freckles."

Years from now, I will look back on 2019 as one of the most unsettling years of my career, if not my life, up until then. Within the span of six months, I lived through a free vortex of events and experiences compelling me to take stock of who I had become, as a child born to immigrant parents from Hong Kong, now a Special Administrative Region (SAR) of China; as a first-generation university graduate, now tenured professor; as one of a handful of art historians of color in Canada; as the sole research chair in a Canadian university specializing in ethnocultural art histories; and as an Asian Canadian, a racialized person working on coming to terms with what Quynh Nhu Le calls "asymmetrical settler racial hegemonies" and identifications, all while on unceded Indigenous lands.

As an Anglophone visible minority growing up in Canada's French-speaking province of Quebec, I am not often mistaken for being anything other than Asian (read: foreign), encapsulated by that proverbial question, "But where are you *really* from?" My parents emigrated to Canada half a century ago and met at Expo 67. Like in many immigrant stories, there was a Chinese restaurant in the picture, but it went bankrupt soon after I was born. In my adult life, I regret that my parents did not force me to attend Chinese-language school on the weekends. My brother and I go months without uttering a single Cantonese word, never mind being able to read or write Chinese. But then, my parents, with twenty dollars a week to feed a family of four, didn't have the resources to pay for lessons anyways.

My mother was a nurse-midwife before she came to Canada and likes to say that she brought 129 babies into this world. She left Hong Kong on August 8, 1967—in the midst of the bomb-strewn riots between pro-Communists and the British colonial government that had erupted three months earlier. Fifty years later, she has not returned. She tried to, in 2019. She was to join me for my birthday while I was teaching at the new Tai Kwun Centre's summer institute. But her flight was canceled for three days. The city's massive anti-government protests against the controversial extradition law proposal, Article 23, had forced the unprecedented closure of the Hong Kong International Airport that weekend. I was heartbroken. Since then, the weekly demonstrations have turned violent and have gone on for months. As the SAR yearns for liberal democracy, Indigenous boat dwellers on its coasts face eviction by real-estate developers. This embroiled history of Hong Kong's future is going on live, now.

As it happens, I was invited to teach on the topic of future commons based on my research on Hong Kong media arts I had begun twenty years ago for my doctoral dissertation, even though I had never visited the city until then. I ended up living there for four years. I made ends meet much the same as I did when I was in Montreal as a poor graduate student—taking on multiple short-term admin jobs and the occasional sessional teaching. That summer in 2019 was a homecoming, so to speak, not just for me but for my mother as well; only the reasons why she left and was not able to return could not be more ironic.

Teaching during a historic protest movement largely driven by young people is unnerving, to say the least. There was a city-wide strike on my first day at the institute. I am still surprised that my 27 students, some of whom joined the frontlines on a nightly basis, came to class at all. To be fair, my topic was on resistance and protest, in search of an alien commons in contemporary art. Most of the participants were local, a few international and diasporic; all were Asian—a class where all the students looked like me. I had ambitiously pulled together a program that was, I felt, the creative culmination of the seemingly eclectic art histories I had been writing about over the years. There were three main sections: Afrofuturism and the Antarctic, Indigenous futurisms and the North Dakota Pipeline, and Asian futurism and the case of Hong Kong—three flashpoints connected by the downward-spiraling metrics of global climate change.

I often get asked by colleagues and students of color how my parents let me go into art history. They didn't at first. I have a science college degree, despite graduating from a fine-arts alternative public high school. The undergraduate art history program I undertook only had historical period courses on Western art up until 1960. Midway through, I had petitioned, unsuccessfully, to do a minor in African studies. It was not until my MA that I would first encounter the term "postcolonial" and be exposed to contemporary art, Indigenous art, and Foucault. In Canada, identity politics and anti-racism initiatives in the arts were at their peak in the 1990s, with an ebb in the 2000s and a resurgence in the past decade, although there remains a scarcity of scholarship on this period.

In December 2019, I was invited to do a public lecture in Toronto reflecting back on the topic of my MA thesis, the groundbreaking 1989 exhibition *Black Wimmin: When and Where We Enter*, which was celebrating its 30th anniversary and a renaissance of Black Canadian art. *Plus ça change, plus c'est la même chose.* It reminded me in a jolt of the many trying angles that still need to be addressed, about the sonar ping of legacy exhibitions that beckons reflection, fluid gender spectrums, and the persistent economic, political, and social conditions of colonization on people of color and Indigenous Peoples.

As much as the 2015 Truth and Reconciliation Commission of Canada's Final Report and its "94 Calls to Action" to redress the state cultural genocide against Indigenous Peoples have been taken up in the form of rote land acknowledgments for official events across the country, much work remains to be done in all sectors on building just relations between Indigenous Peoples and Canadians, given the history and legacy of settler colonialism.

Across the Americas, colonial and settler colonial art history has focused primarily, if not exclusively, on the art of contact and post-contact dynamics between European white settlers and Indigenous Peoples in the Americas and elsewhere via different forms of empires and racial hegemonies. This focus has rendered virtually invisible or irrelevant the ethnocultural art histories of intercommunity and intercultural relations between racialized "visible minority" communities and other nonwhite or Indigenous communities. Recent theories such as Iyko Day's triangulation of Native, white settler, and alien categorizations (the latter denoting non-Indigenous, nonwhite bodies) have flushed out at times heated debates and discussions on the appropriate use of the term "settler" to refer to racialized minorities in an extremely complex terrain.

These identificatory processes range from white privilege and its companion, white fragility, to settler privilege and fragility—the pairings are similar but not the same in terms of applicability, although shaming seems pervasive in both. In hallowed halls of progressive institutions, on smoke breaks and walks home, anguished voices express how Black people in Canada cannot be considered settlers on this land when their presence is inextricably linked to the history and legacy of slavery, some preferring the term "forcibly displanted"—a portmanteau of the words "displaced" and "replanted"—while speaking of African heritage in Canada. In 2019, Statistics Canada released a study on the growth of the "Aboriginal identity population," complicating the already complicated First Nations, Métis, and Inuit designations and raising the stakes for white-presenting Indigenous Peoples, darker-skinned Indigenous Peoples, mixed-race people of all ancestries, and, it must be included, ever-fraught becoming-ally efforts.

Throughout all of this are the discussions of complicity, hesitant beneficiaries, and the Asian model minority myth in which I am personally deeply implicated, kicking and screaming. In 2019, to a packed room of Asian and Indigenous scholars, I introduced myself by telling, for the first time, my personal story and how I did not, like many of my Indigenous colleagues, know anything about my ancestors to speak eloquently of and probably never will; access to that information was cut off long ago. It's unlikely I preempted any reciprocal interest in me or my sense of diasporic unbelonging—that work is a longer-term project.

My work on Asian Canadians in visual culture, the journal *Asian Diasporic Visual Cultures and the Americas*, Asian Indigenous relationalities in contemporary art, and, more recently, the convergence of Indigenous Afro-Asian futurist aesthetics aims to account for the misreadings, missed opportunities, and reimaginings that the above entanglements with difficult knowledge have obfuscated. I realized early on that in order for ethnocultural arts to be a legitimate field of study, I had to take active part in making its history as a researcher, writer, and curator. No matter how thankless, exhausting, and excruciatingly painful it can be, I think it is about aspiring for critical relationalities, self-determination, and sustainable futures.

I hope I have conveyed that, in my story, the path taken has not been a straight one, although it may appear so on paper, read as a series of milestones and achievements, parsed into various stages, periods, and (pre-)occupations. I remain wary about how (to draw from Le) redress and reconciliation, and their terms and conditions, can be instrumentalized by a liberal multicultural state to bring unsettling differences into collusion with colonial settler narratives of civil progress and leave intersectional hierarchies still in place. The sine multiplies, but the cosine inhabits the same footprint (or area)—that is, their biopower has not increased, despite the increase of response mobility and repair.

> *Do I continue to look for sines? In trigonometry, the sine formula helps to find the unknown angle, thus solving the triangle. But that is only if the length of the sides of said triangle—if, in fact, it is indeed a triangle—is known, which is to say, there are trying angles that make it impossible to look for sines, as in sine qua non, "without which is not possible": because they are simply not triangles, and change is hardly ever in a straight line.*

Be water.

AMELIA JONES

Part I: Formation

A scholar trained in art history, now working in an art school within a major university (Roski School of Art and Design at the University of Southern California [USC] in Los Angeles), I have become increasingly distanced from the discipline partly because its normative manifestations have not served my creative energies. And, in short, I could not get a job equal to my research needs in an art history department in the United States, hence ending up, after a sojourn in British and Canadian art history and visual studies departments, teaching critical studies to art and design students.

Art history had initially appealed to me as a naïve undergraduate in the early 1980s at Harvard University because it seemed accessible (the intro survey class was playfully called "darkness at noon") and offered itself as an interesting way to access history and the literary, both of which I loved. I was driven from my initial goal of being a fiction writer by a fear of the inchoate nature of the career (and of my probable mediocrity in practicing it) and from my secondary goal of majoring in marine biology and getting a job at Duke University's Outer Banks Marine Lab because all the students in the intro classes were male premeds. I instinctively ran in the other direction, not realizing that, by running to art history like so many other young women have done, I was acceding to the gender terrorism that inculcated ideas about the impossibility of women being scientists.

I came to this life in the humanities academy also as a reader and a daughter of a dad who was a professor (of psychology) and an activist mother, a student in North Carolina and New Jersey public schools, who had seen almost no visual art until I found myself in the darkened classrooms of the elite and conservative department of art history at Harvard. Before Harvard, I had had no access to high art whatsoever, aside from a painting by my dad's Duke colleague Bob Broderson, and the one coffee table art book my parents had, which I remember most for the titillating quality of its images of naked women (of course). And my sister Caroline Jones—now an esteemed art historian herself—had majored in art history seven years before me, so that put the discipline on my radar screen. Given the limits of public schooling in exposing students to the arts, I was not sophisticated (or entitled) like the private-school-trained students I encountered in droves at Harvard, although of course I was aware of academia as a possible career because of my father's profession.

As a kid in Durham, North Carolina, in the 1970s, I had been what I am tempted to call a "privileged outcast"—a white kid bussed across town to 90 percent African American public schools in the American South. I was both highly visible as a white "Duke kid" or "Dukie" (per my Black classmates) and marginalized from social life at my schools. To put it bluntly, I was an object of fascination, but also socially outcast; from my limited point of view, it felt as if I could only appropriate coolness, never inhabit it. A huge fan of funk music and polyester pantsuits, I—without a social life to speak of—developed a rich reading life, balancing my love of African American fiction (from Zora Neale Hurston to Richard Wright) with an obsession over romantic French nineteenth-century novels by the likes of Alexandre Dumas (little knowing that Dumas himself was part Black). I gloried in and obsessed over the gorgeous technicolor dream of Renaissance Europe presented in Franco Zeffirelli's 1968 movie of *Romeo and Juliet* while also being riveted to the television melodrama *Roots*, engaging directly at my school in the fallout of the series and its crude but effective anti-racist politics. The kids around me gained confidence but also a reignited rage as they learned more about the stories of violence and abuse narrated in this timely show about the history of

Black life in the United States from slavery into the twentieth century, based on Alex Haley's story of his family.[1]

This incongruous set of identifications haunts me to the present day and explains my continued allegiance to the *historical*, in spite of art history's very common and often critiqued forms of conservatism, as well as my insistence on pushing against the normativity of the discipline—in my case, by looking always at art by those artists marginalized from canonical histories (a big issue in the 1990s when I emerged as a professional into the field) and working through feminist, queer, and critical race theory to redress exclusions. I was driven to examining and historicizing contemporary modes of queer and feminist performance (including performance art)—the latter developed through self-training as a performance studies scholar—as key ways of resisting the art historical and art critical tendencies of suppressing temporality, embodiment, and feeling from consideration. As disciplines, art history and art criticism had long been threatened by time-based media and embodied works of art, which thwarted the traditional concepts of "disinterested" interpretation and formal aesthetics still dominant through the 1980s, when I was in school.[2]

These strange alliances of my youth perhaps also go some way toward explaining my odd position as a curator, historian, and theorist of art and performance who always seeks to redress the systemic exclusions of the art and art history worlds and to insist on bodies and performances in spaces mostly still intended for static objects (museums and galleries). These stories of my earlier life perhaps explain some of the contradictions in my thinking and some of my choices of creative community, odd within art history—cutting across art and academic and performance worlds, mostly feminists, queers, many people of color, and other "outcasts" from the privileged centers of the official art world and academia.[3] I am a closet romantic who nonetheless eschews romantic ideas attached to art (which privilege white, heteronormative male subjects); who finds art and its marketplaces increasingly depressing in their instrumentalization of creativity; who experiences institutions of higher learning—rationalized and corporatized as they have become—as frustrating and often demoralizing. As such, I have maintained two goals as I've risen up in the ranks of academia and the publishing and curating worlds: to do whatever I can to support my own, my colleagues', and my students' research and creativity within otherwise soul-crushing institutions, and to maintain a passionate continued attachment to modes of creativity that are resolutely embodied and thus resistant to structures of easy commodification.[4] Both of these serve the larger goal of interrogating structures of power in these institutions and supporting artists and scholars from communities at the margins of the more official and lucrative centers of the art world and academia.

My choice of going to graduate school in art history, made after a two-year stint working at an art book publisher in New York City as a picture editor, made sense at the time. The implicit glamour of the 9-to-5 job in publishing was dulled by the poor salary (I started at $14K, due at least in part to the misogyny of an industry filled with low-paid women) and by the fact that I was hired by a wealthy white male boss who #MeToo'd me within the first year. I was also repelled by the exhaustion of not having enough interesting things to do, driven by boredom into a Ph.D. program in art history. (What other discipline would I join at that point? I did not know that performance studies was just then being developed down the road at NYU.) I started at the University of Pennsylvania, where I obtained my MA, then transferred to UCLA to finish my Ph.D. a couple of years later. I yearned for what I imagined would be a career spent thinking, teaching, and writing about visual culture (ha! ... little did I know these would happen, but only in the interstices of a lot of administrative work, e-mails, meetings, and institutional trauma). My father's seemingly charmed career (replete with his own office, secretary, grant money, and fawning students at Duke and then Princeton) was the life I imagined for myself.

As for art history, to this day I cannot fully explain why I persisted in a discipline that was, at best, detached from every concern of contemporary life in the United States and from everything I cared about (including the identity politics movements in which I became active and politically engaged by my early twenties) and, at worst, boring, formalist, anti-intellectual, and overtly sexist, racist, and classist. Memorizing dozens of slides, as was de rigueur in traditional art history undergraduate and some graduate classes in the 1980s, was the least of the problem. Disturbing to me from the get-go was the resolute refusal of the discipline in its dominant forms to address social and political context, its refusal to acknowledge the embodied vicissitudes of interpretation (the contingency of meaning), and the exclusion of any artwork that did not obey the formal, static, and authorial imperatives of mainstream Euro-American institutions (i.e., object-based; formalist; made by a white Euro-American man, preferably straight or at least closeted).

At the University of Pennsylvania (Penn), I found myself ostracized when, for example, out of a vague but strong sense of political pique connected to what would become my feminist method, I could not stop myself from challenging Leo Steinberg, who, in a graduate seminar entitled ominously "Picasso's Women," persisted in deploying grossly sexist language as he presented Picasso's "love" of women via fawning analyses of his paintings. Steinberg called me out in front of the class to humiliate me in my inchoate attempts to articulate a feminist critique. (In truth, he wasn't wrong to note my naïveté: I didn't know how to articulate the problem, as I had not yet begun to read the feminist art history that was just starting to be published in the United Kingdom and the United States by Griselda Pollock, Linda Nochlin, and others—needless to say, none of these texts were being assigned in classes in US art history departments.) Steinberg's obdurately misogynistic approach spurred me on: I do have a stubborn side, and instead of acting as a deterrent, his attempts to silence me made me more determined to pursue this line of attack. Also at Penn, Dr. Renata Holod, an Islamic art specialist, saved my connection to the field with her seminar on colonialism and art. This was the first time I was assigned a theory text in an art history class: Edward Said's epically important 1978 *Orientalism*, no less. For the class paper, I was able to turn toward my father's grandparents' history as missionaries in India in the late nineteenth century to explore colonial architecture in South Asia via the lens of my own family's participation in colonialism, including reading my great-grandfather John Peter Jones's *India: Its Life and Thought* (1908), a copy of which I found in the Penn library. This experience convinced me that art history could do something interesting and even politically important with the right shift in frame.

UCLA was a far sight more connected and exciting as an overall intellectual experience—and, through the work of brilliant art historian Donald Preziosi (the first US art historian to integrate poststructuralist philosophy into his teaching and research), Latin Americanist Cecelia Klein, Marxist professor Al Boime, feminist film theorist Janet Bergstrom, and other teachers introducing postcolonial theory such as Teshome

Gabriel in the film department, I started to see doors open in a way that kept me going in the field. The UC system, moreover, was on fire with the introduction of poststructuralism and postmodern theory; grad students and faculty even made pilgrimages down to UC Irvine to hear Jacques Derrida and Jean-François Lyotard lecture in the flesh.

All of this was thrilling. Maybe, after all, I could mobilize Preziosi's insights; the work of Said, Derrida, Trinh T. Minh-ha, and Gayatri Spivak; and the burgeoning debates in feminist art history and visual theory to challenge art history on a deep, structural level. I already knew that it wasn't enough just to *add* missing artists to the canon; these theories justified my instincts of pushing against the rigid boundaries of the discipline as it then existed. After I graduated in 1991, and luckily landed a tenure-track job at UC Riverside, I began to notice a dearth of attention in art historical and curatorial accounts of contemporary art to work by women, people who were openly queer, Blacks, Chicanx/Latinx people, and Asian Americans (not to mention any artists beyond the Euro-American framework)—and saw that this marginalization correlated with the exclusion of performance and embodied practices from consideration. I sought in my early teaching and publishing to introduce work by artists using their bodies, work that had been completely erased from histories of contemporary art due to its refusal to obey the disembodied, apolitical frameworks of modernist art history, criticism, and curating (which were Eurocentric, white dominant, masculinist, and homophobic).

This new move was, as noted, mostly instinctive. I did not have much guidance, and there were almost no available publications tracking these artists' works or putting them in social context. I had to research them via word of mouth, oral histories, art magazines, alternative spaces, and obscure journals in local libraries—which explains some of my long-term emphasis on Los Angeles–based performance and visual art.[5] For example, I cannot remember when I first heard about the radical Chicanx art collective Asco and the work of queer Chicanx photographer Laura Aguilar, but I managed to meet her and Asco's Harry Gamboa Jr. and invite them into my art history classes at UC Riverside. By literally bringing creative bodies into the classroom, I was trying to change the histories to which the students had access. By the late 1990s, too, my work had changed trajectory; through this motivation, I had begun to shift my disciplinary focus toward body art, performance studies, sexuality studies (including queer theory), and postcolonial and critical race theory.

Part II: Creativity is never free: Thinking creatively in the academy

Given this trajectory—my instinctive resistance to accepted norms while being fully ensconced in the academy—I now turn to the question of my creative life. The following expresses some aspects of my emotional connection to (and sometimes repulsion from) aspects of the dominant disciplinary structures as well as the larger structures of power in the university system (both of which I resist but, admittedly, also occupy). Within these ruminations, it will be clear that the leitmotif of all of my work, the theoretical and political thread that unites all that I do, has been an increasing awareness and theoretical highlighting of the embodiment and relationality of the art encounter—both within and beyond disciplines, both of imagery or performances and of their discourses and institutions.[6] Acknowledging this relationality entails an awareness of the contingency of all meaning and value as we make, exhibit, write about, and otherwise engage with art, in and beyond the university. This acknowledgment gives me room to breathe, and the space to acknowledge and even flex my own biases (in itself a political move), while also honoring the fecund and richly complex modes of creativity I encounter through art and performance. My work, I hope, honors the energy and ultimately unfixable meanings generated by these encounters.

My creative life is that of an academic who squeezes creativity into the interstices of time left to me after doing administration and teaching, particularly as I have now become "vice dean" (or "dean of vice" as I prefer to call my position!) of academics and research at the Roski School of Art and Design at USC. I am thus someone who has already acceded to a hierarchical array of systems that siphon what I do into mostly predictable forms (the refereed journal article, the conference talk, the book published with an academic press, the show curated in a space designed for art and performance). And yet …? As I contemplate how to live creatively within these systems, I hope to generate some energy through these words to inspire forms of creative thinking (however minute and momentary) in return. I want to say most of all that creativity, for me, is about recognizing the structures of power I negotiate every day in academia and self-reflexively positioning myself within them in new ways. It is about maintaining a sense of dynamism attached to knowing (or thinking I know) that I am engaging an audience of others, saying something to someone else—again an acknowledgment and making use of the relational. This is how I teach, read, interpret, and historicize art and its discourses critically, but it is also how I hope to affect others through my teaching and writing and curating.

I am attracted to the work of others (artists, writers, scholars, curators) who have a similarly skewed relationship to the everyday norms and institutional imperatives—along the lines of Louis Althusser's concept of "Ideological State Apparatuses"—that constrict us.[7] Universities today are difficult places to carve out space for making, writing, creating that are not fully rationalized by the late capitalist imperatives that structure them (we have all been through and participated in multiple and ongoing merit reviews; we have all applied for grants, within and beyond our institutions). The tension of living a creative life today is even more heightened a challenge due to the ubiquity of e-mail and social media: we live in a time in which we give ourselves far too easily to screens and connections forged in the virtual, with algorithmic networks (themselves Althusserian) invading every layer of our consciousness—and how much more so in the era of COVID-19, where almost *everything*, including teaching, is done primarily online! Not only are we still pressured to define our careers through published research, we now also labor to keep up with the imperatives to brand and circulate ourselves and/as our research and creative work online (we are effectively working as PR agents for our institutions, which demand that we tag them). They like to package what we do, no matter how messy and creatively innovative, as "knowledge transfer." We are never free, creatively unburdened. And yet …?

The inimitable diva Vaginal Davis (writer, performer, artist, and impresario: a veritable paragon of living a creative life) stated in 2016 in a published dialogue:

> *In a nutshell, I don't trust institutions. That tired argument for changing an institution from within doesn't hold any*

> *Babylonian Gorgon with me. If you become too entrenched inside an institution it winds up changing you, and not for the better. [...] The lesson is: Don't put all your hope in an institution. It's no panacea or savior.*[8]

We intellectuals often find ourselves in institutions such as universities where we believe our creative impulses might be nurtured and protected. As I have suggested and Davis asserts, institutions will not save us or encourage our creativity. Rather, as is increasingly common in the late capitalist maelstrom in which we find ourselves, the university can and will attempt to instrumentalize bits of us, often using Silicon Valley-esque terms such as "disruption" and "innovation" to market what we do, subsuming it into their brand. They will pressure us to produce and create objects and texts (especially those sanctioned by grants and awards) and siphon these products into their branding mechanisms.[9]

It took me the first two decades of my career to fully acknowledge that this was happening and that my father's "Mad Men" version of academia (replete with tweed Brooks Brothers jackets and three-martini lunches—how they got anything creative done at all is a mystery!) was long gone. Twelve years in the University of California system (1991–2003), seven years at the University of Manchester in British academia (2003–10, the most instrumentalized of all), five years at McGill University in the Canadian system (2010–14)—to that date, all nominally "public" schools—and now almost seven years and counting in the belly of the late capitalist beast, at the fully private University of Southern California (2014–). Manifesting an extreme version of what the publics yearn to do but often fail at achieving due to the weight of state bureaucracies, USC epitomizes the university as branding machine and is paradigmatic of this set of operations. USC blatantly sells its employees' thought and creative output as part of—as integral to—its brand, as a glance at the school's website on any given day makes clear. The fact that this packaging arguably supports and is supported by white supremacist and classist policies (even those veiled under the guise of "diversity" initiatives) and symbology is horrifying, and it isn't fully clear how to resist or survive in the midst of such saturated neoliberal and corporate ideologies other than writing—while supported by a USC salary—about the institutional racism that surrounds me.[10]

And yet I feel freer at this institution that makes no bones about its aspirational and market-driven instrumentalization of my work than I did at places such as the University of Manchester, where the gloss of independent thought was and continues to be polluted by insidious structures of state ownership and assumptions around obeisance to the government. At Manchester, it was made crystal clear that anything I produced as an employee paid by the government was therefore the possession of said government. The London-based offices of higher education continually projected their insidious tentacles of creativity-killing bureaucratese into the hearts of artists and intellectuals who had signed on the dotted line (as if the power dynamics weren't obvious enough, my letter of appointment began with the line "Pursuant upon the approval of her Majesty the Queen"!). The state knew and never let us forget that we had acceded to a life of tick-box-festooned forms aimed at reducing complex thought to terms such as "units of resource" (as my dean at the time called students), "input" and "outflow" (the money made from, say, a conference in relation to money put in), "assessment criteria," "innovation," "buy-out," "research outcomes," and so on.

This kind of thing destroys your soul, one checkbox at a time, defeating the very "creativity" it asserts it is calling forth. British academics are completely exhausted and demoralized, just as (one imagines) the government hopes to achieve. Rumor among browbeaten academics had it that Conservative Prime Minister Margaret Thatcher was the original developer of such tactics and "labor" PM Tony Blair their perfecter (obsessed with "accountability" as his regime was). Thatcher's goal, according to this lore, was to keep intellectuals so busy that no revolution could or would be fomented. This is a brilliantly devised strategy that seems to have worked like a charm. The instrumentalizing mindset results in Orwellian processes such as the UK-wide "Research Assessment Exercise" (RAE)—now called the "Research Excellence Framework" (REF), in an even more deadly bureaucratic application of the law of opposites (where that which destroys excellence is touted as maintaining it). Here, the research and creative "output" of every scholar and artist working at a British university is reduced to a series of numbers, which, added up and combined with other "scores" across the department, determines the funding allotted to that department.

It took collaborating with someone such as Vaginal Davis herself to break these codes and work them against themselves. My initial interest in Davis's work has always been emotional, scholarly, and creative, linked to the dynamics I noted above. But I was also, admittedly, motivated by a secondary goal (I'd say fully achieved) of using the rationalized state culture machine against its own desire to police and control. The cowinner (with fellow professor Laura Doan) of several government grants to support an event called "Theorising Queer Visualities" at the University of Manchester in 2005, I applied for funds to bring Davis to participate in the event and to extend her stay to do workshops with local youth on queer Black experience. With the help of Davis's vast array of identifications and fluid sense of political agency, I obtained a huge Arts Council England grant by making use of these to tick every minority box on the form (Black: check; Latinx: check; queer: check; gay: check; trans: check; lower-income family: check). We were successful in obtaining about £10,000 to fund Davis's two-week stay in Manchester. During this visit, she swanned through the Canal Street club scene (the "queer" zone in Manchester at the time) and engaged with myriad local youth, no doubt vastly improving British culture in the process. A win-win for living creatively *and* exploiting the state to do so. With Davis's help, I was able to feed the maw of the bureaucracy (ticking boxes in my own promotion file: state funding obtained, check), while achieving some important countercultural goals.

The best way to survive the creativity-destroying tendencies of bureaucracies is arguably through such guerrilla tactics. As Davis suggests in her words cited above, performance artists—here artists such as Guillermo Gómez-Peña, Nao Bustamante, and Ron Athey also figure large—are particularly good at developing strategies to use the system against itself. They are often irritated and already marginalized people who have little to lose in doing so.

We agree to be in these systems and we tick their boxes. Some of us even have nominally upper-admin roles such as vice dean. So, as an academic, I must acknowledge that the system is us, or at least we play a key role within it. I'm quite sure most of the British bureaucrats who thought up the RAE/REF started as scholars and artists, each turning into a bureaucratic dominatrix snapping the whip at our backs, capable of producing mind-numbing imperatives as farfetched as those in the movie *Brazil*.

As the mentions of Orwell and *Brazil* suggest, there is a reason the British produce such brilliant satires around the deadening bureaucracy of life in the United Kingdom, addressing the myriad ways in which the institution kills the very thing it loudly proclaims it is nurturing (whether "British culture" or "creativity")—they are experts at producing the culture *and* its critique. What are the "outcomes"? Justify yourself.

Part III: Finding creative agency in the face of clichés

So, being inculcated into every level of institutional obeisance, I don't know if I can access the idea of a creative life as it used to exist, at least for privileged middle-class white late "baby boomers" like me in the postwar United States. It is still violently alive, of course, in our most florid (and nostalgic) yearnings in relation to the visual arts. In this imaginary, we still fantasize that an artist freely expresses herself, that an art historian or art critic can, with objective "disinterest" and the dedication of an eighteenth-century aristocrat on his Grand Tour, convey correct narratives about her area of expertise—these hackneyed ideals are still all too often pulled out from the moldy closets of modernism and dusted off for the pretty little glowing screens of social media (an artist touted for radically exposing circuits of power or racism; a smiling selfie of the ever-modest art historian, curator, or art star in Dakar or Cairo for the latest global art shebang!). Every day I see it somewhere, and often participate in it myself: this seemingly long-lost yet ever-vibrant cliché of the artistic genius who creates spontaneously and thereby breaks free of his mental cages and, in passing, overthrows (casually, like tossing over an unwanted article of clothing or swiping left) bourgeois institutions in one go—or the courageous scholar who bucks the norms to transform the field. We yearn to believe this still exists, somewhere.

My narrative above doesn't avoid this trap. I am aware.

The hardest part of trying to maintain the raw edges of thought without continually succumbing to the pregiven formulae by which this rawness is subdued—if I could describe creativity in that way—is that every level of what we do as scholars is always already institutionalized (as Althusser's model understands and seeks to examine). So, I view my career now as an inevitably partially failed, but never futile, exercise in fully reclaiming the creative life—in the sense of attempting to extricate it from the bodily limits and psychic/institutional habitus that necessarily channel any attempt at creative expression.[11] But maybe this struggle *is* the creative life, misrecognized: the daily grind and the occasionally enlightened stabs at saying or doing something that makes of the old bits and bobs (some admittedly clichés) an ever-so-slightly new collage of thought or expression, one that is always unpredictable in its effects.

We can never predetermine or claim to know how, when, and where the "newness" of what we extrude as our work will be felt, interpreted, and thusly passed along to others. This is the relational pulse that moves me forward.

Creative lives have to be claimed and forged relentlessly, in the face of brutal and oppressive institutions and their internalization as habitus. We must do this in the face of impossibility. There is no other way.

Notes

1. I discuss these experiences briefly in *Seeing Differently: A History and Theory of Identification and the Visual Arts* (New York: Routledge, 2012) and *In between Subjects: A Critical Genealogy of Queer Performance* (New York: Routledge, 2021).
2. I have written about the friction performance art causes to the disciplinary structures of art history in several places, including in the essay "Live Art in Art History: A Paradox?" in *The Cambridge Companion to Performance Studies*, ed. Tracy C. Davis (Cambridge: Cambridge University Press, 2008), 151–65.
3. This allegiance is played out in most of my work of the past two decades. For recent examples, see my coedited volumes: with Erin Silver, *Otherwise: Imagining Queer Feminist Art Histories* (Manchester: Manchester University Press, 2016); and with Andy Campbell, *Queer Communion: Ron Athey* (Bristol: Intellect, 2020); as well as my edited "On Trans/ Performance," Special Issue of *Performance Research* 21, no. 5 (October 2016): 1–141.
4. This is not to say they can, or do, entirely avoid forms of commodification, as the work of Marina Abramović exemplifies; see my exploration of the ways in which her career has instrumentalized performance art: " 'The Artist Is Present': Artistic

Re-Enactments and the Impossibility of Presence," *TDR: The Drama Review* 55, no. 1 (Spring 2011): 16–45.

5. For example, key sources for otherwise obscure information included the *LAICA (Los Angeles Institute of Contemporary Art) Journal*, attached to a short-lived but important alternative space in Los Angeles; Los Angeles Contemporary Exhibitions (LACE) and its archives; and *High Performance* magazine, connected to the performance venue Highways. UCLA's growing complement of oral histories were also a goldmine.
6. On these points, see my article "Encountering: The Conceptual Body, or a Theory of When, Where, and How Art 'Means,'" *TDR: The Drama Review* 62, no. 3 (Fall 2018): 12–34, and chapter 2, "Relationality," of my book *In between Subjects: A Critical Genealogy of Queer Performance.*
7. University art history and art departments and the museum are quintessential examples of what Althusser called "Ideological State Apparatuses," in that they ideologically inculcate us into replicating the "soft power" of ideologies relating to art. See Louis Althusser, "Ideology and Ideological State Apparatuses," in *Lenin and Philosophy and Other Essays*, trans. Ben Brewster (New York: Monthly Review Press, [1970] 1971), 127–87.
8. Vaginal Davis, in Lisa Newman in Dialogue with Vaginal Davis and Del LaGrace Volcano, "'What Have You Done for Me Lately?': The Institutionalization of Queer Feminist Art Histories," in *Otherwise*, 339–40.
9. I note the shift over the past three decades toward universities claiming legal ownership of our syllabi and our research—strong at McGill and USC, in my experience. Fortunately, art historians' work isn't worth much economically, so they rarely follow up on these claims. It must be tricky and stressful, however, to be in the sciences and engineering, where patents can be worth millions. On branding, see Naomi Klein, *No Logo* (New York: Picador, 2000); Klein identifies the shift from making products to branding on the part of late capitalist corporations. Klein's work in this area has been crucial in shaping my critique, and I assign it to my students.
10. I have recently coauthored an article with my former USC colleague Tania Modleski critiquing the White supremacy of USC symbology on campus: "Trojan Horse," *Public Seminar*, July 23, 2020, https://publicseminar.org/essays/trojan-horse/.
11. On bodily habitus, see Marcel Mauss, "Techniques of the Body," *Economy and Society* 2, no. 1 ([1934] 1973): 70–88; and

Pierre Bourdieu, "Structures, *Habitus*, Practices," in *The Logic of Practice*, trans. Richard Nice (Stanford: Stanford University Press, [1980] 1990), 52–65. Habitus is arguably the bodily side of Althusser's Ideological State Apparatuses as they insinuate ideology into our mind–body complex.

YING KWOK

THE ONLY WAY to understand what I am doing, and how and why I do it, is through thinking about the place where I live and work. Ordinary subjects never interested me much during my early school years. They felt like routines with fixed answers and no practical usage: all I needed to do was memorize. But I enjoyed art. It was more open ended, and each piece of homework was a new creation made from nothing. And so, I chose to study fine art at the Chinese University of Hong Kong. In the first lesson of fundamental drawing taught by Professor Lui Chung Kwong, he asked a predictable question: "Who wants to be an artist? Please raise your hand." I cannot remember whether I raised my hand or not. I hesitated because there were no jobs for artists, yet I believed there must be some role in the arts field where I would find my position.

Although I have worked professionally as a curator for the past decade, I still see myself as an artist: an artist co-living with a curator inside one body. I often find myself responding to the world, society, and subjects that interest me in an artistic manner. I always start with a gut feeling, an instinct, before analyzing, then following with fact checking and researching to produce a structured outcome that is more communicable.

I graduated in the millennium year, 2000, from the Department of Fine Arts of the Chinese University of Hong Kong. Two decades ago, the arts scene here was very different. There were less than a handful of art spaces in the city, barely any commercial galleries were interested or willing to work with young artists, and the Hong Kong Museum of Art was interested only in artists of my teacher's generation. Other spaces such as the Hong Kong Arts Centre, Para/Site Art Space, 1a Space, and Videotage were doing some interesting thematic exhibitions from time to time. But for young artists like me, it was so hard to be seen. Most of us chose to self-initiate our own exhibition and host it in some public space available for rental. The process was trial and error; no professional advice was available.

Having won some awards and been approached by a local gallery, Grotto Fine Art (the only gallery designated to the young generation of Hong Kong artists back then), I was among the lucky few who got some positive recognition upon graduation, and I was very keen to carry on making art, which I already saw as my life, a career. As a fresh graduate, I was eager to get my first solo exhibition where I could fully explore my artistic practice and show the "art world" what I was capable of. However, we knew back then that there were no venues or funding support. We needed to contribute our own savings before getting any attention from the industry and the press. When the time came, I knew I wanted to make sure my exhibition would attract art professionals, not just my own friends.

I firmly believed that venue, funding, and press attention were three prerequisites for an artist to share his/her own works with the world. After working in the exhibition department of the Hong Kong Arts Centre for a few months, I got a better understanding of the work involved in organizing an exhibition. There were six or seven of us on the exhibition team at any one time, with each person taking care of a specific aspect: marketing and press, materials/equipment setup, hospitality, and budget. It really required a team to work. What was most important, though, was interdependence and that a professional artist should focus on the artworks and presentation and trust the team in creating the show.

With a better idea of the challenge ahead, I proposed to join forces with four graduated artists: Au Hoi Lam, Sephine Chan, Hui Chui Hung, and Kongee. We each wanted to have our own solo exhibitions, but we worked to share resources and took turns in order to support one another. We named our group *Gifted Young Artists Self-Training Programme (優質青年藝術家自我培訓計劃)*. Five solo exhibitions were staged one after the other in different spaces within the building of the Hong Kong Arts Centre, including the Goethe Institute, the Experimental Gallery, and the Atrium. Suddenly it was not just a solo show of an unknown young artist, but one of the few young artist programs in Hong Kong! After all these years, I still see it as one of the most important exhibitions for me. Not only was it important to me as an artist, but it also planted the curating seed in me. It gave me an early taste of using creative solutions to push the limits and constraints for both myself and my peers.

Under this program, we all got our solo exhibitions. As it was self-organized and completely independent, each exhibition had a unique style and stood out from commercial aesthetics. We did not need to compromise or give in to a theme where an outside curator layers on top of the work. Every single curatorial word was the artist's own. The satisfaction and feeling of being completely honest without holding back was so powerful, allowing us to pursue our visions without regret. It might not be the best exhibition I have ever been in, but the sense of empowerment is unmatched. It gave me the confidence to carry on with my own artistic practice, while also encouraging me to *organize* exhibitions for my peers. Interestingly, I did not think I was curating back then. Those loose curatorial experiences had awakened the curatorial cells in my body and became important track records for me to get my first full-time curating job in the Centre for Chinese Contemporary Art (Manchester, UK) shortly after I graduated from the MA Fine Art program at Chelsea College of Art in 2004.

The job was out of my league, but it was my dream job at that time. The UK art scene was mind-blowing; after living there for two years, I still found that there was so much to see and learn, and nowhere could my home city compare. I wanted to be part of the scene and not just a visitor or guest. I wanted to bring back all the experiences, knowledge, and connections from the United Kingdom back to Hong Kong. The art scene in our city was insignificant in comparison, but I had faith in the artists and art practitioners working here. I eventually moved back to Hong Kong after twelve years in the United Kingdom, in the Christmas season of 2014, and started to work as an independent curator.

My primary academic training as an artist has had a lot of influence on my curatorial approach. I truly believe good art speaks for itself. In all the exhibitions I curate, I tend to put artists' interests as the first priority, to show the best of them without too much interpretation. The solo exhibition is one of my favorite exhibition forms. I believe it can fully illustrate the artist's thinking. Sometimes one single work can tell a multilayered story, but most often, the story is better illuminated with a series of works. This also helps the viewer to better understand the context of the work and why the artist has made it in such a way.

Fast forward to 2014, and the Hong Kong art scene had undergone some dramatic development. By this time, Art Basel Hong Kong was running its second iteration after a very successful launch, putting Hong Kong on the international art map. Famous foreign commercial galleries started moving into Hong Kong, and new museums and art spaces were developed by the Hong Kong government to synergize with the West Kowloon Cultural District. I was invited to curate an exhibition in a new art space called Oi! Street, in a converted heritage building in North Point, Hong Kong.

I named my exhibition *Collector Club*, the idea being to investigate in detail the values of art in terms of its public consumption and perception. Encouraging critical thinking and initiating effective discussions around the values of art, the exhibition takes a "club membership" approach and serves as an incubator for a committed audience to further their knowledge and engagement. An impermanent "Collector Club membership scheme" ran until the end of Art Basel Hong Kong in the same year.

Alongside *Collector Club*, I also started *Art Appraisal Club* with the "member room." It was presented as a piece of work in the exhibition to facilitate art discussions with the members. They receive monthly newsletters with articles contributed by local art writers such as recommended exhibition lists, exhibition reviews, and thematic articles. The writers are experienced professionals working on the frontlines, including Chan Sai Lok, Anthony Leung Po Shan, Jeff Leung Chin-fung, and Yeung Yang. They have kept up with the art developments in Hong Kong for a long time, and they understand artists' work in both personal and professional aspects. Apart from providing insider information and perspective to interested parties, I want to emphasize the importance of discussion and dialogue among local art critics.

The *Art Appraisal Club* idea was well received, and there was a strong demand from members, peers, and ourselves to carry on. In view of the commercially driven art world developing rapidly in Hong Kong, we needed space to cater to the local market, focusing on the local artists through honest constructive criticism. We have a strong desire to continue communicating with members and the public, and to facilitate professional art comments in order to raise the standards of the audience, who, in return, will demand more quality exhibitions. Apart from sharing our writings online, we aspire to produce a printed journal for circulation. Funding is always an issue, particularly in the beginning before people recognize our work. Public funding in Hong Kong is more in favor of exhibitions and workshops, where the audience can be quantified. Our intellectual works and intangible output are tricky for quantitative assessment in this context. Quite often, we have to package it as an art project or event for fundraising. But, most importantly, we have persevered for five years so far. I work in a specific place, and the setting in all its nuance determines much of what I and other artists, arts writers, and curator peers are making.

In mid-2019, Hong Kong experienced an unprecedented social movement that changed the city forever. Various protests continued for eight months, and then came the threat of COVID-19, and then the new national security law that took effect in July 2020. We are undergoing a new phase where we have to unlearn our ways of life and reestablish new ones. I cannot help but think, what is the role of art in times of social unrest? How can we respond to the current situation, and where should our work sit between awareness raising, activism, and art?

I believe people who work in art perceive the world with a certain sensibility and aesthetics, while staying true to themselves and trying to influence others with an artistic manner. To me, it is the fundamental spirit of art to preserve memories for the society and make sure our values and beliefs can be seen, which is why I think art professionals have an important role to play during these troubled times.

MIRANDA LASH

MY CURATORIAL EMBRACE of regional complexity and my belief in the role museums play in supporting artists are intricately connected for me. Great artists embrace complexity—they challenge the way we see the world, often in ways that defy easy categorization and explanation. The artist Mel Chin once described art to me as a "catalyst for thought," a definition I wholeheartedly agree with. President John F. Kennedy promoted artists as the guarantors of a freethinking democracy. Why? Because artists inspire us to think differently. They are the dissident voices and questioners that shake society out of somnolence. As an art historian, my calling is to try to make the most profound and complex ideas surrounding art accessible to the public in a way that allows them to actively engage with art's intricacies. My goal within the museum is to encourage institutions to see these nuances as assets and, ultimately, their salvation. People come to our buildings to find the poetry in life, fresh perspectives, perhaps a chance encounter with beauty, and a place to look and talk about what they see and are processing with others. There is always a new world waiting and wanting to be born, even within the world we already live in.

My convictions surrounding the role of art within museums stem from many places, but two pivotal influences are my mother's family and my time spent living in New Orleans. My mother, strangely enough, is not in any way affiliated with the art world, but her values are foundational to my approach as a curator. I spent my formative years in the 1990s growing up in Los Angeles and Fresno, California—cities where my mother practiced as a doctor serving immigrants largely from Mexico and Central America. Born in Mexico herself, my mother moved to the projects of Pacoima, Los Angeles, as a teenager and committed herself to becoming a family physician dedicated to her community. Almost all of her patients were first- or second-generation immigrants, many of them undocumented migrant workers. She tirelessly served the people who needed her most and continues to do so to this day. My mother's gift to my siblings and me was membership into a large, close-knit, loving Mexican American family. Although my grandparents were poor when they came to this country, they carried with them an abiding sense of dignity and a high esteem for education. We were told that Velascos are "hard working, strong people—we treasure knowledge because it can never be taken away." It was powerful to have these qualities articulated to us as children not as aspirations but as statements of fact. As a result, I regard knowledge as one of the greatest gifts I can give to others.

My family's background relates to art history in the fostering of two qualities that ground my work as a curator and an arts leader—a sense of higher purpose (which my mother had) and a doggedness when it comes to facing challenges and obstacles. The older I get, the more I believe that the path to an extended career as a curator and impactful arts leader pivots not just on brilliance but also on resilience. The simple act of not losing the will to persevere and remain true to your beliefs is essential. I believe that all persons should have the right to access the epiphanies offered by art, without having to wade through content that has been unnecessarily "dumbed down" or oversimplified due to a lack of faith in many publics' abilities. Effective communication that endeavors to bridge ideas across different backgrounds takes extra work, research, listening, and insight, but it is something every citizen deserves. If I had to explain where my commitment to equal access to art stems from, it is probably from my family—the way they live is driven by a sense of fairness and generosity and a great pride and seriousness toward what it means to be a responsible citizen.

For me, as well as for many of my colleagues, one of the most challenging parts of the profession is when it falls to the curator to be the moral conscience of the museum. This may involve advocating for the artist's needs, or bringing forward ethical concerns related to a collection's proper care, or navigating a patron's desires, or pushing for greater equity in terms of how the exhibition calendar and acquisition program is shaped, or arguing against discrimination in the treatment of museum staff. Every experienced curator knows that speaking up can result in very real and at times harsh personal and professional consequences. I have deep respect for my curatorial colleagues who have been bold in advocating for needed change, especially when it has come at a steep cost.

I did not foresee having to be an advocate for paid parental leave, but in 2015, when I was the only curator to have been pregnant in the Speed Art Museum's recent history, I found myself in the position of pushing for paid leave as a moral imperative that matched the progressive branding my museum was presenting to the public. Many female employees at my museum had been pregnant before, but as a curator who visited the homes of patrons and attended their events, I unintentionally became a visible provocation on the subject of paid leave. I was often asked by patrons, trustees, and docents how much time I intended to take off to have the baby. When I explained that I would be taking as little time as possible, due to the lack of paid maternity leave in the museum's employee policy, my director at the time accused me of "embarrassing the institution." I was expected to celebrate women in the programming I presented at the museum and quietly go into financial debt in order to have a child. Pooling information among my colleagues in the museum field regarding other institutions' paid leave policies was an incredibly helpful strategy, even though it quickly revealed to me the sad reality that parental leave benefits are often largely based on state disability laws (and many states, as of 2020, offered no provisions for paid leave).

I struggled with thinking at times that this issue was my problem to solve alone, when in retrospect I could have done more to galvanize like-minded colleagues within my institution to advocate for change, build a broader network for advice and emotional support, and welcome a wider ownership of the issue. Ultimately, after several years of advocacy, the leave policy at my institution changed for the better, but perhaps one of the greatest takeaways from this experience for me was understanding the importance of coalition building and information sharing. Coalitions can not only hasten the process of change but can also ease the toll of a stressful and perhaps professionally compromising experience.

Thoughtful curation is not just the practice of looking closely but also opening yourself up to the broader emotional, political, and spiritual resonances at stake in the artwork. The kind of sensitivity that makes for great art historians and writers can also make the recurrence of injustice and indifference difficult to bear. The most effective bulwark I have found against despair has been staying connected to the community of my colleagues and artists, whose work never fails to reinvigorate my thinking—which leads me to New Orleans, the most stimulating, inspiring, and challenging place I have ever lived. I moved there in late 2007, when the city was very much still in the throes of post-Katrina recovery. My husband is from New Orleans, and together we had watched the destruction of the levee failures unfold in 2005 on our television screen from my graduate-school apartment at Williams College. We wanted to aid the city in its recovery as much as we could, but it took over two years to find jobs that enabled us to move there permanently. In 2007, I was working in Houston at the Menil Collection, a private collection known for its modern masterpieces, housed in an impeccable Renzo Piano building. When I heard that New Orleans Museum of Art (NOMA) was endeavoring to launch a contemporary art program, I seized the opportunity and signed on to be the first curator of modern and contemporary art in the museum's then 98-year history. I was warned it would be a bumpy transition leaving the comforts of a well-endowed private collection, and I will confess that the initial shock led me at times to question the wisdom of my decision. Before the hurricane, NOMA had over a hundred employees; immediately following Katrina, the city reduced the museum's staff to fewer than ten people. When I joined in 2008, the staff size was hovering close to 50, less than half of what it had once been, and many of my coworkers had suffered the loss of their homes, and in some cases their neighbors, close friends, and family members. It became clear that one of my unofficial roles as the museum's first post-Katrina hire was simply to listen to survivors' stories, both within the museum's walls and in the community beyond.

Known for being a staid stronghold for old wealth before the storm, NOMA embarked upon a consistent contemporary program in the hopes of tapping into new audiences and infusing the building with fresh energy. Together with my colleagues at the museum, I worked to create a space of refuge, creativity, and escape. We offered a sense of normalcy amid the chaos, but perhaps more importantly, the museum was part of many concurrent endeavors throughout the city that offered hope that New Orleans would not just survive but also thrive. This experience solidified for me that at its best, the museum is not merely a luxury or a bauble for the elite—it can be a necessary hub for a city's cultural life and a platform for the virtues of inclusivity.

If we adhere to the idea that art is a catalyst for thought, then museums should embrace exhibitions, publications, and projects that embrace and honor art's complexity. When I signed on at NOMA, then-director John Bullard gave me a remarkable degree of freedom in deciding what direction the contemporary program should take. It was a challenging time for the city, as many New Orleanians were still facing acute challenges after Katrina. New Orleanians had experienced so much hardship and had so much to say about their Katrina experiences and their love for the city, it felt like an appropriate time to listen and be open to what the community was thinking and feeling. I felt a responsibility to provide the city with content that in some way felt connected to Louisiana through either the artists represented or the subject matter addressed. This was not because I felt that Louisianans could only relate to content that was about themselves or (as one curatorial colleague erroneously assumed) because I was being "forced" to work with local artists. Rather, it was a way of asserting that the cultural, ecological, and historical legacy of New Orleans mattered and that its creative fruits were relevant to the rest of the country. This was at a time when the feasibility of rebuilding this region was being seriously debated. The citizens of New Orleans did not regard the return of their city as inevitable but rather as something that needed to be fought for on a daily basis.

While I endeavored to create content at NOMA that was relevant to the community, I also wanted to challenge the stereotypes typically associated with the city. We had high attendance numbers for exhibitions that challenged traditional conceptions of New Orleanian culture, which addressed topics ranging from punk rock (*Skylar Fein: Youth Manifesto*, 2009) to queer vogue performances (*Rashaad Newsome: King of Arms*, 2011), from tackling coastal erosion (*Camille Henrot: Cities of Ys*, 2013) to building a live music recording studio in the galleries

(*Parallel Universe: Quintron and Miss Pussycat Live at City Park*, 2008). I wanted NOMA to become known for debuting national and international artists' work, and I endeavored to provide my audiences with access to the most current ideas in circulation. Prizing innovation and emerging ideas have their challenges, as I often showcased artists without commercial galleries that could foot the bill for exhibition costs. Nevertheless, I felt that I was doing my job best when I was pushing my museum forward in some way, either by negotiating a boundary that had not been previously crossed or by brokering a relationship that did not already exist. Although I believe strongly in the role of museums as professionalized protectors of objects, I would argue that ultimately a museum's role is to help us constantly rethink how we understand our past and our future going forward.

Another key source of inspiration from this period came from watching artists rebuild their practice and their studios, in many cases becoming more ambitious than ever before. New Orleans showed me that when all the comforts of life have been stripped away, there is a fascinating and hard-won opportunity to envision a new realm of possibilities. I watched artists repurpose buildings that had to be completely gutted and stripped down to their studs. I watched New Orleans Airlift create an incredible Music Box Village out of the wreckage of a historic house and repurposed materials. The international art triennial Prospect New Orleans launched its inaugural edition in 2008, bringing busloads of critics, curators, and collectors into the city. Several groups of artists formed collaboratives (the Front, Good Children, Antenna, and Staple Goods, to name a few) that are still exhibiting today, over fourteen years later. The vitality of the local scene inspired me to create a series of exhibitions at NOMA, which in part served to bridge the gap between the museum and the artist scene in a way that had not existed before. New Orleans would not have recovered in the same way without its artists—and neither would NOMA.

It is impossible to grasp everything there is to know about a region, even if you spend a lifetime living there. I never planned to spend an extensive amount of time in the South, but the longer I lived in that part of the country, the more it surprised me. The diversity I witnessed within this region made the stereotypes I had grown up hearing about the South seem underinformed and, as I quickly discovered, damaging to the artists and curators practicing here. My fascination with the realities and mythologies surrounding the American South led me to partner with Trevor Schoonmaker, then the chief curator at the Nasher Museum of Art at Duke University (now the Nasher's director) on curating *Southern Accent: Seeking the American South in Contemporary Art*, 2016–17. The exhibition was an expansive look at the many ways the South is depicted through art, music, and literature, using William Faulkner's concept of the South as an "emotional idea" rather than a geographic place. Our commitment to showcasing an in-depth approach to the South as a fluctuating concept with an undeniably dark past, a rich cultural output, and a constantly evolving future satisfied our desire to capture how the South has shifted (and at times stayed the same) in recent decades. It was particularly important to us that we expand the typical dialogue on race in the South by including works by Native American, Asian American, and Latinx artists. The 24 contributors we asked to write for the exhibition catalog (among them poets, activists, musicians, artists, historians, and foodways scholars) were similarly chosen to reflect a more expansive constellation of views on the South than is regularly depicted.

By untangling the South through this project, we hoped to map routes for audiences through their questions about the roots, causes, and perpetuations of regional preconceptions. By offering a fuller presentation of the South's visual and cultural output, we hoped to offer a more nuanced understanding of what it means to be an American. And there lies one of the surprises I arrived at over time from studying a region's history. In the end, the questions that have to be asked in order to understand the specific heartbreaks and triumphs tied to a place ultimately reflect back on the endlessly complex and universal nature of being human.

VIỆT LÊ AND WASEEM KAZZAH

Collaboration

What follows is a conversation in poems and pictures of sorts that put into conversation Waseem Kazzah, a Syrian refugee—whom I met at the Global Asia/Pacific Art Exchange (GAX) in Montreal convened by Alex Chang and Alice Ming Wai Jim—with my deceased father and myself. Waseem and I identify as artists, scholars, and curators.

This is a dialectic about forgetting/remembering refugee lives.

Việt Lê and Waseem Kazzah (Conversations in Poems)

The art of forgetting

Refuge, refuse, refusal
rememory and forgetting:
we are artists, scholars, refugees, bound through space
  and time.
      Let's connect our journeys:
          Waseem, our families, and I
leaving and return

I never learned
how to hold my own
I never learned how to hold my own voice

I felt worthless for a lifetime

It's time to own our worth. I hear
your silence through the years, your voices, still.

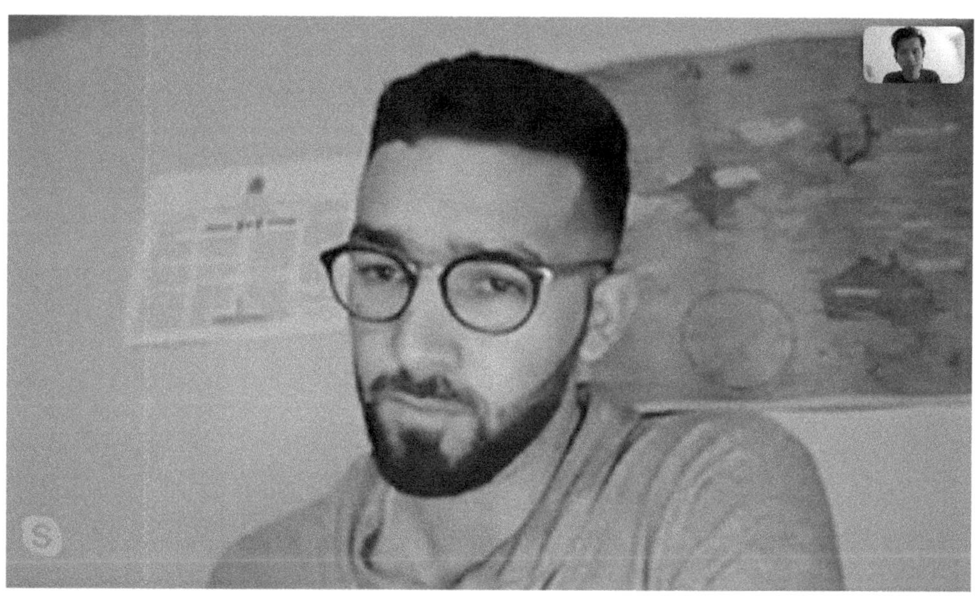

ح ياتي

حياتي الآن بين الطِّي والندمَ والنسيانَ
فقط لأنني خُلِقتُ ببلاد الشامَ
حيث علموني الذُّلَ والندمَ والعصيانَ
حتى غربت إلى بلادِ الأغرابِ والثلج والضجران
حينها حاولت محي الذكريات
حاولت محي ما تبقى من ذاكرتي
من ذاكرةِ الألمِ والهوان
حاولتُ محي ما تبقى من هويتي لكي أنام
ففي نومي تتحول الحقيقة الى أحلام
فلا يبقى الحُزن حُزنا ولا الألم ألماً إلا ماضياً وسراب بلا احساسِ
ولا هواء
عشت حياتي في قالبينَ إثنين
ففي خارجي إنسان و في داخلي آخرٌ بشكل الإنسان
فقدت الروح والاحساس
علموني حُبَ الوطنَ منذ الصغر و يا ليتهم ما علموني

علموني أن أهوى الجدران
علموني أن أعشق الارضَ
يا ليتهم علموني أن الوطنُ له بشرٌ أعز منه ومن الأرضَ فلا وطنٌ بلا إنسان
يا ليتهم علموني أن لا وطنٌ بلا إنسان فعندما أكبَرُ أولُ شيءٍ يشغَلُني هوَ روحُ أخي الإنسان
وعندما أتغربُ اشتاقُ لسلامةِ هذا الحيوان
لن يفهموا معاناتي
لن يفهموا اصراري على فضحِ الحقيقةَ ففي ذاكرتي ما يعجز عن وصفه الوصفُ ولا حتى اللسان
كنت غريبا في وطني وما زلت غريبا في وطن ليس بوطني
سأقول لكم إذا القلبُ هجرَ الأرضَ فلا ينفعُ حينئذٍ أيةٌ ذِكرى فالقلب يهوى شيءً واحداً آلا وهو الآمانَ
كان يسمى وطنا و مازال يسمى وطنا
لولا لم يتخلى عن قضيةِ الإنسان

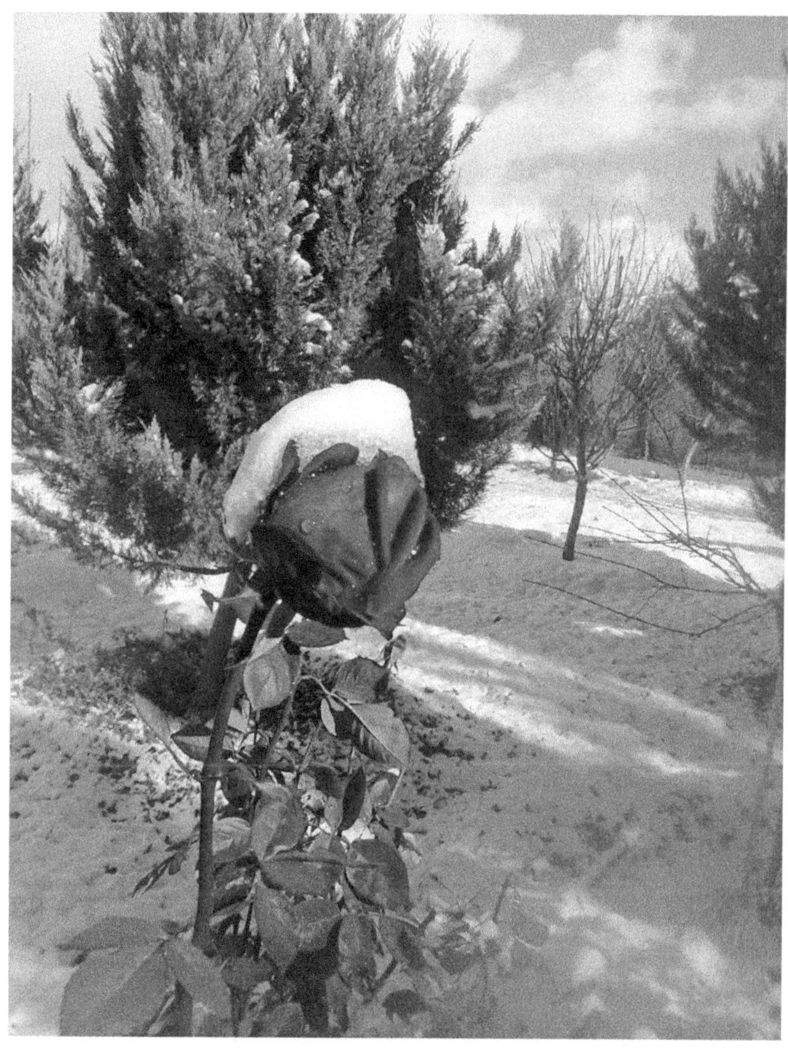

Khan Alsheh, Damascus countryside, 2013. Last "home" for me in Syria.

My Life

Because I was born in Syria, where they taught me
humiliation, bitterness and regret, my life is shattered now
between forgetting, regretting and letting go.
Then, I had to move away from my homeland and roots to
countries of boredom and strangers.
I tried to erase my memories …

When I left my home, I lived in a country of snow and loneliness,
I tried to erase what is left from my memories …
Memories of sorrow and pain …
Once again, I tried to erase what is left from my memories to be able to fall asleep …
Sleep was my only escape, where my reality turned into fiction and mirage,
Where there is no room for desolation and mourning but a tasteless past full of emptiness.

As a bipolar person I had to live
A smiley mask I had to wear for a dead soul pilling sadness and grief,
I am a human being on the outside and another being on the inside,
I lost all my senses but I am still, somehow, alive.
Since I was raised to this life, they taught me how to cherish my land, how to love its soil and to remember its walls,
I wish they had taught me that the land is not worth living if it does not protect its people.

Injustice in this life, I don't know how long I can be patient for!
No one can understand my pain,
No one can understand my perseverance in revealing the truth,
My memories cannot be described by poets nor can it be articulated by tongues.
I was a stranger in my homeland and I am a stranger in a land that is not my home.
Can you tell me the difference between one human being and another or between one land and another?
Let me tell you the difference, it's a fortress mentality that stopped to think or listen,
But it even stopped to beat and it turned into a statue that is lost in memories.
If there is something I know for sure, it would be the fact that if a heart leaves its homeland, memories can't help.
No one loves a country and leaves …
A soul loves only one thing, which is peace.

They called it homeland, and it is still named as such if it did not abandon the human cause.

Oh my beloved ones, you taught me how to smile, why didn't you teach me how to cry?
Oh … my beloved land, why did you teach me how to love, then leave me when my heart became attached to you? Tell me … why?

Text

Each one of us has his/her own way of coping with difficulties. Mine was untraditional but effective in one way or another. My coping mechanism was to forget my past, identity, language, and culture. Forcing myself to stay away from the old me was not a choice but a force by nature. I got a scholarship to study business and political science in Canada as part of a resettlement program. Arabic music, news, and my spoken language itself weren't the same. I was no longer able to listen to them. I didn't want to remember because my heart would ache. A photo of a Damask rose covered with snow might be the last picture I took in my last home in Syria.

Snow …! Here I am in Canada, the land of snow and ice. Is it a coincidence? I do not know. That Damask rose was cold and shy. She was hiding her beauty by closing her eyes and wings to protect herself from the harsh cold snow and sorrow. Are you still following my scattered thoughts?

The oppressors occupied my land and I care no more. It is not my land anymore. Do not tell me how. Art was a healer. A healer to my broken soul. I can express my oppressed voice and scream through images. Through art, I connected with others who can speak that language. That language where my heart is full, my body is loved, and my soul is fully understood.

The only way to survive a trauma is to pure yourself from everything this life has. The only way to survive such pain is by detaching oneself from this life. My people asked for freedom and dignity, but they were not able to get it. It is a privilege to be free. Do not wait; liberate your mind and set your soul free.
Sinsyrianly yours,

Waseem Kazzah, 2019, London, Canada

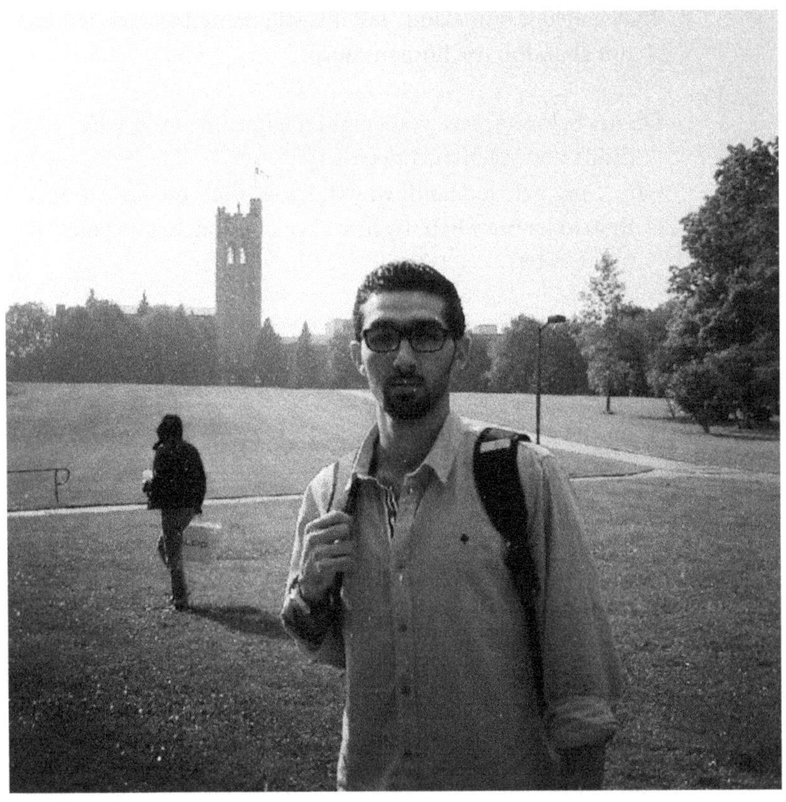

Waseem Kazzah, 2014, London, Canada (my first day in Canada)

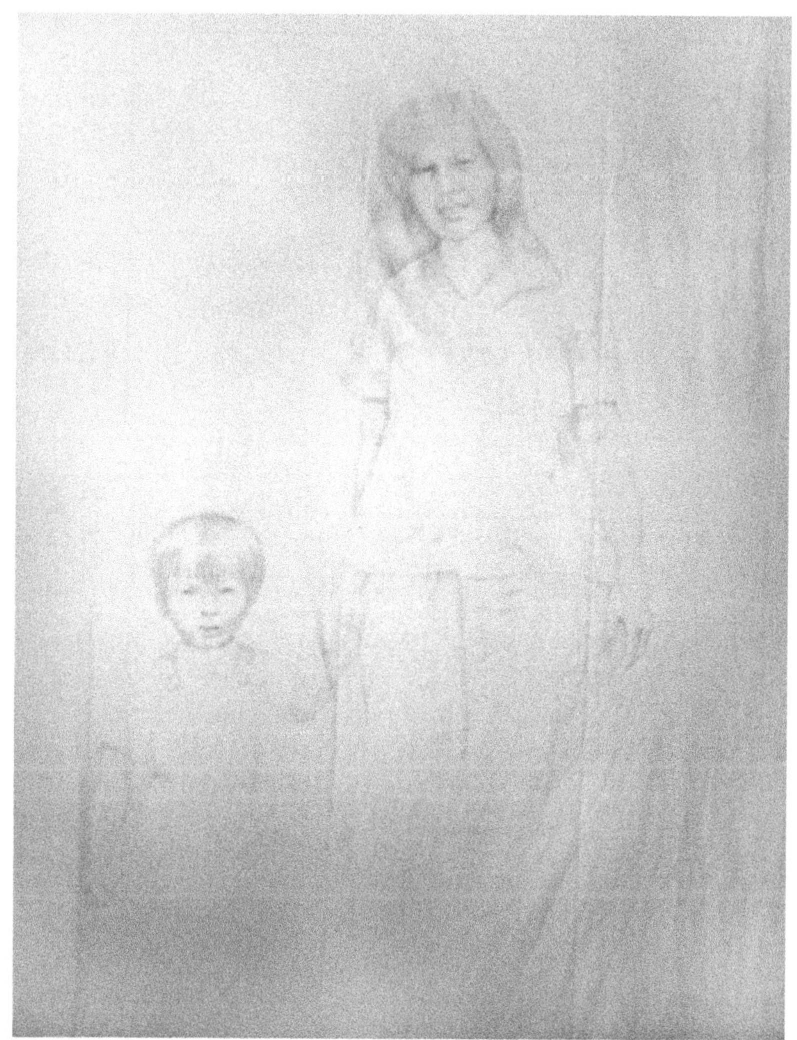

PAROLED PURSUANT TO SEC.212(d)(5)
OF THE I & N ACT TO:
Indefinite
PURPOSE: Viet. refugee

Employment Authorised
(Port) (Date) (Officer)
SEA Aug 28 1979 220

…Y WHEN LEAVING
S—SEE REVERSE
FORM
I-94

PAROLED PURSUANT TO SEC.212(d)(5)
OF THE I & N ACT TO:
Indefinite
PURPOSE: Viet. refugee

Employment Authorised
(Port) (Date) (Officer)
SEA Aug 28 1979 220

…Y WHEN LEAVING
S—SEE REVERSE
FORM
I-94

Việt Lê, *untitled (temple)*, from the *vestige* series; Lê Kim Loi's (Việt's father's) refugee papers.

Tết này thơ gởi cho con

Tết nầy con Bố lên năm
Bố không còn dẫn đến thăm mọi nhà
Bác Thuý gần, Bác Tú xa
Dẫn ra góc phố mua quà cho con
Bố đi, mắt mẹ héo hon
Khuất sau cánh cửa, con còn vẫy tay
Tưởng xa tháng một, ngày hai
Ngờ đâu từ biệt lại dài hàng năm !
Bố mua manh áo, tấm quần
Gởi tình xa xứ để dành cho con
Hình con, đôi mắt ngây tròn,
Bố lồng trong ví, chập chờn cơn mơ
Chuyện con, mẹ kể trong thơ,
Bố đọc trăm bận, lại chờ thơ sau !
Nhớ con lúc khỏe, lúc đau
Nhớ con về ngoại gục đầu ngủ ngon
Nhớ mẹ ghẹo : "Bắc Kỳ con"
Nhớ đi nhà trẻ bị đòn kêu Ba …
Xuân nầy ai ngỡ xuân xa
Tết nầy ai ngỡ chia lìa bố con!

*

Bên nhà còn mẹ, còn con,
Còn cờ phục quốc, Bố còn quê hương.

(Tết Canh Thân 1980)

This Lunar New Year, a Letter for My Son

This Tết you are five
I'm not here to take you to visit every relative's house
Aunt Thuý is close, Uncle Tú is far away
take you to the corner to buy presents
I leave, your mother's eyes wither
Behind the door you still wave
I thought for only one month or two days
Who knew the distance stretches for years!
I buy a shirt, pants
sending you distant love
Your picture, eyes wide and round,

your picture in my pocket, your image wavering like
  a dream
your stories your mom writes in letters
I read a hundred times, waiting for the next one!
Remembering you when healthy, when ill
I remember you, head tilted in deep slumber
I remember your mom teasing: "Bắc Kỳ con"
Remember you being scolded in kindergarten, calling out
  for your dad ...
This spring who knew, a spring far away
This spring who knew we'd separate

*

Homeside, mom and you are there, still
still the flag, I still have a home.

(Tết Canh Thân 1980)

—Lê Kim Lởi, 1980, Orange
translated by Hồ Thị Hồng Hoa and Việt Lê

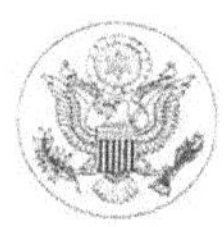

EMBASSY OF THE
UNITED STATES OF AMERICA

Singapore

Date: 22 August 1979

TO: ALL CARRIERS AND IMMIGRATION OFFICIALS

The person(s) listed below, whose photograph(s) is/are affixed hereto is/are travelling to the United States under the auspices of the Inter-governmental Committee for European Migration (ICEM).

The provisions of the United States Immigration and Nationality Act, as amended, requiring all persons to present a valid passport at time of admission to the U. S. has been waived pursuant to authority contained in 22 CFR 42.6(f).

Name	Sex	DOB	POB
Le Kim Loi	M	Aug. 14, 44	Hanoi, VN

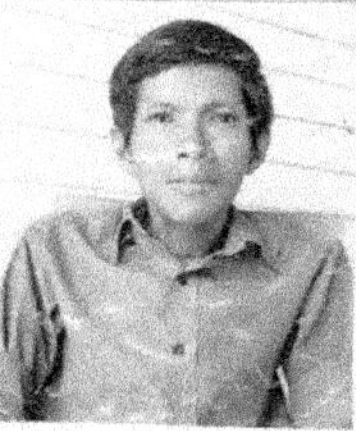

This authorization is valid for thirty days.

ANNE M. HACKETT
Vice Consul of the United
States of America

Samsara
(A prayer for Geshela Gyeltsen)

Fly droning in the suburban temple
suddenly stops.
Do you believe in reincarnation?
Geshela asks. You've been my mother,
brother, father, sister through thousands of lives.

Sitting on crimson
pillows on crimson carpet—
not my blood

relatives, these strangers
nodding, yes.
What forms does one take

after a lifetime, after exhaustion?
Who believes in countless cycles
of winged joys and hunger, circling samsara
not remembering—slow buzzing,
then shedding of husk, another life.

I willfully forget my reincarnations
this life: high school dropout, angry
son, refugee insect, unfaithful
lover, sparrow-child; let me begin

again, let me forge myself anew, a believer
in small kindnesses
under the gaze of this dying

Tibetan monk. I forget and forget.
Light shifts across walls,
Sunday again.
Endless suburban lawns midday:

sprinklers hissing thousands
of small sorrows remembered,
spraying arcs that leave no trace

but green and void,
yes, tell me again and
again.
—Việt Lê, 2019, San Francisco

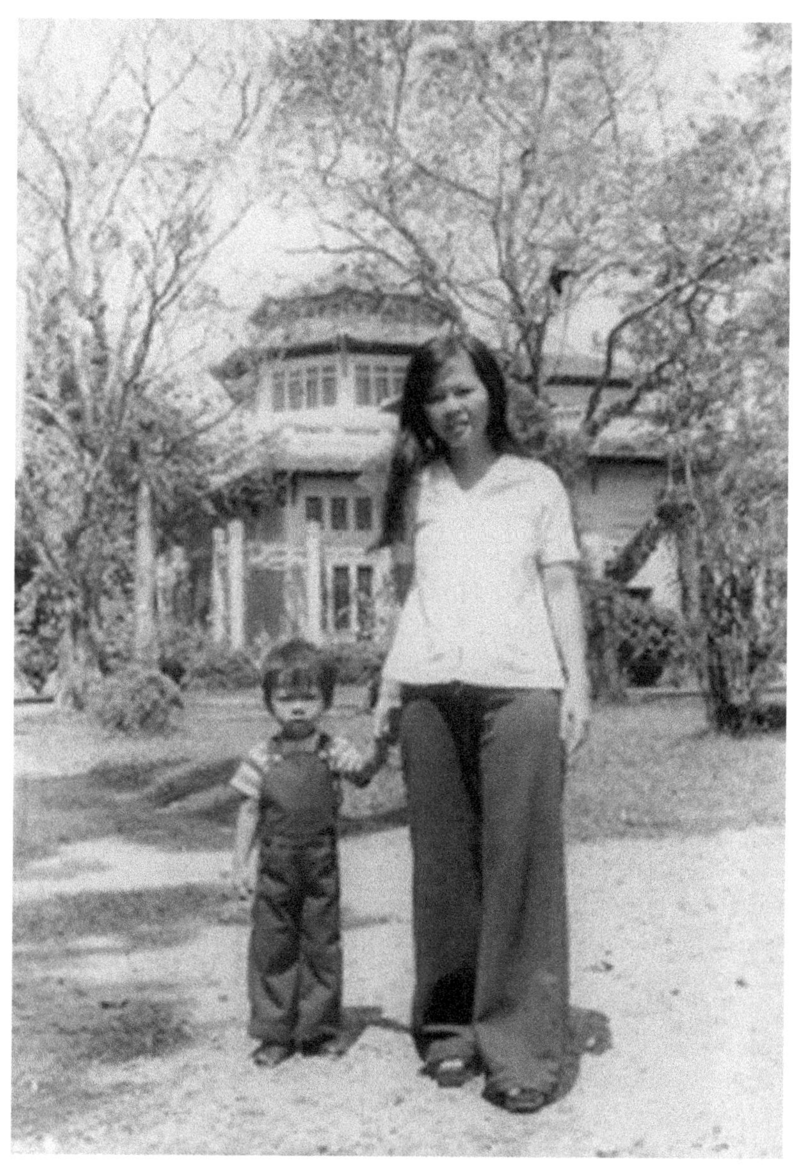

PAWEŁ LESZKOWICZ

TO DO QUEER art you need to be lucky, free, and supported: that is, lucky to have and grasp opportunities free of normalizing oppressions, fears, and professional routine, and supported by people who share your values and are already in the system. I was lucky in all these areas, and my timing was great as well.

I had dreamed about curating queer exhibitions before I started organizing them. And from the very beginning, I knew I would be able to fulfill them at some point in my life. Sooner or later. I have drive and passion, but people have also helped me along the way, and this text is about these people, because *they* enabled me to begin and pursue the curatorial and research path that in the early 1990s seemed to be a bit embarrassing, dangerous, and, for many, impossible: difficult almost everywhere, especially in Eastern Europe, where I am from.

First of all, I was lucky to start my study of art history in the early 1990s, in a postcommunist Poland at a time of radical transformations, when all seemed to be opening up and blooming. The beginning was optimistic and dark at the same time: there were many new possibilities—gay and lesbian organizations became legal and active, and sexuality and culture was already an academic subject—but on the other hand, a new totalitarianism steered by religious fundamentalism started to engulf us. And, of course, postcommunist poverty and massive unemployment were a burden. Additionally, the dominant ideology was based on national, not individual, liberation. Thus, a career in art history and, what is more, the specialization in "queer art history" was a very risky path. But I couldn't stop myself. I still remember the grimaces on the faces of many academics and fellow students. Strangely enough, despite the smirks, I have never felt marginalized or dissuaded from my work. I have fellow travelers. In hindsight, my beginning was easy given the politics and a cultural shift to the right in Poland. The struggle came much later!

But this text is about the beginning and the formation of the energy that has driven me until today. It all began in the Department of Art History at Adam Mickiewicz University[1] in Poznań, a medium-sized Polish city with a great university and Fine Art Academy. Poznań is not the capital of Poland, but it is big enough and close enough to Berlin to assume a more Western feeling than much of the rest of the country. This played a large role in my work and sense of being. There I encountered a professor of art history who is unique in the entire Eastern Bloc: Piotr Piotrowski (1952–2015), whose religion is freedom, democracy, and the power of art—of which he is a true believer! Piotrowski became the supervisor of my MA and Ph.D. theses, where the history of sexuality and art are intertwined, and contemporary art is at the center.

In 1995, I wrote my MA thesis on American gay art of the culture wars during the 1980s and 1990s. I was obsessed with art, politics, and sex, with the "new" salacious and intelligent images. I had access to all the major resources, because our library (before the internet!), thanks to Piotr Piotrowski, was truly perverted. Nan Goldin was my goddess, surrounded by equally major gods: Félix González-Torres, David Wojnarowicz, Robert Gober, Peter Hujar, and, of course, Robert Mapplethorpe. This is where I came from, plus, of course, the wonderful and truly pioneering American gay art histories written by Craig Owens, Douglas Crimp, Jonathan Weinberg, Jonathan D. Katz, Holland Cotter, and the British art historian Emmanuel Cooper.[2] Through their writing, I devoured their interpretations and learned about the history and contemporaneity of homosexuality in twentieth-century American art. Then, around 1995, I had a moment of revelation: there is almost nothing about the topic in Polish art history, about Polish gay and lesbian art—and my work began. My vocation was to queer the history of Polish art![3]

After years of reporting on American gay postmodernism and art around AIDS for the Polish art press, I published my first text on Poland in 1995, "Power-Art-Sex: Erotic Art under Communism," tracing queer contexts, codes, and images. In 1999 it was followed with "The Gender of Contemporary Polish Art."[4] I have covered such pioneering artists as Krzysztof Jung, Wojciech Cwiertniewicz, and Izabella Gustowska. At the time I was writing, transparently gay and lesbian exhibitions seemed impossible in Poland, so instead I was composing conceptual art shows. I would eventually learn that I was wrong and that there were a few exhibitions with gay and lesbian subtexts organized in the 1970s. As a young scholar, I was overly dramatic and ignorant, but the inspiration of Piotr Piotrowski was pushing my research further and deeper.

Piotr Piotrowski's philosophy and practice of socially engaged art history encompassed broader sociopolitical forces in postwar Central and Eastern Europe, such as the struggle with communist totalitarianism, postcommunist nationalism and religious fundamentalism, and the strive for democracy and human rights in the region after the collapse of the Berlin Wall. Hence, the title of his 2012 book is *Art and Democracy in Post-Communist Europe*, where he sees art and art discourse as a force for democracy and civil society in the region.[5] It is therefore a useful model of art history for newly free societies grappling with democracy.[6] As a straight left-wing intellectual, Piotrowski inspired and enabled feminist and queer exhibitions and research. He thought and acted in the tradition of Eastern European dissidents in opposition to many dimensions of power, especially in the relation of art to heteronormative sexual politics and conservative museology. It was his version of twentieth-century resistance and dissonance that I needed and could accept while formulating my own concept of love dissidence.

When years later, in 2010, Piotrowski became for a short time the director of the National Museum in Warsaw, he invited me to curate an LGBTQ exhibition, to realize his aim of turning the institution of national heritage into a critical museum involved in current public debates. My show, *Ars Homo Erotica* (2010), queered the entire collection of the National Museum by presenting it through artworks dating from antiquity to the twenty-first century juxtaposed with contemporary queer art from Central Eastern Europe.[7]

Running parallel to this powerful exposure and opportunity to research and express queer art histories, I was deepening my internal, emotional, romantic self. In 1996, I happily fell in love with my husband of 25 years, Tomasz Kitlinski. We met at a performance art festival in Ustka, a small Polish city by the Baltic Sea—I have always loved the Baltic Sea—where he was performing a peculiar psychoanalytic piece on parenting. At the time, he had just received his postgraduate degree (D.E.A.) supervised by Julia Kristeva at Université Paris-Diderot (known as Paris 7), and he was back in Poland as a performance artist and a young academic promoting his journal devoted to queer feminism and art: *Counter-Art Revia*. Since then, we have often published and curated together on the theme of LGBTQ culture and rights in Poland and internationally. Our recent project from 2019 was a public art festival in Lublin on the theme of "hospitality," with many sculptures and neons in the city center referring to the Jewish and queer histories of this intercultural region.

In 2003, we participated in the public art project *Let Us Be Seen*, a series of photographs of same-sex couples by the artist Karolina Breguła. The social and visual campaign was organized by the NGO Campaign against Homophobia. The portraits were of 30 real Polish gay and lesbian pairs holding hands and standing in the streets in winter. We were one of the pairs, and we are the only couple that is still together! We published a book to reflect on the experience: *Love and Democracy: Reflection on the Homosexual Question in Poland* (2005).[8] The photo-project was initially planned as a public art campaign displayed on city billboards. This was the first coming out on such a scale in the history of the country. However, the billboards were destroyed by far-right militias. Since the streets proved inhospitable, art galleries functioned as alternative platforms for exposure. It was a very successful touring photo show that enabled my own curating.

Everything, the writings, the shows, started because of collaboration. Again, I was lucky with people. In 2005 and 2006, I organized two editions of a political and erotic exhibition and research project, *Love and Democracy*, in Poznań's private Old Brewery Art Center and Gdańsk's public Bathhouse Center for Contemporary Art. My first exhibition was the most queer that I have ever organized, as it was a show of mostly feminist and a few gay artists concerned with the pluralism of love and identities.[9] *Love and Democracy* was possible because of my collaborations with exceptional women artists, collectors, and curators at a time of another far-right siege in the country. The first and smaller version of *Love and Democracy* took place in 2005 as part of the Art Festival in Poznań, sponsored by the Fine Art Academy. I was invited to curate by Izabella Gustowska, the artistic director of the fair: a pioneering Eastern European feminist multimedia artist and curator who since the 1970s has portrayed female sisterhood and intimacy. Because of the danger of censorship and far-right violence in public galleries at the time, my show was located in a well-protected private contemporary art center—the Old Brewery Gallery, owned by a liberal, enlightened, and supportive businesswoman, Grażyna Kulczyk, who is the main female collector of contemporary art in Poland.[10] Thus, erring on the side of caution, for security reasons, hesitation and concern created a situation where public funds were used for a show located in a popular private space. After a positive reception, a bigger version of the show and its catalogue and conference were produced in 2006, at the invitation of the artist and curator Robert Rumas, at a public venue, the Bathhouse Center for Contemporary Art in Gdańsk (by the Baltic Sea), thanks to the hospitable director Jadwiga Charzyńska. Piotr Piotrowski, always a fighter, participated in this historic conference although already sick with leukemia.

I have been lucky, but my country is not; the premise of *Love and Democracy* is still a dream here. The country endures a shift to the right, like many other nations globally. Today, in 2020, Poland is under the rule of a far-right fundamentalist party, Law and Justice. Cultural institutions are under their supervision; homophobia is the official sexual political stance under the influence of the Catholic church. Economic oppression is used to keep everyone in line. The National Museum, which hosted *Ars Homo Erotica* in 2010, now censors feminist art from its permanent collection. Queer curating is truly countercultural and oppositional: it is against the cultural policy of the current government, which combines extreme nationalism with religious fundamentalism and openly questions EU values. The challenges are big, heavy blocks, but still, young curators are sometimes lucky. Surprisingly, queer exhibitions are being organized through crowdfunding, often by city galleries based in oppositional cities, those not run by the ruling party. These are brave cultural institutions that still dare to develop gender- and sexuality-related projects at the cost of losing state financial support as a punishment. Nimble tactics, queer subversions, percolate through culture and activism, yet increasingly, many have stopped questioning their fundamental conditions for saving our declining democracy. In 2020, I am a professor in the Department of Art History at Adam Mickiewicz University in Poznań, Poland, lecturing in modern and contemporary art. Miraculously, I am still able to teach courses on LGBTQ art and rights, and occasionally I curate queer projects. But with the failing state of local democracy, the constant threat of religious fundamentalism and limited funds for progressive exhibitions, I plan to migrate again, to find freedom and equality not only in art and art history but also in real life.

Notes

1. Since 2000 I have worked in the Department of Art History at Adam Mickiewicz University, on and off.
2. Probably for me as a young scholar, the most influential books were Craig Owens, *Beyond Recognition: Representation, Power, and Culture* (Berkeley: University of California Press, 1992); Jonathan Weinberg, *Speaking for Vice: Homosexuality in the Art of Charles Demuth, Marsden Hartley, and the First American Avant-Garde* (New Haven: Yale University Press, 1993); Douglas Crimp and Adam Rolston, *AIDS Demographics* (Seattle: Bay Press, 1990).
3. So far, the main books on the male queer tradition are Pawel Leszkowicz, *The Naked Man: The Male Nude in post-1945 Polish Art* (Poznań: Adam Mickiewicz University Press, 2012) (in Polish with English summary); and Pawel Leszkowicz, *Art Pride: Gay Art from Poland* (Warsaw: Abjekt, 2010) (in English and Polish).
4. Pawel Leszkowicz, "Power-Art-Sex: Erotic Art under Communism," in *Sztuka i erotyka (Art and the Erotic)*, ed. Teresa Hrankowska (Warsaw: Stowarzyszenie Historyków Sztuki [Association of Art Historians], 1995) (in Polish with English summary); Pawel Leszkowicz, "The Gender of Contemporary Polish Art," Magazyn Sztuki (The Magazine of Art) 22 (1999) (in Polish). The two texts were later summarized in English in Pawel Leszkowicz, "The Queer Story of Polish Art and Subjectivity" (2006), https://artmargins.com/the-queer-story-of-polish-art-and-subjectivity/.

5. Piotr Piotrowski, *Art and Democracy in Post-Communist Europe* (London: Reaktion Books, 2012). His other major book in English is *In the Shadow of Yalta: Art and the Avant-Garde in Eastern Europe, 1945–1989* (London: Reaktion Books, 2009).
6. See Elżbieta Matynia, ed., *Grappling with Democracy: Deliberations on Post-Communist Societies* (1990–1995) (Prague: SLON, 1996).
7. On *Ars Homo Erotica*, see Katarzyna Murawska-Muthesius and Piotr Piotrowski, eds., *From Museum Critique to the Critical Museum* (Burlington: Ashgate, 2015); Pawel Leszkowicz, *Ars Homo Erotica Catalogue* (Warsaw: CePed, 2010); Jon Davies, "Towards an Intimate Democracy in Europe: Paweł Leszkowicz's Queer Curating," *Journal of Curatorial Studies* 2, no. 1 (2013): 54–69; Maura Reilly, *Curatorial Activism: Towards an Ethics of Curating* (London: Thames & Hudson, 2018).
8. Tomasz Kitlinski and Pawel Leszkowicz, *Love and Democracy: Reflection on the Homosexual Question in Poland* (Kraków: Aureus, 2005) (in Polish with English, German, and French summaries). See also Tomasz Kitlinski and Pawel Leszkowicz, "Let Us Be Seen: Gay Visibility in Homophobic Poland," in *Men Speak Out: Views on Gender, Sex, and Power*, ed. Shira Tarrant (London: Routledge, 2008).
9. See the catalogue: Pawel Leszkowicz, *Love and Democracy* (Gdańsk: Bathhouse Center for Contemporary Art, 2006); Pawel Leszkowicz, "The Power of Queer Curating in Central Eastern Europe," in *Working with Feminism: Curating and Exhibitions in Eastern Europe*, ed. Katrin Kivimaa (Tallinn: Tallinn University Press, 2012), 118–52.
10. In 2007 I had the pleasure to curate the first exhibition based on her collection; Pawel Leszkowicz, *Art from GK Collection* (Poznań: Kulczyk Foundation, 2007) (in Polish and English).

LUCY R. LIPPARD

Vignettes along the path

My mother and I, in a tiny apartment on NYC's far east side.[1] She works as a secretary at a private school on the other side of the Third Avenue El where I'm starting kindergarten. She plays our old upright piano every night. We often go across town to the Metropolitan Museum, and I learn to distinguish between Dutch and Italian Renaissance paintings. My father is an army medic in the South Pacific. In Fall 1945 he appears at our door, a mythical stranger. We move to New Orleans; then Charlottesville, Virginia; then New Haven, Connecticut. In summers we go to the coast of Maine, where my parents (and I) are Sunday watercolor painters. They are (not necessarily avant-garde) art lovers, good anti-racist liberals, agnostics, so in order to rebel, I have to become an atheist and a socialist. At around age 12, I decide to be a fiction writer, because I love to read. But I don't want to major in English in college, because I don't like being told what to do about such a personal passion. I major in art and take a few studio courses. At one point I come home, lay out my latest efforts and say, "Maybe I'll be an artist instead of a writer!" My parents scrutinize the work and agree: "No. Writer."

*

After a junior year in Paris, after a road trip west (hitchhiking and bussing across Canada on the return), after graduating from college in 1958, after a few months working with the Quakers in a tiny village in Puebla, Mexico, I move to the Lower East Side. The stairwell of the tenement building on Ninth Street and Avenue A smells of drains. The toilet's in the hall, but my one-room "apartment" is only $18 a month (luckily, as my weekly take-home pay from the Museum of Modern Art Library (MoMA) is $45). I inherit my pad from an addict, a nephew of Archbishop Cushing, thanks to friends with the *Catholic Worker* who ignore my atheism and inspire my activism. I leave my Yale Law School boyfriend for an AWOL sailor/Bowery bum, who is a converted Zen Buddhist. We wait for him to be picked up, and eventually he is. When I am out really late, walking home through Loisaida in the low light of dawn, I see old Russian or Ukrainian couples sitting silently on benches in Tompkins Square—not homeless, just former farmers, early risers.

For a couple of years I rise early to write fiction. I'm not very good at it and find myself drawn into the Tenth Street alternative gallery scene. Like so many of my literarily inclined colleagues, I become an art "critic" by default. (I dislike the term. I consider myself an advocate, not an adversary.) Almost everything I know about art I learn from artists. Among the earliest: Robert Ryman, Sol LeWitt, and Eva Hesse.

*

I am living with a painter of white canvases on Avenue D, then in a loft on the Bowery, working as a freelance researcher for curators at MoMA. The museum pays for graduate classes in art history at NYU's uptown Institute of Fine Arts, and I receive an MA in art history in February 1962. I start writing for *Art International*, *Artforum*, and *Arts*, and in 1964 I have a son named Ethan Isham. My father complains that he can't understand what I write in art world jargon. I try to clean up my act. Conceptual art in the mid-1960s allows me to use words to collaborate with artist friends, which opens up new territory. (If anything an artist does is art, then anything a writer does is writing.) The founding of the Art Workers' Coalition introduces me to left politics. I repay the museum's generosity by picketing it on several occasions in later years on such issues as anti-Vietnam War, artists' rights, trustee affiliation, staff unionization, and feminist representation.

*

By the end of the 1960s, under the influence of minimal, conceptual, and political artists, I am a divorced single mother living in a raw co-op loft on Prince Street, inching my way out of formalism toward vehement feminism and activism. I write an experimental novel while living with my 4-year-old on the coast of Spain for a few months. In the process of writing, I discover that I am not one of the boys. I am ... a woman! I return to New York a feminist and find hundreds of allies. Many become friends for life. For much of the 1970s I write mostly about women's art. We start organizations and protests and a journal on feminism and politics. I'm introduced to esthetically powerful community arts by a long-time partner. At the end of the decade, my son and I live for a year on an old stone farm in Devon, England. I hike across the fields every day and discover megalithic art on the Dartmoor. It reminds me of contemporary land art and throws me back into what we call "nature," as though we were not a part of it ...

I write and talk about escape attempts, reflecting my failed desire to escape the increasingly commercial art world. I've always been interested in broader audiences, though I've never had one. At one point in the early 1980s, I think I want to sell my feminist comic strips on street corners, but my heroine, Polly Tickle, never makes it off the page. We start an activist artists' group and initiate a lot of street and demo art, trying to escape to places where art writing of any kind, no matter how lucid, is impotent. Public art and public actions interest me, especially when no one knows it's art, when the public just comes upon something inexplicable and responds, or gets the message. Content and context become my bywords. Over the years I become more and more of a populist, in the true rather than the Trumpian sense of the word. I've never been a theoretician; I like to say that theories are ideas with hardening of the arteries, but it may also be that I'm too dumb or too lazy to engage with all the complexities and wordiness of esthetic theory. I cofound a center for artists' books. I organize on behalf of Cuba and Central America. I consider becoming a real journalist, but it's too late.

*

The rest of the story is a restless history of unaffiliated freelance writing, 25 books—on Hesse, Ad Reinhardt, conceptual arts, social change art, feminist art, multicultural art, Native American art, land and place and climate change, archaeology, and history. Freelancing is highly recommended for those who, like me, have an authority problem. It's been a good life. I've always been able to make a living. My advice to aspiring writers: keep your standard of living very low ... then you can do what you like. And now, in the Trumpian era of cruelty, greed, bigotry, and climate chaos, my Depression-era childhood's lifetime addiction to the second-hand—clothes, cars, furniture ... even men—runs counter to the impossibly endless growth of capitalism. Downsize or die.

I receive more awards than I deserve. I start spending time in the West, where my grandparents were raised. My parents die. Suddenly I have some money. After 35 years in Lower Manhattan, I build a little house (dubbed "the shack by the creek" or "the Smurf house") on a patch of overgrazed pasture on the edge of a tiny Hispano village in New Mexico and move there for good, hoping to escape not art, but at least the art world. I decide to devote myself to the local, to our fire department, water board, planning committees, and a community newsletter I began 25 years ago, still going strong. However, the ripples from local to global are inescapable. Books are my favorite form. I still write full-time. Freelancers die with their boots on. With fascism hovering over us, my old age is personally happy, professionally ineffective, and politically despairing.

*

Why did I choose this path? I'm not sure I did. When asked about my working methodology, I always say, "One thing leads to another." That's the story of my life too.

Note

1. This essay was completed prior to the 2020 US presidential elections.

MARGO MACHIDA

BRIDGING MULTIPLE SITES and communities, my involvement in contemporary Asian American art and art history has followed a circuitous route. While an academic colleague playfully remarked that I pursued my university career in reverse, in retrospect, my trajectory over the past four decades as an artist, curator, arts writer, cultural activist, educator, and scholar developed organically since my 1968 arrival in New York City from Hilo, Hawai‘i, at the age of 17. Moving straight from a small, semirural island community with a predominantly Asian population to attend New York University as an aspiring writer, I was unexpectedly overwhelmed by a vertiginous sense of displacement. As a Hawai‘i-born Japanese American woman, I was abruptly thrust into a completely unfamiliar environment: a vast urban setting in which I knew no one and where I found myself, for the first time in my life, sharply aware of being primarily perceived as a member of a racialized minority group who also was considered exotic, since the Hawaiian Islands were commonly known through tropical imagery from Hollywood films, television, and tourist brochures. This radical change, and the fact that my background and experience were incommensurable to many people I met, acutely affected my sense of self, as I was increasingly made conscious of, and compelled to grapple with, issues of otherness and difference.

For most of my childhood in the 1950s, Hawai'i was a US territorial possession. Hawai'i did not become a state until 1959, having been acquired in 1898 following the overthrow of the Indigenous monarchy by American settlers. While local culture was certainly suffused with American values and expectations, Hawai'i is unique among the 50 states for its Asian-majority population. This palpable Asian influence, alongside the significant presence of Native Hawaiians, is interwoven in many aspects of daily life. The confluence of multiethnic demography and a geographic location midway in the North Pacific has complexly generated and shaped Hawai'i's distinct character, oriented as much toward Oceania and coastal East Asia as toward the US "mainland." In addition, when I left the islands in the late 1960s, a grassroots Indigenous movement to revive traditional Hawaiian language and culture, and to seek self-determination and sovereignty, was gaining momentum. Growing up in an environment distanced from, yet ineluctably enmeshed with, the US presence in the region, I later realized that this background closely informed my outsider/insider view of American society.

Furthermore, I was rapidly caught up in a surge of activism upon arriving in New York. With the antiwar, counterculture, feminist, Black Power, and Young Lords/Nuyorican movements in full sway, there was a powerful sense of urgency on my campus to mount highly visible public responses during that pivotal moment in American history. One especially memorable event I attended was the massive 1969 antiwar demonstration in Washington, DC, to protest escalating US military involvement in Vietnam.

At the same time, I was increasingly drawn to Manhattan's downtown art scene, especially to alternative art spaces on the Lower East Side, where many artists of color exhibited, and to the Studio Museum in Harlem, newly founded in 1968. While I had been drawing since childhood and had taken art lessons in Hawai'i, contacts and discussions with the African American artists and curators inspired me to actively take up painting and later to pursue an MA in fine arts at Hunter College, CUNY (1978). Among those influential figures was the art historian and curator Lowery Sims, an early visitor to my new studio. Through these relationships, I became aware that parallel art worlds, support networks, and budding institutions existed alongside the largely White-dominated art "mainstream." Yet my direct involvement with Asian American art and artists only began a decade later after relocating to a loft in Manhattan's Chinatown. By the late 1980s, I also gained the friendship and support of feminist scholars, especially Moira Roth, whom I met when taking part in *Autobiography: In Her Own Image* (INTAR Gallery, New York). Organized by African American artist, educator, and activist Howardena Pindell, the exhibition featured works by twenty women artists of color.

In Chinatown, I increasingly had dealings with cultural activists in the local community arts movement, especially with members of the pioneering arts organization Basement Workshop. The late poet and artist Fay Chiang (1952–2017), its former director, first encouraged me to write about fellow Asian American artists. Basement was formed in the matrix of multiculturalism, the rise of ethnic studies, the antiwar movement, feminism, and anticolonial struggles of the 1970s. Since the images and histories of Asians in America went largely unrecognized by society at large, Basement's members regarded art as a means of collectively "coming to voice." Guided by an expansive ethos in which activist artists assumed multiple roles as documentarians, critics, educators, curators, and organizers, I was similarly emboldened to take on such responsibilities. Yet the period also coincided with the surge of Asian migration that followed the 1965 Immigration Act's upending of the miniscule immigration quotas that had long curbed the Asian presence in the United States. The abolition of the quota system based on national origin, alongside the enactment of Vietnam War–era refugee statutes and the establishment of diplomatic relations with the People's Republic of China, led to a vast Asian influx. The differing perspectives and priorities of the newly arrived would radically transform the terrain and internal dynamics of Asian America. Thus, my first published art writing in 1985 was for *Myths*, an exhibition at Basement Workshop of work by New York–based Chinese émigré artists from the Epoxy Art Group.

By 1988, I curated my first thematic exhibition, *Invented Selves: Images of Asian American Identity*, for the Asian American Arts Centre (AAAC) in Chinatown. Shortly thereafter, the precedents set by Basement Workshop and AAAC in bringing Asian American art, artists, and issues into public discourse fomented the establishment of Godzilla: Asian American Art Network (1990–2001), which I cofounded in 1990 with artists Ken Chu and Bing Lee. Deliberately departing from existing community models, Godzilla was a loose-knit collective and forum where artists, curators, and writers of different Asian backgrounds and generations shared their work and ideas. Choosing not to institutionalize, or to be based in an ethnic enclave, Godzilla moved freely among artist lofts and alternative spaces throughout New York City with its open slide shows, public forums, and exhibitions. Beyond routinely attracting hundreds of artists, Godzilla gained early notoriety by sending an open letter to major New York City museums that challenged the lack of Asian Americans in the 1991 Whitney Biennial, resulting in a meeting with the Whitney's director and curators.

The resonance of this formative period, in combination with an uneasy experience of internal migration to the continental United States, would underpin my emerging interest in themes of diaspora, circulation, settlement, and cross-cultural convergence and conflict. Indeed, my conversations with Asian American and Asian artists—especially diasporic and émigré artists—often raised references to global, transnational, and oceanic linkages between maritime Asia, Oceania, and the Americas. In also seeking to examine conjunctions and tensions between Asian migrants and Indigenous peoples across the Pacific, the scope of my inquiries over the past decade has gradually extended to artists of Asian and mixed Asian-Native ancestry and cultural heritage throughout Oceania and Australia.

Negotiating the academy

While much of my work is currently known through academic publications, I never aspired to become an academic, having written about and organized shows featuring Asian American artists well before I began to teach full-time. The academy began to assume an important role in advancing my efforts only in 1989, the year I received a Rockefeller Foundation Humanities Fellowship from the Asian/American Center at Queens College, CUNY, under the leadership of historian John Kuo Wei (Jack) Tchen.

This fellowship enabled me to conduct the interviews and studio visits with Asian American artists throughout the East Coast that yielded the thematic structure for my first national curatorial project, *Asia/America: Identities in Contemporary*

Asian American Art (1994–96). Organized for the Asia Society Galleries in New York, this traveling show featured work by twenty foreign-born émigré and refugee artists of East, Southeast, and South Asian heritage. Shortly after *Asia/America* made its debut, on the strength of the research behind the exhibition's extensive catalog essay, I entered graduate school in my mid-40s to earn a Ph.D. in American Studies from SUNY Buffalo, focused on the use of oral history in the arts. My doctoral dissertation developed into the monograph *Unsettled Visions: Contemporary Asian American Artists and the Social Imaginary* (Duke University Press, 2009). In 2002, at the age of 51, I got my first tenure-track teaching position in art history and Asian American Studies at the University of Connecticut, from which I recently retired.

My academic trajectory therefore owes a major debt to the initial support and mentorship of Jack Tchen, who went on to become the founding director of the Asian/Pacific/American (A/P/A) Studies Program and Institute at New York University, with which I maintain an ongoing relationship. Spearheaded by art writer and curator Alexandra Chang, far-reaching arts initiatives under the A/P/A Institute's auspices proved vital in taking my research and projects into the international arena. They include the Diasporic Asian Art Network (2009–) that I cofounded, the NYU Global Asia/Pacific Art Exchange (2013–), and the *Asian Diasporic Visual Cultures and the Americas* journal (Brill, 2015–), for which I serve as an associate editor.

The groundswell of exhibitions and writing devoted to Asian American art, and the formation of Asian American art history as a field of study, have been largely due to the multisited efforts of artists, activists, curators, critics, archivists, and scholars with kindred interests, both within and outside the academy. This collective move to foreground the work and wide-ranging concerns of artists of Asian heritage has served to counter prevalent views of Asian American art as a narrowly specialized interest area primarily associated with domestic identity politics and minoritarian issues. Moreover, while seeking acceptance from the academic "mainstream" was never the principal arbiter or validator of my research, in my experience the often dismissive attitudes of conventional scholars, and their impact on acquiring adequate institutional resources, can be stultifying. In hindsight, the uncommon path of functioning both inside and apart from dominant institutional systems has made all the difference. Being able to draw on both nonacademic and academic voices and networks has effectively provided a more productive foundation for my artist-oriented work, allowing me to actively pursue open-ended projects from markedly differing angles of view.

Art and dialogic exchanges

Ultimately, what has long captured and sustained my attention in writing about art is the intensive use of dialogic exchange with artists about the work they produce. Employing this often-demanding interpretive methodology, I gain considerable insight into how visual art functions in negotiating and projecting the artist's complexly layered presence, heritage, and position in the world as a social actor. Not unlike the journalistic interview, individually focused inquiry opens a capacious space to explore the personal realm and the ways in which an understanding of real-world experience can be manifested through the intervention of art. Over time, I therefore developed an artist-centered interpretive approach that I term "oral hermeneutics." Integral to this collaborative interview process is the production of transcripts derived from digitally recorded conversations. By closely analyzing and comparing these interactively generated texts, it is possible to mine the substratum of associations and concerns that undergird specific works of art, while also identifying broader themes that conjoin bodies of work and different artists.

For me, as an American-born writer and fellow artist, the initial impetus for pursuing this dialogue-based approach appeared to be a natural step, as a pragmatic response to the challenges I found in apprehending the particular contexts, histories, and cultural references that foreign-born Asian artists drew on in their work. Beginning in the mid-1980s, my first dialogues were project-driven, when I interviewed artists Ken Chu and Y. David Chung for curatorial essays to accompany exhibitions I was organizing. The richly detailed material resulting from those early conversations provided a strong sense of what such an approach might yield.

Looking back on the path my practice has taken, I certainly consider myself fortunate to have found supportive spaces and to have developed relationships with people pursuing congruent interests at key moments. These links, built up over time, and ongoing exchanges with artists strengthened the personal and intellectual commitments that continue to drive my work forward. Yet much remains to be done to advance my field of study. Indeed, I am often reminded of the obstacles that younger scholars still face in establishing a career in Asian American art by the difficulties my former graduate students encountered in finding academic programs and knowledgeable advisors willing to sponsor their research. Drawing on experience, my advice to anyone in the arts working on noncanonical and marginalized areas is that the impetus to pursue such work must ultimately be generated and maintained from within, since institutional validation and backing cannot be assumed. As the field of Asian American art history has been brought into being through sheer acts of will by dedicated individuals despite considerable odds, it is indispensable to recognize that personal interventions do count and that our task necessarily requires a tenacious commitment to cultivating interest and alliances within and across a range of communities.

AMALIA MESA-BAINS

THESE POSTCARDS TELL stories from the past to describe how I'm doing. The postcards cover life events, artistic development, public activism, and personal struggle.

#1 Baby art and the mysterious pencil

My first encounter with art was actually my first use of a pencil. I recall learning to hold a pencil, and the moment I put it to paper, something magical happened. Where I put the pencil, something followed—a line moved with me. It gave me an exciting sense of power.

Observation: Try to keep the magic power.

#2 Dad and the easel

From my earliest childhood, my family understood my desire to draw and paint, and as I realized later, I would become the third generation of artists in our large extended family. It was as though they were waiting for me to show my talent, and their support was immediate. I got my first easel at 7 or 8, and my first studio was on the back porch between the washing machine, with roller wringers, and the dog's bed. My father, who worked in a grocery store, used to collect the ends of the butcher paper roll, which was crimped, and cut them into large squares and put rocks on the paper to make them flat so I could paint.

Observation: Artists are not only born but also made by family love.

#3 High hippy days and self-revelation

In 1967, after my marriage to Richard Bains, we moved to San Francisco. Richard was in a rock band and it was the "summer of love." My studio was in the Haight in a garage behind the Jeremy Ets-Hokin building referred to as the Donald Duck Towers. We used the garage as an artist loft, spent days in the Haight Ashbury, meeting friends and eating piroshkis. These were the days of the first be-ins and when LSD #25 was legal. I was making my first Uvex plastic-molded pieces, sewn and stuffed bird shapes and metal flake structures. It was an age of finding artistic vision, joining festivals and exhibitions, and making a new alternative family of artists and musicians.

Observation: The first steps of an artist's adult life are often utopian and collective.

#4 Teacher Corps and political life

Following the high hippy days, I needed to work, and I found out about Teacher Corps, a program to bring people of color into inner-city schools to teach. It was a revolutionary program at San Francisco State University, which was part of a national movement. We spent part of the time in public schools and community organizations in the Mission and the rest in classes in the Western Addition, because the Third World Student strike was on campus and we refused to cross the picket line at S.F. State College. The Black Panther Movement also touched us because a number of our colleagues in the program had ties to the movement, and we learned first-hand about the government's COINTELPRO.[1] I was so fortunate that my team leader, Yolanda Garfias Woo, became my mentor and changed my life and introduced me to the *Dias de los Muertos.*

Observation: Politics can be a bridge to your future even when you do not yet know it.

#5 Chicano Movement and the Galeria de la Raza

In the early 1970s in the Mission district in San Francisco, I had my first formal introduction to the Chicano Movement through community galleries, and while helping with the first exhibitions, I met other artists such as Carmen Lomas Garza, Ester Hernandez, and Patricia Rodriguez of the *Mujeres Muralistas*, who became my *comadres* or co-mothers, and that was the moment of belonging. I never really felt truly Mexican because I was born in the United States and had never even visited Mexico because my father's family had left under such a traumatic and ruptured moment in the Mexican Revolution. I also learned very quickly through discrimination and racism that I was not "American" (White), so I simply longed for a sense of self that fit. Through the *Galeria de la Raza*, I met other Chicana artists, and I was born into a new collective identity through the connection between social justice and the arts. This sense of purpose and meaning has never really left me—it is the basis upon which I have built the many layers of my art and work.

Observation: We always have a second chance at a meaningful life, no matter the obstacles.

#6 Days of the dead

Even though in my family and childhood we never forgot the dead and spent many weekends at the graveyard, I had never celebrated the Days of the Dead. Through my close friendship with Oaxacan artist and teacher Yolanda Garfias Woo, I learned of the tradition. She taught me the difference between the home altar, which was the permanent ongoing record of the family, and the *ofrenda*, an offering dedicated to the dead. My first *ofrenda* was dedicated to five women: my grandmothers, Amalia and Mariana; my *Tía* (Aunt) Angelina; my dear friend Susana; and my newly discovered icon, Frida Kahlo.

Observation: You never know when history will overtake you and direct your future.

#7 Frida arrives

For much of my art career, I have had a connection to the art and life of Frida Kahlo. In the mid-1970s, I learned of the work of Frida Kahlo through artists at the *Galeria de la Raza*, including Rupert Garcia, Ralph Maradiaga, and René Yañez, who all knew a great deal about her life with Diego Rivera and their visit to San Francisco in the 1930s. In 1971, I went to Mexico and made my first visit to the Blue House in Coyoacán, and I saw in her diaries the drawings and words with their frenetic quality that was overwhelming. I found myself going out in the garden frequently to recover my emotions.

> *A cabinet with all her toys, yellow pages, small glass figurines, dried flowers, the bed with the plate of butterflies, the globe hanging—a nest of her own. How could anyone live in the shadow of such a man and bring to light a life of her own?*[2]

Like Frida, I was unable to have children and worked to create the life of a woman artist. Through the *Galeria de la Raza* and under the leadership of Ralph Maradiaga, I was able to work with other Chicanas to interview the women in the San Francisco Bay Area who knew her in the 1930s. The women interviewed included Pele de Lappe, Emmy Lou Packard, and Lucienne Bloch Dimitroff. Eventually we produced an exhibition as a homage to Frida Kahlo, and for me personally, it began a lifelong connection to her work and life.

Observation: Even the dead can be your model for an artist's life.

#8 Finding a new form: Expanding sacred spaces

My most significant artwork began with the home altar and the *ofrenda*, or Day of the Dead offerings, through my role in the Chicano cultural movement of the 1970s. Over time, I reinterpreted the *ofrenda*, the home altar, in a more contemporary form by amending furnishings, even using the women's vanity and emphasizing the life of women in homages through altars. The *descanso* (resting places seen as roadside shrines) and the *Capilla* (little chapel-style home yard shrines) also became part of my expansion of the sacred form.

Ironically, after almost twenty years within the Chicano orbit inventing my own form in isolation from the larger art world, when mainstream installation art became in vogue, my work was discovered, and I began to be seen within the context of the installation form even though that was never my intention.
Observation: The art world will find you when you least expect it.

#8 Not Again, Chicano Art: Resistance and Affirmation (CARA), 1990 National Endowment for the Humanities

Chicano Art: Resistance and Affirmation was a historic and comprehensive national exhibition of art of the Chicano movement, undertaken by UCLA's Wight art gallery. This traveling show was the first large-scale examination of the social and political civil rights and culture movement. Nevertheless, the catalog proposal was reviewed by four different panels and approved each time, only to be ultimately rejected and vetoed by the chair of the National Endowment for the Humanities, Lynne Cheney (Dick's wife) because the term "Chicano" was unacceptable as it was "too political" and should be changed to Mexican American. I think she missed the point.

Observation: Art historical knowledge is needed.

#9 Caribbean Cultural Center/African Diaspora Institute: Cultural Diversity through Cultural Grounding Series, 1989, 1991, 1993

In the era of appropriation, reclaiming First Voice meant distinguishing our efforts from the mainstream through cultural grounding. The multicultural group was part of a self-determination movement based on First Voice leadership and practices to combat the mainstream distortions. Through Marta Moreno Vega's visionary leadership, we established a diverse collective, hosting a series of conferences and publications, including *Voices from the Battlefront: Achieving Cultural Equity*. These collective efforts built a foundational network that still exists as one of the constant groups invested in collective action for social justice.

Observation: Collective struggle is critical to self-determination.

#10 Learning to live with the studio after the MacArthur (or get out of the garage)

The year after my long illness, I received the MacArthur fellowship, and it seemed the gods were sending me a message of renewal, so we bought a studio and I finally had a space to make art, but I still kept using the garage at the new building. My husband finally moved all the art supplies and tools into the studio proper, and I got used to all the space and accepted the permanency of this new way of working. I was 50 years old, and I had finally graduated to a real artist's studio.

Observation: Sometimes the gift comes when you most need it.

#11 Surviving to make art—left-handed drawings

The car crash was a rollover and my body was broken: elbow, wrist, neck, leg, and many other fractures. I endured surgeries, many days in intensive care, and a move to a recovery center, where I faced enormous fear not knowing how I would ever make art again, much less walk and live. I engaged in survival tactics, and my mother helped me build an altar in my recovery room. With only my left hand and arm not in a cast, I worked at learning to draw with my nondominant hand. I sketched my altar and my many flower arrangements that eventually were made into cards to be sent to family and friends who had supported me with calls and notes of love. I tried to draw away my trauma in a self-sustaining practice.

Observation: Art can heal.

Postcard epilogue

These postcards encompass moments in my art life and are also reflections on life lessons. Being an artist begins as a singular practice but flourishes when you grow into a community that supports you and that you support. I have been lucky as a Chicana because the Mexican traditions of collective work and *compradazco*, or shared godparentage for us as women without children, gave us a model for shared art practices. The years as an older artist are tempered by restrictions of the body but enlivened by wisdom of the mind and a love of friends and family. *Art is forever.*

Notes

1. Counter Intelligence Program (1956–71) was a series of covert surveillance projects carried out by the FBI.
2. Excerpt from my own notebook, written in 1971 on my first visit to the Blue House when I was 38 years old.

MARSHA MESKIMMON

SOME TIME AGO, I was talking with a friend of mine about his practice as a studio potter. He was a very skilled and creative maker whose reputation in the field was built mainly upon work he had produced between the late 1970s and the early 1990s. By the time of our conversation in the early years of the present century, he had not produced a substantial body of work for more than a decade. Our conversation turned to this fact, and with some regret, he said that when he had "lost his studio," he could no longer work as once he had. My thoughts have returned on many occasions to the story of my friend's "lost studio," and when I was invited by the editors of this volume to think about living and sustaining a creative life, it seemed an apt point of departure for my tale.

As might be anticipated, I queried the loss of the studio—what became of it, how and why?—and, of course, the answer was not simple. The studio had not burned to the ground, it had not been seized by the authorities, there were no dramatic events surrounding its demise. The studio was a reconditioned outbuilding behind the house my friend had shared with his wife and children for more than twenty years—the years coinciding with the high point of his practice. The children had grown and gone, the marriage had dissolved, and the house had been sold to finance the two separate residences now occupied by the erstwhile couple. The loss of the studio was a sad, but quotidian, tale of change. And yes, there was space to fashion a "new" studio in the present house, and yes again, my friend had access to a well-appointed cooperative studio, one that sustained the professional practices of a number of other ceramic artists. Yet, when all was said and done, it remained the case that my friend had lost his studio, and with it, his creative practice.

You will already have apprehended the fact that the lost studio was much more than a physical space or technical facility; "the studio" signaled the very conditions for making art. It was, hearkening to Virginia Woolf, "a room of one's own," the locus from which a creative life could be lived and sustained. The reference to Woolf here is apposite. This story lingers in my imagination because it exemplifies *both* the importance *and* the privilege of "the studio/room of one's own," a trope that I would like to reconsider and imagine differently here, through a contingent and creative feminist ecology.

Hearing the tale of the lost studio saddened me; my friend pined for the past and I, in turn, felt acutely his loss of future creative potential. However, I also found (and continue to find) the tale frustrating, since it can be told only from a position of extraordinary, *naturalized* privilege that takes as read a certain form of individual creative capacity. For starters, this is a tale that normalizes entitlement so effectively that "the studio" is posited as a bare necessity when, in fact, it has long been a luxury enjoyed only by very few people, more often than not White men with a degree of economic independence. When, in 1928, Woolf was writing the lectures that would be published as *A Room of One's Own*, very few women could command any of the conditions pertaining to the autonomy of thought and action described by the writer's evocative essay title.[1] To "lose" a studio, one must have been in the privileged position of having one in the first place.

It would be easy to take a harsh view of this tale of privilege and loss, *per* Charles Bukowski's "Air and Light and Time and Space" (1992), in which he viciously mocked those who use the quest for perfect creative conditions as an elaborate excuse for their creative inactivity. While the poem is a salutary reminder that creativity can flourish at the very limits of endurance, its sardonic and admonishing tone is not one that I would elect to follow, nor does it get us very far.

Rather, I want to take a lead from two of Woolf's later interlocutors, Alice Walker and Kajsa Dahlberg, both of whom engaged with *A Room of One's Own* in their critical, creative practices. Separated from Woolf's text, and each other, by a considerable period of time, cultural experience, and language, Walker's well-known essay "In Search of Our Mothers' Gardens" (1972) and Dahlberg's photographic bookwork *A Room of One's Own/A Thousand Libraries* (2006) neither ignore the question of economic and social privilege raised by Woolf's imaginative feminist polemic on the possibilities of sustaining a creative life nor collapse their responses into cynical and counterproductive pessimism.[2]

Walker's text eloquently invokes the unsung lives of countless African American women who might have been recognized *as artists* in their own time, and ours, had they not lived under the inhuman conditions of slavery and its enduring legacies of racism, sexism, violence, and economic exploitation. She adroitly "replaces" words in Woolf's text ("insert 'black woman' [...] add 'chains, guns, the lash' ") to extend and emphasize the critical political dynamic of the argument that to claim a room of one's own (with a lock and key, and enough money to live independently) is tantamount to calling for an end to gender, race, and class subordination. Creativity is transformative, and sustaining a creative life is an ethical and political act of transformation.

For me, however, the power of Walker's encounter with Woolf goes beyond bringing a race-critical, intersectional dimension into the text. Rather, it resides in telling an intimate tale of beauty, generosity, and love sustained through her mother's creativity, a creativity expressed by her garden—a room of her own making. Walker comes to acknowledge her mother as an *artist* and, with this revelation, to celebrate an imaginative legacy, a history-in-the-making, of Black women's creativity. Walker does not flinch from the horrific histories that stifled Black women's creative lives, but neither does she accede to the logic that they have not been creative.

Walker's text, like Woolf's before it, asks us to imagine creativity differently and to look in new and unusual places for evidence of lives lived in richly creative ways. These activities are themselves labors of love and solidarity, ones that I share with Walker and Woolf as a scholar who has focused for many years on exploring the cultural legacy of women who make art. Knowing that there is a history, a legacy, of women as cultural producers on a truly global scale is part of sustaining a critical and creative feminist practice, a practice that is not forged upon the singularity of the great male artist and his solitary genius, but on dialogic knowledge practices that create relationships and sustain connective and collective forms of creativity.

Dahlberg's more recent engagement with Woolf's text extends this dialogue to include other readers. *A Room of One's Own/A Thousand Libraries* is a photo-book comprising the annotations and marginalia found on copies of the translated essay in public libraries across Sweden. The heavily marked pages of Woolf's essay compiled by Dahlberg provide a visual and material map of the text's reception during a pivotal period in the development of contemporary Scandinavian feminism, following its publication in Swedish translation in 1958. Like Walker's imaginative textual "insertions" in "In Search of Our Mothers' Gardens," the annotations and underlining found in the Swedish versions of the text demonstrate the particular, local dialogues with feminist thought from which its transnational currency emerges. This work is affective, hopeful, generous, and, importantly, collective. Indeed, Dahlberg's creative encounter with the text verified just this point; one of the most underlined sentences from the texts in Swedish libraries reads:

> *For masterpieces are not single and solitary births; they are the outcome of many years of thinking in common, of thinking by the body of the people, so that the experience of the mass is behind the single voice.*

As a scholar, it is my hope to contribute to a transnational feminist dialogue with/in the arts. To do so means to embrace change, contingency and creative collectivity. Over the years that I have been writing, I have "lost" and "found" many different "studios/studies," some through welcome changes and others as a result of difficult events beyond my control. In every instance, desired and not, my small acts of reestablishing the material and imaginative spaces necessary to work have been supported by the knowledge that generations of women and other marginal subjects had sustained, and continue to sustain, creativity despite sometimes unimaginable obstacles. Living and sustaining a creative life against the grain of the norm depends upon looking *elsewhere* with *others*. Creative thought is emergent and mutable, knowledges are practices, and as a feminist committed to social and ecological justice, working through decolonizing, queer, material posthumanisms, I fashion my tools toward hopeful transformation.

My friend's studio was lost to him because he could not change his singular model of living a creative life, he could (or would) not look elsewhere for the different materials and tools he needed—he ran out of time. The same cannot be said of the creative women invoked by Woolf, Walker, and Dahlgren, and their example is, instead, timely. Yes, we need bread, but we need roses too; in fashioning myriad rooms of our own, we critique both past and present without yielding our creative potential to become otherwise, with and through the love, generosity, and fellowship of others.

Notes

1. Virginia Woolf, *A Room of One's Own and Three Guineas* (London: Collins Classics, 2014).
2. Alice Walker, "In Search of Our Mothers' Gardens," in *Within the Circle: An Anthology of African American Literary Criticism from the Harlem Renaissance to the Present*, ed. Angelyn Mitchell (Durham: Duke University Press, 1994), 401–9. Kajsa Dahlberg, "A Room of One's Own/A Thousand Libraries" (2006), http://www.kajsadahlberg.com/work/a-room-of-ones-own—a-thousand-libraries/.

COMBIZ MOUSSAVI-AGHDAM

THROUGHOUT MY PH.D. program in Art History and Visual Studies at the University of Manchester in the mid-2000s, I was navigating a territory of art history previously unknown to me. As an overseas student from Iran, I confronted a vast area of studies, often with confusion, that sometimes seemed irrelevant to the discourses and trends I had encountered before. There was a gulf between what I knew as the field at home in Iran and in England, where art history over the past four decades had expanded to incorporate the sciences and the broader humanities. As a person driven to conceptualizing and reconceptualizing "phenomena" holistically, I found this all-encompassing discipline fascinating and definitely felt that I found myself in the right space to develop my intellectual life and profession. My program gave me the freedom to immerse in diverse fields, such as art, science, and philosophy. Correspondingly, I made a synthesis of these discourses and intellectual systems and methods.

Before I elaborate on my experience at the University of Manchester, it is essential to give you a picture of my educational background as an art student in Iran. To describe the significant differences between studying art theory and history in Iran during the late-1990s through the early 2000s (my MA program was called "Art Studies") and England, I would need to indicate my then interests, experiences, and goals for the future before starting my doctorate program. To begin with, I chose natural sciences as my high school major, even though I was enthusiastic about art and good at painting and sculpture. I must say I enjoyed studying physics, chemistry, biology, and geology, an endeavor that I am not regretting now. Later, this scientific background helped me with the topic of my Ph.D. thesis, which explored the relationship between art and entropy at psychosocial and philosophical levels.

I was meant to become a medical doctor and not a doctor of art history! In the 1990s in Iran, being an artist or studying in the humanities was not approved or favored by middle-class families such as mine—especially after the 1979 revolution in Iran, when there was less attention paid to art in society, since the new state authorities discouraged many cultural activities and artistic practices. On the heels of the Cultural Revolution in the early 1980s, the universities were shut down and when they reopened the curriculum had adjusted to the Islamic theological doctrine, filtering out those students and lecturers of all ideological groups who seemed to be unfaithful to the premises of the new state. In this condition, studying art lost value. Courses such as music, sculpture, dance, and interior design were considered un-Islamic, bourgeois, corrupt, or vain and omitted from the university curricula. This led to the immigration or marginalization of many artists and humanities scholars.

I studied agricultural engineering and painting for my undergraduate studies simultaneously, going back and forth between two universities. The experience of studying in these two different spheres made me think about the overlaps and divergences between art and science, the area I chose to work for my MA and Ph.D. research. The artists teaching us were promoting abstract art based on formalistic modernism. This frame of mind could be considered an attitude of resistance against a kind of ideological social realism advocated by the Islamic state.

In the mid-1990s, several years after the end of the war with Iraq, the relationship with the outside world was still very restricted and there was not much chance to receive information from other cultural events and changes from the outside. I took a free course on art history in the late 1990s to improve my knowledge in the field (there was not, and still is not, an independent art history discipline in Iran). Ruyin Pakbaz, a unique figure who doubtlessly deserves to be called the father of art history in Iran, taught us a linear history of art. Based on survey textbooks such as Helen Gardner's *Art through the Ages* and Arnold Hauser's *Social History of Art*, Pakbaz's theoretical framework was the combination of traditional Marxism and formalism. Despite being classical in his view toward this field of study, he was influential in structuring my mind through his linear narrative of art history.

Upon my arrival in England, I was shocked with a new cultural and academic environment. On the January 26, 2003, I left Tehran for Manchester, a few months after completing my MA in art studies. This geographical change was a turning point in my life. I found myself in an entirely new atmosphere, with a new language and culture. However, for me, this new adventurous world was more fascinating than fearful. I had made a big effort to pass the exam back home to get a grant from the Ministry of Science in Iran. It has been a privilege for many Iranian students to study in an "advanced country" such as England. Therefore, I found myself quite lucky in this regard. Apart from studying in the "center," having the experience of a free and open society was too precious for me. This acknowledgment was what helped me get through all the difficulties in all aspects of my life.

As noted before, in Iran, our education in art and theory was mainly based on a combination of traditional Marxism and formalism. Before 2003, the year I began my Ph.D. in Manchester, neither had I heard of postcolonial theory or queer and gender studies nor did I know much about the psychoanalytic and phenomenological approaches to artistic practice and theory.

In the first year at Manchester, I participated in some courses to learn about the new methodologies of art history and whatever else I had missed during years of study in Iran. I wondered how such subjects in the humanities could be related to art and how all these could have impacted me as a "non-Western young person." Regarding my studies in art and science, I found our department a place in line with my interests, where there were various seminars and conferences in related fields. And my supervisor, David Lomas, had also established a center on Surrealism for the study and research of philosophical and scientific aspects of the movement. I had never thought of Surrealism beyond a modernist movement in the past and that it had importance in the contemporary art scene, too.

Without a doubt, the most useful course I deliberately participated in together with several of my colleagues was Amelia Jones's Art History for MA students in 2006. In a review of the treatment of the history of art, we were encouraged to read the texts from the establishment of the discipline to the contemporary period. Later, after I returned to Iran in 2010, I planned to teach a course in a similar structure, translating and delivering the texts from two leading textbooks by Donald Preziosi and Eric Fernie, to my students. From then on, I began to be critical of the ways the discipline had developed in its European context.

This was the second chapter of my intellectual life in England. I came to understand that beyond my mere fascination by Western life and culture, I would never fit into that society—not without suppressing my differences. I remember one day, Stephanie Koerner, a lecturer in our department, told me, "Combiz, you won't be able to use your knowledge and experience [from Iran], maybe not more than ten or twenty percent of it, in this culture." Her revelation was formative. I understood her declaration, her assertion that "You must learn my language. It is not the other way round!" Funnily, I did not take this comment as condescending. She was, in fact, right. Stephanie could understand me as an outsider. She comes from a family of Jewish Austrian immigrants who were victims of the Holocaust. She could see how I was struggling to express myself in English and more generally, more importantly, in the cultural environment.

At the same time, I was emboldened to explore the discrepancy between the (Western) contemporary and the non-Western, the center and the periphery: this became my main preoccupation. Of particular interest was considering how a person from the non-Western world could be modern and contemporary in her/his own life. Here, I am not going to discuss the theoretical issues related to contemporaneity and otherness. What I would say is that today in the so-called global village, the opportunities for people are far from equal. This is traceable in both mainstream historiographies and histories of individuals and societies alike. The outsiders of all walks of life must make a huge effort to integrate in the developed communities and, in my case, in Euro-American academies. To be able to think, talk, and act as a superior Westerner was the primary goal of many of us in the first place. Considering art historical practices at the academic level, we also need to train ourselves to view these through the eyes of Euro-American scholars and learn how to utilize the methods they offer. The straight White male Christian middle-class Westerner still casts shadows on the resilient and conservative discipline of art history.

Upon returning to Iran in 2011, I started teaching at the Art University in Tehran. I began focusing on the development of "Iranian modernism" in the 1960s, while examining methods of art history in the contemporary Iranian context. Over the past ten years, I have taught students new methods of art history and critical theories—beyond the obsolete formal and iconographic versions of image analysis. I have also attempted to find and formulate new questions, frameworks, and methodologies for interpreting Iran's artistic practices, regarding its particular culture and history. Learning and using, and at the same time being doubtful about, some axioms of the mainstream scholarship, under the rubric of either postcolonialism, Marxism, or feminism, have occupied most of my career in the past few years.

In this short self-referential anecdote, I have tried not to self-censor myself and to be frank and honest in depicting my life experience. While I avoided conveying feelings of self-victimization as a member of the Global South—or the formerly used expression "Third World"—my path was not an easy one. Yet, practicing art history has unexpectedly shifted the course of my life journey.

DEREK CONRAD MURRAY

I WAS DRAWN to art history from a young age. My father had a small but substantive collection of art history books that were dominated by two primary obsessions: European and American modernism and twentieth-century African American art. My interest in his books—which I read cover to cover—was further bolstered by regular (almost weekly) trips with him to local galleries and museums. These excursions continued into my adult life, until my father's passing in the mid-1990s. Our shared love of art and its histories continues to drive much of my passion for visual art.

Before embarking on graduate study in the history of art, I attended art school at ArtCenter College of Design in the 1990s, with a focus on painting and theory. It was during my time there that I first became aware of racial disparity and marginalization in visual arts education, as Black artists (and artists of color in general) were completely absent from the histories and theories being taught. In fact, at the time, African American artists like Glenn Ligon, Lorna Simpson, Carrie Mae Weems, Lyle Ashton Harris, Fred Wilson, David Hammons, and Ellen Gallagher (among many others) were receiving critical acclaim, major exhibitions, and mainstream exposure—but they were absent from my studies. Within the walls of that institution, it was as if they didn't exist at all, despite their increasing prominence. I found this dismaying for obvious reasons, but also incredibly motivating and sustaining, giving me a mission and a sense of purpose—and ultimately leading me to embark on a career as a scholar. Since that experience, I have wanted to challenge the erasures and myopic value systems that make such exclusions possible. My aim was to transform the field and broaden its methods to be more honest, inclusive, ethical, diverse, and intellectually expansive.

To that end, I have chosen to be a theorist, as opposed to an historian. I underscore this rather obvious point because I have, on occasion, been regarded as a "bad" historian, while my theoretical approach can appear somewhat foreign, if not opaque. This has been a primary point of tension in my writings on African American art, because of my decision to operate independently, to engage with continental philosophy, and not to participate in the field's often nontheoretical brand of recuperative commemoration. In fact, my methodology is interdisciplinary, drawing from cultural studies, critical race theory, feminist studies, queer theory, philosophy, and sociology. I am also deeply committed to an intersectional approach to the complexity of identity, which necessitates always considering the ways that gender, race, and sexuality are interconnected. And perhaps more importantly, I resist essentializing Black culture and history, and refuse to hermetically seal it away from other histories of social and political struggle or other intellectual and creative traditions. My embrace and implementation of intersectionality has its roots in critical race scholar Kimberlé Crenshaw's original formulation, though I have developed my own methodological approach that acknowledges the complex manner in which identities are entangled and mutually dependent.

My recent work on the ethics of art history has been influenced by three key thinkers, all of whom engage with critiques of liberal tolerance in institutional and intellectual contexts: Slavoj Žižek, Sara Ahmed, and Wendy Brown.[1] Approaching theoretical questions in this manner has forced me to both broaden and deepen my knowledge base, but also has served to challenge my own biases in productive ways. A major concern that informs my work is the discipline's enduring reticence around the troubling realities of social discrimination (i.e., homophobia, racism, sexism, transphobia, and anti-immigrant bias), xenophobia, economic hegemony, and global crises—in favor of an area studies–based, historically and methodologically isolationist, and regressively formalist approach that often resists disciplinary self-criticality.

I appreciate art from all historical periods and geographies, but my enthusiasm has continuously been impacted by the myopia, entrenched biases, and outmoded methods that, in my opinion, have hampered the discipline of art history, threatening to push it into obscurity and intellectual irrelevance. I don't say this lightly, and my intention is not to malign the work of my colleagues, many of whom do brilliant work and are deeply committed to rigor and excellence, not to mention equity and fairness. My concern for the discipline has to do with its continued investment in a regressive Eurocentrism, combined with an often-disingenuous liberalism that is steeped in political correctness yet overwhelmingly disinterested in bringing about equitable change. The combination of these elements has created the conditions for socially committed and progressive scholarship (especially research dedicated to anti-racism, anti-homophobia, and anti-gender discrimination) to be marginalized and regarded as tangential to the discipline's central concerns. As a result, scholars whose research takes on such interests tend to be regarded as anomalies and are all too often relegated to the periphery of the field. These challenges are well known and have been taken up by scholars for several decades, yet they remain a central struggle well into the twenty-first century.

The challenges of which I speak have not impacted my passion and desire to be in the discipline—and the forms of resistance I've personally encountered have generally not been particularly formidable, so they have not mounted much of a challenge to my professional, intellectual, and institutional ascendency. That said, my interest in the problems of the discipline has more to do with the core ethics of art historical scholarship and the vitality of its discourses. What good is a discipline of study if it has no moral conscience and no desire to take on the most pressing concerns that have impacted human culture throughout history and into the present? The intent is to ponder why it is that the histories of art—and the value systems and methodologies that construct them—have been formulated through a pernicious colonialist set of logics that persist with minimal challenge.

The discipline has fallen behind the academy at large in terms of its ethical considerations, to the point that scholars throughout the humanities and social sciences largely ignore art historical work, even if they themselves study visual art. One must ask why this would be happening. Since the multicultural era and the identity debates of the 1980s and 1990s, many of the most prominent art historians and critics have rigorously theorized identity-based art (and socially engaged art practices) as regressive and degenerative—ultimately characterizing such concerns as ethnographic, exploitive, and ultimately tangential to arts development. For the past fifteen years, my work has been committed to challenging these framings while simultaneously formulating methodological approaches that reflect a more progressive and inclusive engagement with the visual. My first book, *Queering Post-Black Art* (2016), is one example of such an intervention.

Postwar art history has generally distanced itself from issues of social urgency: institutionalized racism; the persistent global problem of gender discrimination and violence; rampant homophobia and anti-trans violence; the migrant crisis; and colonialism and imperialism. And in its resistance to such concerns, the discipline has positioned socially committed scholarship as nonessential to the development of art.[2] These concerns have taken on even greater relevance in light of the Trump administration and the rising tide of xenophobia, racism, and White supremacist extremism. While academics and universities have attempted to distance themselves from increasing intolerances in culture at large, the prevalence of performative moral outrage, symbolic decency, and political correctness (within the liberal university) has increased exponentially—even while such sentiments are not always reflected in institutional demographics and bureaucratic practices. For many minorities within academia, the liberal progressive university is a space of hostility, noncollegiality, and a lack of hospitality, even while such spaces (and their progressive practitioners) emphatically profess their unwavering support for underrepresented groups. It is precisely this contradiction that warrants urgent and honest consideration, especially given what would appear to be the Leftist belief that structural bigotry and social discrimination exist only beyond the walls of the liberal university. The fallacy of the liberal academic utopia masks a more stark and disturbing reality in which diversity rhetoric and sentimentality actively conceal the presence of continued structural disparity.

The institutional rhetoric of diversity has become codified along the lines of *diverse subjects*, not *diverse spaces* or *diverse methods*. Substantive equitable change cannot occur by simply inserting so-called *diverse* bodies into an institutional space. Change can occur only if the core values and methods are transformed. As it concerns the presence of difference, there is a distinction between presence (as in diverse spaces in which all members are supported and have a voice) versus diversity only in representation. There is a tendency within liberal academia for forms of difference to function symbolically as *the* "subject of representation" in scholarly and artistic work while demographically remaining underrepresented within institutional and intellectual spaces. For the above reasons, I believe that disciplinary transformation cannot be achieved in scholarship alone; rather, it begins by transforming the institutions and departments that foster it. We must also acknowledge that the term "diversity" has become viewed as shorthand for institutional inaction and empty, tolerance-based sentimentalizing.

The aesthetics of tolerance in the academy has impacted my research as well, particularly as it pertains to the issue of diversity. For example, the presence of ethnic and racial minority scholars in art history has not substantially solved the problems of difference (in terms of its absence and nonessential status), largely because there tends to be more of a focus on recovery, commemoration, celebration, and isolation, rather than a direct methodological engagement with the discipline's omissions and erasures. Among minority and underrepresented scholars, there must be a greater willingness to grapple with the canons, the theorizations, the master narratives, and the exclusionary histories. As a result, and bearing in mind a few exceptions, there is a tendency for the historical work of underrepresented scholars in the discipline to methodologically mirror Eurocentric institutional approaches and methods while merely substituting European subjects with ethnically non-European ones. Despite this, I do not place any blame at the feet of vulnerable scholars, because their positions within universities are precarious enough and their choices are often dictated by the very real, if not inevitable, fact that their careers and livelihoods may be threatened by their liberal and socially progressive colleagues. That said, there is a kind of mannered respectability and conservatism within these subfields that have not adequately dealt with a range of intersecting concerns, like queer and trans visualities, or the conjunction of race, gender, and sexuality—not to mention the attempts at theoretical erasures within mainstream debates. These omissions have always troubled me, and I have therefore endeavored to model a set of alternative methods. That said, my aim has always been to enrich American art discourse while resisting the kinds of essentialism that, in my opinion, only serve to hamper its progress and potential impacts. Furthermore, without an engagement with the core debates in the discipline of art history, the work of underrepresented scholars and artists will continue to be theorized out of relevance—and will be perpetually reduced to a prescribed and ultimately marginalized role.

This is also the reason that recent strains in my research have turned away from the object and toward methodological, institutional, and disciplinary concerns. My choice to be a theorist as opposed to a historian was, in many respects, dictated by this very problem—by what I continue to see as a lack of theoretical engagement and criticality (and self-criticality) in the work of many minority scholars, which is often reflected in a retreat into disciplinary appropriateness, and what I characterize as a very celebratory form of recuperation. I see this tendency as motivated more by a desire to cement a place within a conservative discipline, as opposed to a mandate to critically dismantle the discipline's exclusionary practices and values. I, on the other hand, believe that until disciplinary values are challenged and transformed, the discipline will remain largely inhospitable and methodologically closed and will further marginalize identity-specific genres. My most recent book, *Mapplethorpe and the Flower* (2020), presents a set of possibilities for how we might understand the notable artist's flower photographs when considering them through an intersectional lens. There is a tendency in Western art history to act as though artists exist in separate, ethnically distinct universes, whereas their lived realities and histories are comingled. The separation of art's histories into ethnically distinct subfields is a persistent limitation that encourages art historians of color to restrict their work only to the study of cultural production by artists of their own respective identities. The methodological approach modeled in *Mapplethorpe and the Flower* challenges this deeply ingrained presumption.

Furthermore, within art history, identity-specific subfields remain peripheral and unacknowledged by a great many art history programs in the United States, which further impacts their disciplinary legitimacy. As a consequence, their presence has yet to substantively impact the master narratives and driving criticalities of the disciplinary center. While these arenas are successful in their acknowledgment and recovery of that which has been ignored, their commitments are often disengaged from the central debates, theories, and methods that drive both the historiography and criticalities of mainstream art discourse. This occurs because minoritized art historical genres have been formulated as distinct from the frameworks that traditionally have ignored them.

I want to make it clear, however, that in my assessment of certain subfields (particularly in the arenas of African American, Chicano/Latinx, South Asian, and queer historiographies) in art history as methodologically adrift, I acknowledge a larger problem in academic culture: institutional values and practices that create discrete identity-based groups, each lobbying for its own respective interests and arguing for space for themselves within the academy. Diversity efforts within universities tend to (intentionally or not) encourage racially essentialist approaches, often justified as a celebration (or simple acknowledgment) of differences. For example, in my institutional home, a diversity initiative was embarked upon in which various groups were individually convened to discuss equity issues within the university. However, these groups were distinct according to identity, in that there were separate meetings for Black, Asian, and Latino faculty, and so on. These identities were separated as if their concerns are unrelated or unique, and their institutional experiences distinct. This is not to mention the fact that minority faculty were tasked with finding solutions to problems of institutional equity that were not of their making. Such approaches are not unique to the liberal university and have become *de rigueur* among the diversity and equity mandates within both public and private institutions.

Bearing these institutional challenges in mind, I have never been comfortable with the essentialist values and boundaries so often policed in intellectual work. Within this I include minority discourses, which I fear may become separatist and a means for self-segregation and tribalism, justified as academic, intellectual, and institutional equity. But I also tend to see these discourses as succumbing to institutional values that segregate intellectual labor—often regulating those who are women, queer, or ethnically non-European (their histories and criticalities) to a tangential and peripheral status historically and intellectually, not to mention within the university itself. The problem is therefore twofold: On the one hand, the mainstream tends to either theorize out or outright devalue the contributions of minoritized constituencies. On the other hand, underrepresented scholars often restrict themselves to recuperative and identity-specific efforts that may disengage from the very practices that craft their deprioritized status. The resulting ideological deadlock prevents the discipline from envisioning and implementing a more progressive future.

I have often written about art history's shabby attitudes regarding difference in general and its resistance to the politics of identity. But the greatest trick of the discipline has been its facility to convince us that difference exists beyond the concerns of art: that scholars engaged with such concerns must labor on the periphery—perpetually making a case for its importance and humanity. As a result, a cultural politics of identity (which recovers that which has been ignored) has been the dominant mode upon which the under-acknowledged have waged their battles for recognition. It would seem that the critical project of institutionally dominant art history has been to displace particular identities, subjectivities, and histories—to create a version of art's development that is willfully myopic and limited. Those who have been removed were characterized as different, as Otherness, destined to a perpetual condition of justifying their humanity and value in the face of erasure. However, in the end, what we were given was a set of incomplete, if not entirely illegitimate, histories that have apparently been washed clean of their inherent richness and complexity. I argue that we should not look at difference in art history through an oppositional political lens but discuss its fundamental presence. Moreover, the aim should not be to think of our identities (in scholarly praxis) as implicitly different, but to acknowledge that art history has positioned certain subjectivities as such.

Ultimately, in my estimation, the problem of art history is not its intolerances, or its lack of diversity per se, but its overall absence of social, political, and ethical engagement. The hostility toward difference and the lack of diverse voices are a byproduct of its ethical drought. What takes its place, as I articulated earlier, is a cosmetic performance of political correctness and often empty commitments to diversity, equity, and inclusion. My aim here is not to advocate for some unrealistic and unattainable form of idealism, but rather to begin a conversation that can lead us to dismantle the procedural, methodological, intellectual, and institutional systems that function as hindrances to a healthy disciplinary future. The global protests in response to the extrajudicial murder of George Floyd in Minneapolis, Minnesota, on May 25, 2020, as well as the disproportionate racial impacts of the COVID-19 pandemic, have ignited what appears to be a greater consciousness and sense of urgency around eradicating the enduring scourge of American racism and xenophobia. How this will impact art history (and academic culture in general) has yet to be seen. Yet this moment holds the opportunity for the discipline to take a hard look at itself and hopefully to gesture toward unprecedented change.

Within American art discourses, is the social role of the so-called underrepresented intellectual or artist merely to poetically muse about their suffering, to create beautiful and moving distractions for an unbending, intolerant society? I certainly hope not, but I ponder this nonetheless, because in this questioning is also an acknowledgment that equitable change always occurs by force of will and unbending commitment. It is never truly granted. Appealing to decency and better angels is often a waste of time and misses the point entirely. The unbending chauvinism that grips the discipline is not (and has never been) an expression of its rigor and excellence, nor is it a sign of strength. It is, on the contrary, its greatest weakness and a consequence of an ethical vacuum that subsumes and dulls the more socially engaged work of the progressive practitioners within it. Therefore, those of us who are committed to a more socially engaged art history must take it upon ourselves to endow it with the critical power to emerge as a transformative force for good in a tumultuous time.

Notes

1. For additional reading, see Slavoj Žižek, "Tolerance as an Ideological Category," *Critical Inquiry* 34, no. 4 (Summer

2008): 660–82; Sara Ahmed, "Institutional Life," in *On Being Included: Racism and Diversity in Institutional Life* (Durham: Duke University Press, 2012), 19–50; Sara Ahmed, "The Nonperformativity of Antiracism," *Meridians* 7, no. 1 (2006): 104–26; Wendy Brown, "Tolerance as a Discourse of Depoliticization," in *Regulating Aversion: Tolerance in the Age of Identity and Empire* (New Jersey: Princeton University Press, 2006), 1–24.

2. See, for example, one critique of this in Okwui Enwezor, "Mega-Exhibitions and the Antinomies of Transnational Global Form," *Documents* 23 (Spring 2004): 2–19, at 4–5.

SAMUEL PECK

IN THE 1980s and early 1990s, I grew up a White, cisgender male in a large middle-class family (seven siblings) in Providence, Rhode Island. As a kid, my time was punctuated by moments of great pleasure (art, competitive swimming), heartbreak (my parents' divorce), and trauma (sexual assault). I spent a long time trying to forget my problems using work, alcohol, and anything else to help me push them away and move along with my life. I felt like a dog chasing its tail. I was sleeping very little and dreaming even less. I needed a change but didn't know how or where to look. In 2002, my brother Wes initiated an honest conversation with me about being survivors of sexual assault, and we formulated a plan around what we needed to do to protect our niece and nephew from their father. In this process, it became apparent that in my teens and early 20s, I was trying to run away from the trauma that my brother and I experienced during our childhood when our brother-in-law sexually assaulted us. This discussion wasn't our only conversation on the subject, but it was where we took action and decided to cast off shadows. We began to talk with each other about what had happened. Up until this point, we hadn't told anyone in our family.

We decided to take the necessary but painful step of disclosing the assault to our family, discussing what needed to happen to protect everyone, and going to the state police with our story. Eventually, this led to his conviction in 2005. He served time in prison but is now out on parole as a registered sex offender. The last time I ever had to face my brother-in-law was in court as the judge sentenced him. Though justice was served, the judicial process doesn't erase the psychic trauma of that assault, which stays with me and is something Wes and I will be working through for the rest of our lives. The constant outlet I've always had to work through my thoughts and feelings is my artistic practice. Before dealing with my sexual assault, I turned to less productive means of coping. After my brother-in-law was jailed, I focused on art, my relationships, and therapy as my primary sources of healing. One of my main mediums of choice, the visual journal, became the way to explore who I was after facing my demons and to create the same space within my classroom once I became an educator.

Based on my childhood trauma experience, my goal since I started teaching in October 2003 has been to protect and provide opportunities for students to flourish. I have worked to become an artist, researcher, and teacher of the visual arts. I taught PreK–12 and college art classes in Greensboro, North Carolina; Harwood, Maryland; and Minneapolis, Minnesota. Being in an art classroom gives me space to work alongside my students, to think about, around, and through the arts on an everyday basis. My students are interrogating the ideas, ethics, materials, and situations that are interesting to them and me through choice-based art education and Teaching for Artistic Behavior (TAB).[1] I find purpose in the space of being troubled by their lives' phenomena and being provoked to grapple with my ignorance. I work to provide safe, enriching spaces and challenges in the classroom through the three simple core tenets of TAB: (1) Take Care of People, (2) Take Care of Stuff, and (3) Behave Like an Artist. My goal is to move away from teacher positionality of the "sage on the stage" and instead become a facilitator where student agency for discovery, experimentation, and imagination can thrive.

Teaching is a practice that can swallow you up, and I know that to balance myself, I need to pursue the next step in my education as an artist and follow TAB's core tenets myself. I follow every avenue. I am curious. I am challenged in ways I could never have imagined, and I realize the more I drill down and hone my craft, the more I understand how little I know. This expanding of horizons is what my visual journal project, tet[R]ad: Draw and Play Here, can provide for participants: space and a contextual place for the art educator to grow and develop their craft as an artist with the support of another creator. For those with the difficult task of finding time to make, it provides a buddy system to help you stay on track, just like you do with a fitness trainer—a model to help keep you, the artist, within your studio practice.

After finishing my MFA at the University of North Carolina at Greensboro in 2010, I realized I was sitting on a small debt mountain. Financially, although I was making more money as a full-time PreK–12 teacher and adjunct, I wasn't in a place where this debt was going to disappear quickly. I had just finalized a divorce and had significant financial strain and responsibility. I thought through my options, and I felt I needed another income source and the possibility for another job track in case of hard times. The North Carolina Army National Guard became my solution to this fiscal crisis and an opportunity to be civically responsible to my family and community. Ideologically, I believe in serving one's country to give back to what has been given to you. I wanted to put out forest fires, help build homes, and rescue folks from natural disasters. I believe in trying to do what we can for one another, and I wanted to help my community in ways I wasn't already doing. I knew that I would be trained for warfare, as well. I make no illusions to the fact that I am part of the US war machine and complicit in the actions that are taken in my name and through what I help promote. I am not a high-ranking decision-maker, though, just a conscientious soldier since 2013.

The ethical, moral, and social justice issues surrounding the army and education system permeate my thinking. They push me to ask more significant questions of myself and my practices as an artist-researcher-teacher. This thinking also drives my tet[R]ad project to be civically, ethically, and community oriented. Tet[R]ad: Draw and Play Here is an international artmaking exchange envisioned and developed by artist David Modler[2] and myself. The ongoing endeavor of tet[R]rad fosters arts-based learning through one-to-one visual journal collaborations, which are inherently dialogical. A visual journal is an artist book used as a processing tool and a precious object to capture your life through words and images relationally, as I have done. Tet[R]ad hopes to illuminate the structural framework that cultivates a collaborative creative community while addressing relationships of our individual and collective stories. The project is not only a structure or a system to promote sharing and exchange; it is grounded in arts-based research practice.

As tet[R]ad's community grew, and the boundaries to the artistic practices it encompassed expanded, the tickle of curiosity pushed my mind again. My community started to ask questions about whether David or I had done doctoral research on the project. In 2017, I jumped back into graduate school to experiment, investigate, and explore the tet[R]ad phenomena. Through my doctoral program in Curriculum and Instruction at the University of Minnesota, I have learned about and expanded on what it means to be democratic, ethical, moral, inclusive, and socially just as an educator, while increasing my awareness of ways to investigate and discover the world through social science. As feminist scholar Gloria Evangelina Anzaldúa states: "Nothing happens in the 'real' world unless it first happens in the images in our heads."[3] The questions I seek to answer through my research are to explore the multiplicity of the artist-researcher-teacher role in the project;[4] study what, where, and how participants learn through the project; and examine how individual artistic accomplice stories impact cultural development and expansion of their artistic practices in new ways. The visual journal is a vehicle for this artistic action in what it provided for me and how I hope this project can help others.

This journey of curiosity to dig deeper into the visual journal and the tet[R]ad project is a recipe for building connections with others. This space to learn has allowed me to open up and see how the demands for conformity in the US Army and other such systems, my trauma from sexual assault, and becoming a teacher are instrumental in my growth. They set the stage for starting this project, and although I wouldn't want to go through the hard parts again, I would not be who I am without them.

Notes

1. Katherine M. Douglas and Diane B. Jaquith, *Engaging Learners through Artmaking: Choice-Based Art Education in the Classroom (TAB)*, 2nd ed. (New York: Teachers College Press, 2018).

2. David R. Modler is an artist, researcher, and professor from Baltimore, MD. He has a BS and MEd in art education from Towson State University and his MFA in painting from James Madison University. Modler currently works as an associate professor of art in the Department of Contemporary Art at Shepherd University in Shepherdstown, West Virginia. He lives in Rockville, MD, with his amazing wife, Stephanie.
3. Gloria Anzaldúa, *Borderlands/La Frontera: The New Mestiza* (San Francisco: Aunt Lute Books, 1987), 87.
4. Stephanie Springgay, Rita L. Irwin, Carl Leggo, and Peter Gouzouasis, eds., *Being with A/r/tography* (Rotterdam: Sense, 2008).

RAQS MEDIA COLLECTIVE

DELHI, SEPTEMBER 2020 CE

A RECENT WORK of ours, *31 Days*, outlines a world and a home that are getting unshaped and in need of repair, alteration, and reapprehension. Another recent work was the Yokohama Triennale 2020: *Afterglow*, and it asks how to care with and for the toxic. It posits a visit into our collective reservoir of intellectual and cultural resources in order to renew and gather, with auto-didacticism and luminous care.

An account of a collective self is imprinted within the pressures of the moments in which it is written. Today, as we revisit the various formations, gestures, and decisions of the three decades that we have been working together, we are within a ruined economy and a shattered social consensus. News has just arrived that India's GDP has been sliding and is now at –24 percent. Rarely does a generation see this kind of constriction without a civil or territorial war. Ninety-nine percent of TV coverage unrelentingly plays a show trial of a young actress whose live-in partner, a film star, died by suicide. The spread of the pandemic is reaching levels here that make the world nervous. People are restive in unknown ways, and glimpses of this leak through social media inflections and infractions. Recently, our small dream of a backup studio apartment for friends passing through Delhi vanished into thin air. The builder company has filed for bankruptcy, and it is now apparent that it was made of multiple shell companies. The claimants are in the thousands. It makes but a small news story and adds to the evidence of a collapsing world. What has been inaugurated, probably, is an intense phase of *scavenging capitalism*.

Within this context, we can do a rearview mirror look at various decisions, critiques, commentaries, and creations that we were, and are, part of. We approach this with a sense of both excitement and bewilderment. We ask ourselves how to understand the difference between being in a slow time machine and being in a fast time machine, and how to tell stories that we have not heard before.

In an interview with a national newspaper a few weeks ago, we were asked how the 1980s—the decade in which we were stepping out into the world—were for us. Everyone agrees that there were shifts within what we once called the "void years" of the 1980s, shifts that unfolded in multiple directions and dimensions. Now it feels like the 1980s were a *shunting yard* where many rusted wagons and old engines were being discarded and newer ones sanctioned. It was an acrimonious, anxious field. After the fall of the Berlin Wall, we saw a film by a banned documentarist from erstwhile East Germany. The film was entirely an observation of railway wagons coming in and going out, joining and unjoining, in a shunting yard. It was without words and with a foreboding of a flickering time. This was the period when we moved between demonstrations, reading groups, theater rehearsals, film screenings in VHS, art talks, and shared photocopied essays and books. These arenas and intermittent gatherings shaped the way we experienced the unmaking and making of the world.

Looking back, one decision seems significant. Our film school classmates were moving into the emergent, buoyant television industry and going, via that route, into the Bombay film industry. We decided against it. The arena of documentary filmmaking was small and fragile, but vibrant. The nature of the micro-conversations, assemblies around film viewing, and attendant workshops were energetic and questioning. They welcomed critical writing and debates between generations of established and aspiring filmmakers, where there was no separation between the amateur and the specialist, or the local and the outsider. It was in this milieu that we lived the value of intellectual pursuits and affective communities, and we felt the force of gathering and an acceptance of dissensus. To write commentaries, to make films, to assemble, to argue proposals, to create arenas of transcultural ways of thinking, conversing, and making is a continuum and needs to be thought together—this we intuitively grasped in those days.

The 1990s was a decade of refitting of economies everywhere to unprecedented scales, new networks, and accelerated mobilities, leading to institutional mechanisms cranking and croaking, and also exposing various hatreds. Specifically, in our immediate surroundings, upper-caste anxieties and contempt for the life of others, its morbid fear of losing control over resources and infrastructure, and its ability to whip up frenzy of religious belonging were on overt display. On the other hand, thriving practices around technological innovations brought in a density to our media experience. It is within these circumstances that we took two further decisions: one, to delve more into the socio-technological world of practices, from high art to street to neighborhoods, and two, to create gatherings and infrastructures of knowledge. This was our intellectual premise in the making of Sarai, a space that created the possibility of sustained investigation and exchange between many.

We are the generation that had to start the process of living with the World Wide Web. It inaugurated our understanding that infrastructure is decisive, that it needs to be shared, that it grows with an extensive public life, and that it has to be questioned and continuously innovate. Sarai was that place where we activated and created a milieu, backed by a public architecture of sharing, in which diverse languages, dialects, disciplines, practices, forms of speech, and argumentation could contend and nest. It was a practice in thinking as to how nodes are constituted and how they entangle other nodes as they move in epiphytic, parasitic, and morphing ways. This generative and threshold-challenging movement of words, images, sounds, codes, and platforms sustained restive, defiant, patient, and gregarious modes of being.

It was in those days, when the joke about us was that we were Sarai by day and Raqs after twilight, that we got invited to present our work within contemporary art. This was a tremendous boon, as it allowed us to test unconventional modes of documentary image arraying and sculpting arguments in order to delve into the spectral world of shadows and premonitions, and to speculate on the not-yet. Within a few years, a rescrambling of sedimented historical documents and narratives with fictive and undisciplined cartographic moves and playing with devices like clocks and chess boards emerged, and unpredictable itineraries surged.

We made friends, comrades, fellow travelers, and allies in different cities: Beirut, New York, Amsterdam, Mexico City, Mumbai, Barcelona, Ramallah, Athens, Bangalore, Dubai, Johannesburg, London, Hong Kong, Berlin, Shanghai, Kolkata. And it is these alliances that also keep our practice grounded in the world. We brought all into conversation via the Sarai readers and Sarai events and, increasingly, through curatorial maneuvers and measures. Our curatorial ethics developed here: as sites of gathering and as infrastructural gambits that are sharpened through their ability to call in many experiences, intelligences, and subjectivities.

From 2000 onward, there seems to have been a turn in the world toward unbridled and galloping masculinity, and the muscularity of highly productive economies, with their elites riding them. It heralds a new iteration of *rentier capitalism* building its insecurities onto security and surveillance regimes. This inaugurates social media, a medium in the making and being tested from the late1990s onward. In Sarai, with our coder colleagues, we had imagined and proposed what was then called social software. That is, software where you could work with and meet others, and leave a trace of this encounter. OPUS was one among these, one that got global recognition. But soon the turn toward consolidation of social media platforms swamped the million mutinies of code. The idea that code should be free, and free for all to modify, is what we thought the world was going to be, and we still work with it as an ethos. We argued that a culture thrives where all are creators of *recensions*, with no anxiety of originality. We remain curious and cautious about the delirium and disruption afforded by the immediacy of social media. In Sarai, with some of our colleagues, we had predicted that the media will alter the terms of social life. Over the past ten years, popular tumult and rebellions have crested with the ease afforded by the tools that social media has brought into our mutual relationships. It has changed the governed and changed governmentality.

Today, in an ancient urban village in the southern part of our city, there is a studio with a blue floor, and this is where we work. This is where our working table, the stage of our arguments, and our unwieldy anarchive, sits, waiting. For the past many months, this studio has appeared intermittently in our dreams because we haven't been there in person, so it comes to us instead. The lockdown has kept the studio locked in on itself, and we have met, every other day, online: to share ideas, to argue, to plan, to schedule and reschedule everything, including the writing of this text.

Many friends had commented about the awkward word "Media" in the middle of an otherwise poetic evocation of complex cultural and praxeological genealogies in our name. We took a position neither for nor against particular forms, and we let the meaning of the "media" in our middle name slide between medium, techné, and mode of being. Nowadays, that "middle" is often the only discussion in philosophy and arts. That awkward middle has foregrounded itself in a most virulent, poetic, lifesaving, and also pathological way. What does this mean? One of the abiding logics of our practice is the tuning, modulation of, and play with foregrounds. We try to shift focus and change lenses to arrive at different ways of locating a foreground. Hibernating, sedimented, forgotten, misplaced, aborted, or overcharged worlds are repositioned and weighed again. A closed mine, a lost rhinoceros, an old fingerprint, an ancient shipwreck, a broken cup, a hard biscuit, a century-old herbarium, a Cold War bunker, a grainy footage of a shipyard, a handmade dog in an archive, a fable from a workers' newspaper, a collectively rewritten diary, all appear, and sometimes, like a Mughal miniature landscape, merge into each other without fear of perspectival order. Or, shorn of the accoutrements of historical bondage, they come close to possess us and overcome the limits posed by linear time.

This happens to our name as well. This coming decade, all three words will be under varying argumentative pressures. The Islamicate mystic overtones of the word "Raqs" contaminate many an ear even as they reassure many others, the inflammable word "Media" now haunts as infection and as redemption, and "Collective" may be the last bastion of our ability to act with a degree of trust and deliberation. When work happens and conversation grows, it will harness a kind of bioluminescence from a triangulated consciousness of these three vectors.

SHAHZIA SIKANDER

AS A CHILD, I grew up in a multigenerational household in Lahore, Pakistan, where storytelling was a daily ritual. Long participatory conversations over food and family gatherings, involving cousins, uncles, aunts, parents, and grandparents, each overlapping their unique perspectives, commentaries, jokes, anecdotes, fostered an environment of creative intimacies. History, religion, ethics, fantasy, comedy, all sorts of stories converged as we, the children, the many cousins living under the same roof, learned to formulate opinions, observe, and express. I was better at expressing myself through drawing. I don't recall exactly when I started to draw, but I remember that it came to me more effortlessly than speaking up. I have vivid visual memories of early childhood books and their unique illustrations, partly because of my father's enacting of the characters as he read the stories aloud. The amalgam of tales and contexts—from oral Punjabi songs and poems passed on through my maternal grandmother to being read aloud Urdu translations of Korney Chukovsky's Russian stories and of Hans Christian Andersen, from mythic stories about the Greek Alexander (Sikander in its Urdu variant) to the folkloric tales about the Prophet and his encounters with Gabriel, shared by my paternal grandmother—had an impact of wonder and a desire to imagine and be transported to different worlds through image-making.

The languages spoken in our house were Urdu, Punjabi, and English, and though I could speak all three, I was unable to excel in any one of them. In that mix, drawing was critical in allowing me to express complicated emotions and concepts intuitively. As a teenager, I also studied nature to find inspiration. In those years my interest in patterns and obsessions with fractals, biology, the solar system, cartography, and geography was fueled by curiosity for mathematics, especially geometry. For me, math was an integral part of drawing as I studied and drew forms and assembled relationships, painting them, giving them names and characters and devising some sort of role-playing through the forms.

The interactive nature of telling stories has also played a role in my sharing a creative language with my son. When Alexander was two, I would take the simplest idea or element that excited him, and we would create stories about it, taking turns, moving it in any direction we wanted. Bringing characters and stories to life unfolded into collaborative paintings. Sensitivity toward color and form informed our early ventures into painting. Even at 2, he could tell the difference between the child-friendly low-pigment tempera and the dynamic colors of highly saturated inks, choosing those instead. When he was 6 or 7 years old, he would draw for hours, patiently depicting animals, birds, sharks from memory and observation with precise enigmatic expressions and complex lyrical forms. I often let him paint into my large drawings or let him take over my minimally started works. We collaborated on an eight-foot painting for a group show I was invited to, *Scale: Possibilities of Perspective*, at the Children's Museum of the Arts in New York City in 2018. Juggling a child as a single parent while remaining creative has been akin to having a second shot at childhood. It continues to ignite my core belief in creativity and in centering our lives around curiosity and passion, self-awareness, and respect for nature: that it is all right not to be able to solve everything and that some things get resolved through dreaming. It was an epiphany for me as a diasporic individual that instead of fretting over my less-than-perfect Urdu, I could embrace painting as my shared mother tongue with my son.

My work as a visual artist investigates interdisciplinary languages of form, migration patterns, cultural quarantine, and the flux of human identity. I work in a variety of mediums and scales to address the multivalence of ideas. Every artwork I create, I conceive of it as a poem: individually crafted, exploring tensions between material and meaning, people and society, power and powerlessness to engage with the intrinsically beautiful and poignant into the culturally relevant and transformative.

Eurocentrism has been operable throughout art history and history. When we inherit one-sided or polarizing constructions of the past, we often unconsciously keep marching down the same well-preserved paths. The notion of "home" and authentic state is embedded within my practice as an artist but not in any definitive ideology, nationalism, or geography. The multiple juxtapositions, unexpected detours, dissonance, jostling, shifting hierarchies are strategies I have employed in my work since the mid-1990s to destabilize and explode binary thinking in all its forms. The nonbinary gender identity is equally layered in my work, and it is particularly heightened in iconographies of women that are not tied to a heteronormative lineage or to conventional articulations of diaspora and nation. The female protagonists can be equally androgynous, proactive, confident, intelligent, and in their playful stance connected to the past in imaginative ways without glorifying it. They are the antithesis of the fictions of purity and authentic national culture.

Historically, the movement of objects (and bodies), such as in trade, slavery, migration, colonial occupation, and urban patterns of human costs of displacement and pollution, has forced meaning to shift and oscillate with every generation. When one thinks in terms of narratives and how history is determined, how real is that account? All histories are about redactions where often the highest bidder gets to tell the story.

Reinterpreting the past to engage with contemporary social and political issues has been the touchstone of my engagement with art. The 1980s in Pakistan very much shaped me as a young adult. Pakistan had been under Zia's military dictatorship since the late 1970s. During the Soviet–Afghan–US–Pak War (1978–92), the rise of Ronald Reagan and Margaret Thatcher and the US military presence in Afghanistan and northern Pakistan started to seep into Pakistani culture through anticommunist propaganda, the military importance narrative, incessant institutionalization of religion, corruption, and expensive imported US products in the local markets. The diminishing of women's rights, blasphemy laws, the Islamization project, the polarized public and private spaces discouraged dissent and creative expression. I was inspired by women leaders like Asma Jahangir, Pakistan's human rights activist. One of my first mentors was the late artist Lala Rukh. In 1986, I worked with her at the Simorgh foundation, a women's resource and publication center, while studying mathematics at Kinnaird College for Women. She was a founding member of the Women's Action Forum (WAF). Being a part of WAF gave me substantial insight into women's rights and issues, as well as a broader grasp on the intersections of community and art. I was in search of a creative environment to reflect upon the mechanism of power and how women could be agents of change, and the idea of pursuing art and mathematics simultaneously suited my inclination toward logic and intuition.

At the National College of Arts (NCA) in Lahore in the mid-1980s, my interest in miniature painting, an unpopular subject for my generation at that time, got sparked by my own lack of general knowledge about visual histories of the region as well as the prevalent intellectual cultural disregard toward craft-based miniature painting. Mostly mired in its iterations of "tourist kitsch" much more than its "indigenous" status, it had been declared derivative. In those years, "tradition" was a complicated idea readily referred to as inferior and anti-avant-garde by the liberal elite and simultaneously championed by the conservatives. It was also clear to me that the "tradition" in the context of the Indo-Persian visual canon was truncated, at best, and its custodian, the master miniature painter Bashir Ahmad, was struggling to find A+ students to work with. Ahmad's devotion and sincerity to "tradition" was, however, interesting to me as a young observer. Both his teachers—Sheikh Shujaullah and Haji Sharif—belonged to a family of court painters, and there was something deeply powerful about that idea of knowledge being passed through generations. How tradition is defined and how it is disseminated, that performative aspect captured my imagination.

There was no culture of museums when I was growing up in Pakistan in the 1980s. Much of the art was stolen by the English anyways. This is also a time when the art history curriculum at NCA was dated. I recall learning by heart sections from *Art through the Ages* and never fully grasping whatever I was learning, as it never directly intersected with my lived reality. In terms of miniature painting, its precolonial history was written mostly by Westerners from the perspective of Eurocentric nineteenth-century scholarship. A majority of the region's historical art was hiding out of sight in Western museum storages as a result of the colonial histories of plundering and looting, or in private collections yet to be published. Without deep critical conversations about English conquest, dispersion and revival of the arts within the academic institution itself, the identity of a Pakistani art was in flux.

The Scroll (1989–90), my thesis work at NCA, emerged as the tipping point in the local debate around "modern miniature." It received national critical acclaim in Pakistan, winning the prestigious Shakir Ali Award, NCA's highest merit award, and the Haji Sharif Award for excellence in miniature painting, subsequently launching the medium into the forefront of NCA's program.[1] In 1992, I was asked to teach alongside Bashir Ahmad, becoming the first woman to teach miniature in the history of NCA.

Much of the visual history I wanted to research was in India and in institutions outside of Pakistan. Unfortunately, the political climate between India and Pakistan in the early 1990s was such that I was unable to get a visa to study in India. I had also written to the Pakistani ambassador to the United States to support young artists' work, and it led to an opportunity to travel standby on Pakistani International Airlines to showcase my paintings at the Pakistani Embassy in Washington, DC, in 1993. Technically, the show was a one-week event linked to a celebration at the embassy for the Pakistani expat community. No one bought any of my artwork, and the disappointment fueled me to reach out to some art schools to share the work in person. Rhode Island School of Design (RISD) showed a keen interest, and I was able to find assistance with tuition through a Des Moines–based women's organization and juggling many jobs including TA for Mary Anne Staniszewski and babysitting.

I became aware very quickly that America was fundamentally about a Black-and-White relationship, where being Brown was not yet fully visible. The hardest aspect was that no matter how nuanced one's work was, the persistently polarized discourse and the prevalent framing devices would inevitably dwarf complexity. This continuing Samuel Huntington–style commentary of West versus the rest of the world was present even within the feminist discourse, where one would be expected to cull out one's representations in the composite "Third World." The notion of the Other was problematic as it gave overt attention to identity over everything else. This was also a time of post–Magiciens de la Terre decentering-the-Eurocentric-art-world commentary. Though it stands in stark contrast to where the global aspect of literature and art are now, the United States in the mid-1990s did not have much diversity.

The Euro-American canon dominating the field of painting and art history was still very much Eurocentric in the early 1990s. Even though the big theme emerging after the fall of the Berlin Wall and economic transformations was globalization in the art world, contemporary art from South Asia was still not visible in exhibitions or in gallery representations. Reading art journals and art history books that did not relate to or represent one's experiences, one had to use imagination a lot.

My iconography started to breach national boundaries. I wanted to intersect with Pakistani feminists, writers, and poets, like Fahmida Riaz, Ismat Chughtai, Kishwar Naheed, Parveen Shakir, and with Julia Kristeva, Luce Irigaray, Hélène Cixous, and bell hooks, to understand my own engagement with feminist forms and in turn explore language from specific points and places of women's narratives. I was dislocating context and intimacy across race and sexuality to reread the texts from new perspectives that I was experiencing. By reorganizing the framing devices of center and margin within the miniature painting, I could open up the narratives of gender and sexuality simultaneously. The female forms that started to emerge in my work were monstrous, playful, explicit, evocative, precise, and determined. The work started to embrace a state of homelessness, not as an exiled or diasporic artist, but as a female agency rupturing through abodes of patriarchy and militarism across national boundaries, cultures, and histories. Anarchy, lack of sovereignty, and constructions of femininity and beauty started to dismantle the orthodox representation within the visual tradition of the Indo-Persian miniature.

After RISD, I moved to Houston in August 1995. I had started to read about the American civil rights movement and Black power. The Jim Crow battle, though an American story, resonated with the struggles and freedom movements of colonized people around the world. To read and learn about the intimacy of violence in the history of slavery and genocide and imperial wars was a starkly different experience from the two years in Providence's international student environment of RISD and Brown. The American landscape, to me, could not be separated from my understanding of US foreign policy—American involvement across the globe as it affected the geopolitical education of one's identity as a Pakistani.

It was not surprising for me to find a natural place of connection at Project Row Houses in Houston. It was a shining example of the African American community and collectives operating outside of the traditional spaces of power and narrative, where the local and the everyday functioned as sites of transformation, where women, students, Third Ward residents, artists of color, thinkers, poets, musicians, and social activists would come about and engage.

Challenging colonial ways of seeing and knowing is a concerted effort. Finding alternative ways of being, creating unexpected juxtapositions between seemingly oppositional ideas and histories to imagine visual forms that challenge fixed narratives, that aim to reorganize histories and geographies of inequality, keeps my work moving forward. My work is not about hybridity. It is not fusing cultures or aesthetics. By reflecting upon gender, race, class, and language differences as a means of contact, it seeks overlapping diasporas in the American landscape, analyzing the legacy of colonial imperialism, highlighting the politics of provenance, ownership, and narration by taking a closer look at historical works, documents, and unarchived materials to use as inspiration for a new direction in art history and a contemporary visual idiom.

Promiscuous intimacies

The ideas encapsulated in this sculpture, which takes its title and description from Gayatri Gopinath's essay on my work, are part of the DNA of my work.[2] I first sketched out the concept in 2000 for a banner for MoMA, when I worked with the curator Fereshteh Daftari. At that time, it was not important for me to declare the content through a 3D form. I was culling art history's classicism and ethnocentric reactions to Indian art as per Johann Joachim Winckelmann's doctrine. I was also making a point by entangling mannerism, the anti-classical impulse within the Western tradition, alongside Indian art, both as accomplice witnesses of a one-sided history, and the drawing I had sketched with the two protagonists sufficed. In 2017, I had the opportunity to be part of the NYC Mayoral Advisory Commission on City Art, Monuments and Markers, and during that process of hearing differing public opinions and studying public monuments, their complicated histories, historical reckoning, and tensions between communities regarding representation, I felt the urge to respond to the overt male representation of historical monuments through an anti-monument. I decided to cull out the protagonists in my paintings and reengage them in a sculptural format.

This sculpture, with its sinuous entanglement of the Greco-Roman Venus and the Indian Devata, explores the "promiscuous intimacies" of multiple times, spaces, art historical traditions, bodies, desires, and subjectivities. In their suggestive embrace, the intertwined female bodies bear the symbolic weight of communal identities from across multiple temporal and geographic terrains.

They evoke non-heteronormative desires that are often cast as foreign and inauthentic and instead challenge the viewer to imagine a different present and future. The sculpture with its backward glance demands that we understand "tradition," "culture," and "identity" as impure, heterogenous, unstable, and always in process, disrupting taken-for-granted national, temporal, and art historical boundaries.

From the Indus Valley excavations to the Chola bronzes, bronze and metal casting has had a long history in South Asia, where the sacred and tangible objects often interacted in essential and functional ways with human activities and socioeconomic practices. My work in bronze colored in various patinas highlights that classical painted statuary was polychromatic and not necessarily "lily white" as often constructed over time in popular imagination. "Color prejudice," points out the historian Sarah Bond, reveals that "how we color (or fail to color) classical antiquity is often a result of our own cultural values."[3] For me, connecting the patina to these larger discussions on color in classical sculpture also links the issue of classicism with American monuments and memorials, which are often revered as symbols of patriotism in their classicism aesthetic. When asking what stories and whose perspectives get commemorated in public spaces, black, Indigenous, and people of color (BIPOC) and especially women of color are the least represented. It is precisely these multiple urgent cross-currents of reexamining colonial and imperial stories of race and representations that *Promiscuous Intimacies* engages.

Notes

1. Salima Hashmi, "Studies in Excellence," *Newsline*, March/April 1992, 113; Rina Saeed Khan, "The Best Art to Have Come Out of NCA in Two Decades," *Friday Times*, February 27–March 4, 1992, 1; Salima Hashmi, "Youth – Shahzia's Miniatures," *Libas International* 5, no. 1 (1992): 108–9
2. Gayatri Gopinath, "Promiscuous Intimacies: Embodiment, Desire and Diasporic Dislocation in the Art of Shahzia Sikander," in *Shahzia Sikander: Extraordinary Realities*, eds. Sadia Abbas and Jan Howard (Munich: Hirmer, 2021), 118–29.
3. Sarah Bond, "Whitewashing Ancient Statues: Whiteness, Racism and Color in the Ancient World," *Forbes*, April 27, 2017, https://www.forbes.com/sites/drsarahbond/2017/04/27/whitewashing-ancient-statues-whiteness-racism-and-color-in-the-ancient-world.

LOWERY STOKES SIMS

ON THE WEBSITE of the Metropolitan Museum of Art, the credit line for two works on paper by McArthur Binion that I acquired for the collection late in 1979 acknowledges the contribution of a group of "various donors." The purchase itself was an act of desperation born out of frustration on my part as I grappled with what was then, for me, an intractable system that tended to disregard artists of color, women, and certain White males who weren't enshrined in the hallowed halls of art stardom. The timing of the accession also coincided with what would be a key moment in my curatorial career, when my temporary stewardship of what was then the 20th Century Art Department was drawing to a close. William S. Lieberman, a long-time fixture on the curatorial staff of the Museum of Modern Art, would soon arrive at the Met as the new departmental chairman.

Lieberman's arrival at the Met culminated a tumultuous sixteen-month period after Thomas Hess, distinguished art critic and editor—who assumed the position after the founding departmental head Henry Geldzahler left the Met to assume the position of commissioner of cultural affairs of the City of New York during the first term of Mayor Ed Koch—died suddenly of a heart attack in the office on a beautiful day in July 1978. Yours truly was therefore put into the situation where she was appointed assistant curator, acting in charge (or, as I like to title myself, acting-like-I-was-in-charge) of the department. The purchase of the two drawings by McArthur Binion would not have been sanctioned by the administration during my ad hoc tenure as department head. But the addition of two other funds on the credit line indicates that since I'd taken the initiative to fundraise for the acquisition, the administration decided to support it with additional monies. For the most part, I was given the clear impression that I was really only tasked to keep things moving on and continue projects that Tom Hess had put into place, not to get any ideas about anything else more ambitious. I would not have permission to spend monies from any of the several standing acquisition funds for the 20th Century Art Department, although I remember engineering a few donations here and there.

At that point in 1978, I had been on staff at the museum for six years, three as an educator in what was then the Community Programs Department and three as a curator. It was a momentous moment because I realized that I would have to cope with a very steep learning curve about the true nature of museums, the administrative foibles of the institution, and deciding whether or not I was going to continue in the field.

My sister, Benna, used to complain that I had a book on every alternative career I had considered since I started working at the museum. My experiences up to that point had left me in a skeptical frame of mind. I blabbed about taking up geology or astronomy (with which I had flirted as an undergraduate at Queens College), archaeology (a childhood obsession from which I was discouraged by my mother, who declared that you had to be both rich and White to pursue this career, only to realize later that being a curator was tantamount to the same thing), or even underwater archaeology—notwithstanding the fact that I was and am not a great swimmer. I had taken lessons in my twenties, trying to disprove stereotypes about Blacks not being good swimmers, on the supposition that we had bad memories of the sea voyages we endured in the trans-Atlantic slave trade—but I never got really good at it, though I can do a decent dog paddle or float on my back and do an awkward backstroke. My young cousin Marin has proven to be the real swimmer in the family, drawing important inspiration from Simone Manuel, whose gold-medal performance at the 2016 Rio Olympics was a stupendous event.

During the late 1970s, however, in the midst of the particular phalanx of challenges presented to me, I would earn my chops as a curator at the museum and learn a lot more about how to navigate the system, to the extent that I dug in, decided to stay with it, and ended up working in three different museums in New York City over a period of 43 years. I don't remember the catalyst that particularly fired me up about purchasing McArthur's works on paper. It might have been because he needed the money, or because I liked them, or because I felt that aforementioned desperation to act, or a combination of all three. But I remember going home one night, cold-calling a number of friends and friendly collector types I had gotten to know over the previous three years, and asking each of them to send me a check for $100.00 so I could purchase the drawings. I don't remember how many responded, but evidently it was enough—maybe ten or so—that when the accessioning information was transferred into the museum's database, whoever input it couldn't be bothered with so many names. Or so I'd like to think, in my customarily paranoid and cynical frame of mine.

I thought about all of this some 35 years later when Mary Sabbatino, director of the New York branch of Galerie Lelong of Paris—and a long-time professional colleague and sometime Wifredo Lam cohort—contacted me to write an essay for the catalog of an exhibition of McArthur's work they were planning at the gallery. I accepted on the condition that she subsidize the trip for me to visit McArthur in his studio, since it had been over twenty years since I'd last seen him. While I'd had noticed his work popping up in art fairs showcased by the Chicago gallerist Kavi Gupta in the 2000s, I had not had any dialogue with him about what was happening with him and his work. Although I had done a lot of writing on painters and sculptors after I left the Met—to be first a museum director at the Studio Museum in Harlem and then a curator at the Museum of Arts and Design with a new portfolio of design and craft—I was curious why Mary had thought to ask me in this instance. She told me that she had seen my name, address, and telephone numbers (home and work) on the reproduction of pages from McArthur's address book from the 1970s in one of his more recent paintings, where he rotated copied segments from the book onto the surface and dug a grid pattern over it.

This was, in fact, the second time in the spring of 2015 that I had been in contact with an artist I had first met earlier in my curatorial career but had been out of contact with for a number of years. The Studio Museum in Harlem had also asked me to contribute to one of their publications: an interview with Stanley

Whitney for the catalog of the exhibition of paintings they were organizing for the summer of 2015. My resulting dialogues with both artists revolved around our common experiences of being African Americans in the art world of the 1970s and 1980s and the special challenges they both faced as abstract artists in an environment dominated first by the presumptions of formalism and then by the self-reflectiveness of postmodernism. In both cases, they had to navigate issues of identity that would be imposed on their artmaking, the perception being that they were too subsumed by a Black identity to be accepted in the mainstream or were avoiding acknowledging their identity by doing abstract art. So, it is not without a pervasive sense of irony that I witness the widespread, if belated, recognition and promotion of abstract artists who have preserved since the 1960s and 1970s in the art world. The roll call includes William T. Williams, Sam Gilliam, Howardena Pindell, Oliver Jackson, Mary Lovelace O'Neal, Mildred Howard, Stanley Whitney, Mel Edwards, and Jack Whitten.

The conversations I had with McArthur and Stanley covered a range of topics: the nuances of theoretical and critical concerns, their own strategies for navigating that liminal space between experience and imposed presumptions about their selfhood, and their success in finding ways of avoiding being pigeonholed either by blackness or by abstraction. I had faced similar challenges as a curator, so I supposed it was this shared experience among McArthur, Stanley, and me that led both the Studio Museum and Galerie Lelong to engage me in their catalog projects. I could certainly provide a useful perspective to writing about their work in terms of both the past and the present. I guess that is why and how I ended up staying in this field: to provide perspective and a sense of experience and analysis. Returning again to this period 1978–80, I realized that my baptism by fire in the senior administrative echelons of the art world was intense and rapid fire. In addition to coping with the politics of the museum, I was also given access to another level of social and political interactions than even an ad hoc position would have given me. Some were enlightening, others vexing, but none were boring.

JAUNE QUICK-TO-SEE SMITH

Confederated Salish and Kootenai Nation MT

Tribe and community have always been fundamentals in my work and activism. My worldview is that we must "give back" lovingly when we can and receive graciously when we are in need. We must come to understand that individualism and fossil fuel have gotten us into the mess we are in, and neither one works.

Everything I write, paint, draw, or speak is about my tribal philosophy, my worldview. We must care about one another and our living planet. There is no other way if we are to survive.

I call myself a cultural arts worker; I use humor and satire to examine myths, stereotypes, and the paradox of American Indian life in contrast to the consumerism of American society. My work is philosophically centered by my strong traditional beliefs and political activism.

My work, both on paper and on canvas, has been narrative and still is. Stories move back and forth across history and present day with no beginnings and no endings, using written words and symbolic images.

The tactile surface of the work has been and still is composed of all sorts of collage, such as newspaper, tea-stained paper, fabric, photocopy images, oil crayon, acrylic, charcoal, and oil paint, often whatever is handy in my art debris and will help me tell a good story.

A good story matters in the work. Stories about respect for the natural world. *She*, after all, is who gives birth to us and who will subsume our bodies when we're done with them. Stories concerning the treatment of animals, climate change, women's rights, war, justice, more war, and never-ending war fill the spaces of both canvas and paper.

War is a major issue in the downfall of humankind, besides lack of potable water, a planet covered in cancer-causing pesticides, internationally powerful agri-growers ruining our organic and indigenous seed, plastics and chemical pollution, overpopulation, deforestation, and climate change.

Things were different when I was a little kid; we drank water from rivers and creeks wherever we were. My dad grew a garden, and we had a cow and chickens. We churned butter, canned food, ate our own beans and potatoes, and made bread. We shopped once a month, and every two months for coffee and flour.

When I was really young, my mother left my sister and me with the Plumleys, an elderly Native couple who lived near us, and she took off with the migrant workers. Her intent was to make enough money to return and steal us away while my dad was at work as a farm hand.

My dad, Salish and Metis, at age 40 had raped my mother when she was 14 and living with her Cree father. My dad and my grandfather drank together. My mother was afraid of my dad, so she never made it back to get my sister and me. But surprisingly, my father raised us, which was highly unusual for a Native man in those days, especially since he was illiterate.

I remember some of the places we lived. We had to move all the time; dad looking for work, figuring out a way to care for us. Sometimes someone would report him for being drunk and would find that we girls didn't have anything to eat. Then a sheriff or a social worker would put us in a welfare home.

Sometimes we stayed on a reservation; in those days, these were one-room cabins for two or three families. No electricity, no running water, and we slept on the floor against the wall rolled in our blankets so the adults wouldn't step on us.

I started work when I was 8 as a field hand to help my dad. I worked year round for the Nisei who returned from the internment camps to rent their land that the government had confiscated and sold to White people for pennies on the dollar. In high school, I worked as a waitress and in the canneries in Puyallup, Washington. My intent was to go to community college in Bremerton.

The boys' basketball coach was my counselor for scheduling classes. Even though I told him I wanted to go to college, he told me that Indians never go to college, so I needed to take vocational courses. I went to college anyway, working in the school library, cleaning apartments, and working as a maid for the family who owned the apartment I rented. I had to make up the math and language that I had missed by taking the vocational course. I majored in art, but at the end of my second year, the instructor informed me that women could not be artists. He suggested I go into teaching.

Between the racist, misogynistic advice, personal economic issues, and raising children partly alone, it caused a struggle that I faced by attending a series of schools, moving, dropping out, and taking one class at a time. I spent 22 years to finally end with a master's degree at the University of New Mexico. There, I was told that Indians don't go into fine arts and was told to go into art ed. Against all odds, I gave up on the MFA, and after four years battling the system, I took the MA and my dignity, and left. By the time I graduated, I had a New York gallery, the Kornblee, and a review in *Art in America*.

In 1976, while I was in graduate school, I began organizing a Native American group that Navajo artist Larry Emerson called the "Grey Canyon Artists" for the city streets and buildings that formed concrete canyons. I searched first for exhibit spaces in New Mexico, then began writing to museums outside the state. Within six years, we exhibited in many places but most remarkably in San Marco Gallery on the Plaza in Venice, Italy; the North Dakota Museum of Art; and the Portland Art Museum in Oregon.

During this time in the early 1980s, I searched far and wide for Native American photographers. After four years, I had gathered about 10, not all of whom were professionally trained. Most photos were the small Brownie type. Rosemary Ellison, director of the Southern Plains Museum, allowed me to show the photos there in Anadarko, whereas all the galleries or museums in New Mexico and Arizona had turned me down. What? No Indians with feather bonnets or dancers in costume? What? Only a table with a sack of Blue Bird flour sitting on oil cloth and an out-of-date John F. Kennedy calendar hanging high on the wall? No, we have no interest in your so-called Genre scenes is what I heard over and over.

With the help of lots of artist friends, mostly Natives, I toured the photos for two years in a little wood box. This was the first touring exhibit of Native photography made by Natives in America. At each stop, Indians came to see the show and told me they took photos too. I kept adding from each stop, and at the end there were 60 Native photographers in the show I titled "The Peoples Show," which ended at the Heard Museum.

A decade later, I found venues in Scotland, France, and two in Germany. I titled this exhibit "Positives and Negatives, Contemporary Native Photography." Again, these photos were likely the first made by Native Americans to exhibit there.

Before I completed this photo exhibit in the 1980s, I started working on a Native women's exhibit, with the help of Harmony Hammond and Lucy Lippard. I located 30 women of all ages, from 20-something to 80-something. I wanted work being made at that time by living Native women artists, such as beadwork, photography, sculpture, quilts, jewelry, painting, and ceramics.

This was a groundbreaking hit in the Native community, and with the help of Peter Jemison, then director of the American Indian Community House in New York, we opened with a big crowd, Spiderwoman Theater performing in the afternoon, and a big outdoor dinner after that. The exhibit was called "Women of Sweetgrass, Cedar and Sage." I chose those plants because we use them in ceremonies. I've had complaints about not adding tobacco to that list, but I was going by the sound and how it would be remembered, and indeed, it has been remembered in the Native community in the United States and Canada too.

From the 1970s into the 2000s, I organized and curated 30-plus Native American exhibitions for nonprofits, small museums in rural areas, and galleries especially in the Northern Plains states such as Montana, the Dakotas, Minnesota, and Wisconsin, as well as Midwestern states. Some of the notable exhibits were "We the Human Beings; Our Land Ourselves" and "The Submuloc Show or the Columbus Wohs." A few had catalogs, some had brochures, and some had no documentation at all, only residing in our memories.

While doing this work, I served on many boards for Native American arts organizations, including the tribal college on my reservation, Salish Kootenai, which was a great honor. I was also voted onto the Board of Trustees for the College Art Association, the first Native American to serve in that role.

In the 1980s, I served on the IAIA (Institute of American Indian Arts) Board of Trustees and was disappointed in the facilities that Native students had to deal with, such as hot wires sticking out of the walls of the old barracks, no ventilation for jewelry or etching, broken windows covered with cardboard, and toilets stopped up for weeks at a time.

So I flew to DC on my own and met with Bill Richardson's staff, as well as the staffs of Dale Kildee and Pete Domenici, to discuss making the school freestanding. This elicited congressional legislation was written by Alan Lovesee, who worked for Kildee. I led a letter-writing campaign with my friends Linda Lomahaftewa (Hopi) and Karita Coffey (Comanche), and this endeavor moved the Indian college out of the Bureau of Indian Affairs to become federally chartered, like Gallaudet University for the hearing impaired and Howard, the African American university.

Through the 1970s, 1980s, 1990s, into the 2000s, my husband and I were raising children and grandchildren while I was traveling to exhibitions, both my own and those I organized. I was serving on panels and giving lectures at museums and universities, attending board meetings, painting, drawing, and making prints at various shops. I was traveling four months out of the school year but only one, two, or three days for each trip.

In the 1980s, I worked with a group on my reservation to research and build a small museum for both tribes, the Salish and the Kootenai. But it eventually came to be used as a classroom because each tribe wanted to build their own facility. So, back to square one, I now would like to see a living-learning center on the Salish Kootenai College campus that my cousin founded and which serves 75 tribes. This facility would allow all tribes to participate in exhibiting and crafting while learning business strategies and conservation of Native art materials.

In the 1980s, I also consulted with the Heard Museum and encouraged them to educate their viewers about contemporary Native art by promoting an ongoing exhibit like the Whitney Biennial and also collecting from the exhibit to expand their contemporary collection.

Ten years later, I consulted with Jennifer McNutt at the Eiteljorg Museum in Indianapolis and encouraged them to do the same thing. The Heard dropped theirs after 10 years, but the Eiteljorg named theirs a *fellowship* rather than a biennial and has continued to exhibit and purchase for their collection, which has created a sizable contemporary collection.

In the mid-1990s, I offered to give the Missoula Museum a modest amount of money and my life's work in prints in order to begin a collection of contemporary Native art. That process is still going strong and now has a wing of the museum dedicated to nationwide contemporary Native art, with revolving exhibits and a growing collection. Laura Millin may be the only director in the United States to have designated space for living Native artists and not antiquities as is so often the case.

We, Natives, are so often written about and spoken of in the past tense, as though we've vanished, according to myth-making by this country's Euro-hegemonic society and historical White guilt. My prime concern in speaking about and showing images of other Native artists, every chance I get, is to show that yes, indeed, we are alive all over this country and creating some of the most meaningful art of our times.

PRZEMYSŁAW STROŻEK

I AM NOT a sportsman and not an artist. I am a football (American soccer) and sports fanatic, and at the same time I am a fanatic of art and art history. These two spheres, sports and art, are not mutually exclusive forms. Rather, they form an inseparable unity and shape the art histories I write. Starting in 2000, I would often travel to cities and countries to see live sporting events live at stadiums: I was connected to the "Ultras group" of Polonia Warsaw football team, and I traveled around Poland to see them play. For a few years, I was closely involved in the life of Polonia supporters—I often went to away matches, even experiencing clashes between hooligans from different teams. I've often been asked why I went to the away matches if they were so dangerous and you never knew how it would end. But it seems to me that my fan life has somehow influenced who I am today—not in traditionally accepted intellectual terms, but certainly in terms of overcoming certain extreme situations, learning about yourself and your behavior in uncontrollable circumstances, which occur when you find yourself in the crowd. I not only support Polonia Warsaw but also go abroad to see my other favorite teams from other parts of Europe: for example, in the 2000s and 2010s, I went to Hamburg to watch football games by my beloved FC St. Pauli, to Madrid to watch Rayo Vallecano, and to Milan to watch games by Inter at the Giuseppe Meazza Stadium.

While traveling to other countries, I also did art history research in different archives all over the world and went to see the permanent collections in the museums—both arts and sports—where sport-themed artworks are also to be found. Very often, I combine my sport and art fanaticism within one journey: for example, in 2017, during documenta 14, I watched a football game in Athens (Panathinaikos vs. Panionios), and during Art Basel Miami, I watched a basketball game (Miami Heat vs. Atlanta Hawks). Traveling to other countries and seeing both sporting events and art events live (like biennials and art fairs) is an intrinsic part of my life. During my travels, I try to learn as much as I can about the city life, artistic life, and how the local society interacts with cultural and sporting events. I also visit historical sporting buildings, which enable me to think about the past of sport fever. The most interesting are the sites in Eastern Europe, filled with Brutalist stadium architecture and a fanatic atmosphere.

In 2011, after I received my Ph.D. on the 1920s–1930s historical avant-garde, I realized that I wanted to focus on topics that are closer to my daily fascinations: this is when I explicitly combined my sport and art history fanaticism. I started to deal with the research on sport and the avant-garde in 2012. That very year, the most important sporting event that has ever been organized in my country took place—namely the UEFA European Football Championship in Poland and Ukraine, the so-called Euro 2012. The football fever flourished in Poland during Euro 2012, and I started to write articles around the topic of football and socially engaged art. I realized that football and sports are not only about winning or losing in a physical contest. Sport has almost always been, and in fact still is, about politics, cultural and visual propaganda, social problems, nationalisms, as well as gender, race, political performance, and activism. It can tackle both liberation and discipline at the same time: gymnastics, for instance, can be seen as a liberation of the body through innovative dance experiments, but it can also be seen as a disciplining force, such as when it is connected to military training. Sport is like a lens through which you can research the cultural problems of given societies. When I travel to other countries to collect materials on this topic, I always visit artistic and sport archives. Recently, during my trip to Buenos Aires, where I planned to curate an exhibition on the historical avant-garde, I went to the Espigas Foundation's Document Center on the History of the Visual Arts in Argentina, looking also for artistic material related to the 1978 World Cup. I would like to use this amazing material in my future research on sport, politics, and art during the Cold War.

Since January 2020, I've been an associate researcher at the Archiv der Avantgarden, a research institution focused on the history of avant-garde movements in the twentieth century, which is now a part of the Dresden State Collection. Next to art-historical documents, the archive also contains a lot of material dedicated to sport, and especially the worker sport movement, which was propagated by leftist avant-gardes. In my current research, sport and sporting events, rather than particular artistic trends or styles, provide the starting point for my analysis of sport-themed artworks. With my focus on the "visual turn in the history of sport," I consider paintings, sculptures, photographs, illustrated sport and art magazines, ephemera, fan memorabilia, and graphic design as source documents to discuss the importance of sport and art (or, more broadly, sport and visual culture). In my recent book, *Modernizm–Sport–Polityka* (2019), I demonstrated the extent to which sport-related artworks in 1920s were influenced by factors including the geographical context of sport policy in the respective countries and the promotion of sport through art exhibitions. In my practice, I combine sport history with art history to create a balance between those two disciplines, taking a nonhierarchical approach to both. I publish my research in both sport and art-historical magazines and books.

In the environment of artists and art critics, it is not easy to find people who have a shared experience of supporting a club, going to away games, or loving football more than life. One such example is Daniel Haxall, who invited me to write for his book *Picturing the Beautiful Game* (2018). We went together to see England versus Macedonia at Wembley in London, one day after the conference on sport in which we participated at the National Football Museum in Manchester in 2013. Recently, I have been also asked by Marcin Dudek, a contemporary artist, to write an essay for his catalog about my experiences of being a football fanatic. It was the first time I focused entirely on sporting spectatorship and did not write about art. And to be honest, it was a great experience, but I would rather write about art.

GLORIA SUTTON

STARTING IN 2016, one of the consistent refrains among my contemporary art historian colleagues was the need to alter our teaching methods to counter the ways that the election manifested more latent forms of racism and misogyny that shaped daily life in the United States. My response then, as it is now, was the fact that my own lived experience continues to serve as my radical pedagogy. If 2016 marked an uptick in feminist consciousness-raising among my contemporary art historian colleagues, it also confirmed that very little has changed in the field. As the only tenured person of color in my Art + Design Department at Northeastern University, my presence in the front of the lecture hall or on the hiring committee is always the exception to the rule. And as a woman from a working-class, mixed-race background, I remain one of the only contemporary art historians tenured at a private university who received her Ph.D. from a public one.

Public = civic

In addition to opening a pathway for me to enter an art world that is bounded by layers of exclusivity and restricted access (personal and institutional), the American public education system also instilled an ethos of porosity that frames my scholarship and a belief that civics and art history are intertwined, which grounds my teaching. My identity as an American was the first privileged position I occupied, a status that was made paramount every day by having to show my military-dependent identity card at the various army bases—from El Paso, Texas, to Schwäbisch Gmünd, Germany—where my White father was stationed with my South Korean immigrant mother in the late 1980s. My father's rank as an enlisted soldier rather than an officer meant that while I went to school with children whose parents had college degrees, we lived in separate housing complexes with different playgrounds. Those were just the overt markers of class distinction. Growing up as a military brat not only prepared me for the peripatetic life of an academic but also made visible the invisible codifications that reinforce class, gender, and racial divisions. And now, reflecting back, I can draw direct connections between how both the military and academia rely on an invisible control structure that implicitly shapes how you live, work, and learn, which turns on "white body supremacy," a term Resmaa Menakem introduced as a way to think about the racialization of everyday experience in his 2017 book, *My Grandmother's Hands: Racialized Trauma and the Pathway to Mending Our Hearts and Bodies.*

In tandem with my government-issued education, the other public resource that shaped my entrance into the field of art history was the many national, regional, and municipal art museums that offered open talks, free tours, access to collections, and library privileges that afforded me an international world-class art historical education not because I was a card-carrying member, but simply because I was a citizen. And importantly, my status as a resident could be confirmed. The need to carry validation was imprinted on me early since my countenance and coloring remained ambiguous as well as contextual. In Europe, for example, I read as Asian as it did not (and frequently still does not) compute that I could be both American and Asian at the same time. During my undergraduate studies in North Carolina (1990–94) and graduate work in California in the early 2000s, my lack of a discernible accent meant for many of my peers and professors that I did not count as a minority, and my work in museums signaled that I passed as middle class. These experiences made me highly attuned to the contextual background against which individuals like me figure, setting up my long-term investment in understanding the political stakes of visual representation and how the understanding of identity is a mediated one. For these reasons, I specialize in contemporary art history and media art and prioritize publishing in exhibition catalogs that, unlike academic journals, do not require subscriptions or reside behind paywalls. In fact, my career began at *Afterimage: The Journal of Media Arts and Cultural Criticism* (1995) in a one-year editorial position funded by a grant from the Nathan Cummings Foundation that allowed me to enter a field that is typically sustained by nonfunded internships. Subsequently, my publishing record over the past two decades has taken shape through books, journals, catalogs, magazines, web platforms, and other accessible forums of public engagement. Developed by UCSD Professor Grant Kester, who was then the editor of *Afterimage*, the funded editorial position was aimed at mitigating chronic minority underrepresentation in arts criticism. Yet, arts criticism is still "largely segregated" as Elizabeth Méndez Berry and Chi-hui Tang wrote in their July 15, 2019, *New York Times* article, "The Dominance of the White Male Critic," arguing that "at a time when inequity and white supremacy are soaring, collective opinion is born at monuments, museums, screens and stages—well before it's confirmed at the ballot box."[1] It is for these reasons that I also dedicate much of my time and energy outside of the classroom to giving public lectures, participating in panels, and contributing to the public life of public museums and the communities they serve.

Marginality as method

As a scholar who specializes in two emergent fields, contemporary art and media art, I am often asked about the relevance of art history's methodologies to subjects that are inherently tethered to the new and the now. My response is that contemporary art historians do not occupy a position of remove and this inherent proximity to our subjects heightens the ethical stakes of our practice. We are absolutely complicit with the curators, editors, critics, archivists, conservation experts, dealers, and especially, the artists themselves, who generate the primary source material and the interpretative network that coalesces into the historical record. The political and ethical stakes that motivate my participation in an art world, which by definition traffics in exclusivity and restricted access, is a conversation I am prepared to engage. But more disconcerting is how often my own positionality becomes assumed or circumscribed by the fixity of what art historian Huey Copeland has precisely termed as "identarian formations" in his study *Bound to Appear: Art, Slavery, and the Site of Blackness in Multicultural America* (2013). The way, for example, that art historian colleagues ask me to teach topics on Asian art history simply because of my own Korean American identity, which is often followed up with the rationale that "we are getting so many of *those* students and they would like a class about *their* art," echoing nativist anti-immigrant rhetoric. Likewise, rather than seeing the work of artists of Asian descent bearing on—let alone influencing—contemporary art more broadly framed, it was suggested by colleagues at peer-reviewed journals to publish texts on these artists in specialist volumes geared toward geographic specificities. These experiences have helped me see the renewed stakes for my current book project on the New York–based artist Shigeko Kubota (1937–2015), which in turn mirrors the artist's own art historical reception.

Specifically, in 1991, New York's American Museum of the Moving Image presented a nearly thirty-year survey of Kubota's artworks. On view were objects from Fluxus events produced when she migrated to New York from Japan in 1964, up to her groundbreaking video sculptures—hybrid objects that merged the durational qualities of time-based media with the formal elements of the built environment—produced from the 1970s through the 1990s. In an interview, Kubota noted that it was fitting that her mid-career retrospective would be at an institution devoted to media art and located in Queens—"the place of immigrants" and "different ethnic groups"—suggesting that, even if the square footage and lighting control existed in Manhattan to accommodate her large scale sculptures and videos, she "couldn't have a show anyway: the Whitney is only for Americans and MoMA is too slick; and also I'd have to die to have a show there." Kubota's comments conveyed a false modesty. In fact, MoMA's own pivotal media art curator Barbara London acquired the artist's 1976 sculpture *Duchampiana: Nude Descending a Staircase* in 1981, making Kubota the first artist to have a video sculpture enter MoMA's collection. But Kubota's assessment bore itself out—only after her passing will the artist be granted a solo exhibition, curated by Erica Papernik-Shimizu, which will open at MoMA in 2021 following a retrospective throughout Japan with contributions by New Jersey City University professor of art history Midori Yoshimoto.

I am basing my contribution to *The Storytellers of Art Histories* on this anecdote for several reasons. First, it underscores the way that media art developed through a network of institutions that operate in close proximity but distinctly adjacent to those that often define what gets to be categorically defined as modern or contemporary art. Second, Kubota's sentiments convey the way that media art has always been an inherently international enterprise and one of the only fields in which women and immigrants have predominated as both artists and curators from the outset. And, more pressing, it is a marker that even in 2019, representation of work by women artists, and women of color in particular, still remains marginal within museums and other collecting and exhibition organizations, and even more so in the academic institutions and funding bodies that are charged with telling the broader story of art history. In particular, my voice was given space because curators and artists, including Rosa Barba, Jennifer Bornstein, Anna Craycroft, Henriette Huldisch, Laura Owens, Eva Respini, Sara VanDerBeek, Kerry Tribe, and especially Renée Green, advocated for my inclusion on their panels, public conversations, or Tables of Contents.

Another key reason I am choosing to focus on Kubota's work now is the fact that my recent criticism has centered on more established international artists who overlapped with Kubota and whose own foundational narratives are currently being recalibrated against new critical scholarship produced through public exhibitions that I contributed to in 2018. For example, rather than recirculating the biographically overdetermined narratives around Yayoi Kusama, my contribution to the Hirshhorn catalog for *Infinity Mirrors* curated by Mika Yoshitake demonstrated Kusama's "systems thinking" and focused on her lesser-known Expanded Cinema works. Likewise, when art historian Eva Ehninger invited me to contribute to the scholarly reader *Bruce Nauman: A Contemporary* for the Schaulager, I framed his work in terms of Stuart Hall's theories of encoding and decoding meaning. Most aligned with the way I am approaching Kubota's work is my essay on Elaine Summers for MoMA's *Judson Dance Theater: The Work Is Never Done* at the invitation of Thomas Lax. I not only presented Summers as a visual artist who developed the concept of Intermedia but also pointed out the ways the Experimental Intermedia Foundation she created to support the work of other artists would become a hallmark of feminist media art. Eschewing the trope of "recovery," I argue that Kubota juxtaposed technological and kinetic processes alongside organic/biological and human/social ones, pointing to a model of what we can understand as radical commensurability, a reciprocity between bodies of knowledge and bodies marked by lived experience.

Ultimately, my stakes as an art historian are to demonstrate the ways that the lived experiences of race, gender, class, and ability not only regulate and legislate bodies but also shape and condition the reception of artists as well as scholars. Rather than continually inscribing concentric circles around *qualifiers* of visual art such as "feminist," "Asian," or "video," I am invested in making visible the ways that contemporary art history is subjected to cycles of conformism and acts of erasure. When we claim our own stakes rather than only follow the field's often narrow, predetermined ones, we can critically recuperate marginality not only as a subject but also as a compelling methodology for art history.

Note

1. https://www.nytimes.com/2019/07/05/opinion/we-need-more-critics-of-color.html.

ACKNOWLEDGMENTS

We thank editor and writer Hrag Vartanian for introducing us to Sharon Louden, the series editor. And Sharon for having the foresight to bring us together. We did not know each other before this project, but now we see our ideologies as productively entangled.

We are in awe of how our publisher, Intellect, and Tim Mitchell, have kept this project on track. Also, we thank Sean Kelly Gallery, whose namesake waived their fees to reproduce the work of our contributor Shahzia Sikander on our cover.

Most importantly, we are so grateful to each of our contributors who agreed to share their stories with us and the public. During a worldwide pandemic, each person worked on multiple drafts. We cannot thank them enough for their commitment to the project, and we dedicate the entire volume to all of these brilliant artists, archivists, art historians, and curators.

Finally, telling stories also involves listening to those who read them—you! We plan to animate some of the issues brought up in this book among a variety of audiences. We look forward to ongoing conversations and further storytelling.